Photomediations: A Reader

Photomediations: A Reader
arose out of the Open and Hybrid Publishing pilot,
which was part of Europeana Space,
a project funded by the European Union's ICT Policy
Support Programme under GA n° 621037.
See http://photomediationsopenbook.net

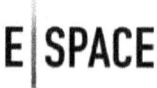

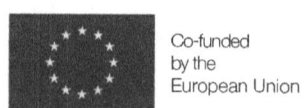

Photomediations: A Reader

Edited by Kamila Kuc and Joanna Zylinska

In association with Jonathan Shaw,
Ross Varney and Michael Wamposzyc

O
OPEN HUMANITIES PRESS

London, 2016

First edition published by OPEN HUMANITIES PRESS 2016
© Details of copyright for each chapter are included within

This is an open access book, licensed under Creative Commons By Attribution Share Alike license. Under this license, authors allow anyone to download, reuse, reprint, modify, distribute, and/or copy their work so long as the authors and source are cited and resulting derivative works are licensed under the same or similar license.
No permission is required from the authors or the publisher. Statutory fair use and other rights are in no way affected by the above.
Read more about the license at http://creativecommons.org/licenses/by-sa/4.0

Figures and other media included with this book may have different copyright restrictions.

Cover and design: Michael Wamposzyc, 2016 CC BY-SA
Cover image: Bill Domonkos, *George*, 2014 CC BY-SA

Typeset in Fanwood Text, a free OpenType font by Barry Schwartz.
More at: http://www.identifont.com/show?2DMD

ISBN: 978-1-78542-020-7 PDF
ISBN: 978-1-78542-002-3 Print

Open Humanities Press is an international, scholar-led open access publishing collective whose mission is to make leading works of contemporary critical thought freely available worldwide. More at: http://openhumanitiespress.org

Contents

Photomediations: An Introduction   7
Joanna Zylinska

I   PHOTOGRAPHY, OPTICS AND LIGHT

1. A New Kind of History?
   The Challenges of Contemporary Histories of Photography   21
   Ya'ara Gil Glazer

2. Painting with Light: Beyond the Limits of the Photograph   48
   Melissa Miles

3. Why Burn a Photograph? A Film by Hollis Frampton   64
   Alexander García Düttmann

4. Processing Color in Astronomical Imagery   75
   Kimberly K. Arcand, Megan Watzke, Travis Rector, Zoltan G. Levay, Joseph DePasquale and Olivia Smarr

II   THE IMAGE IN MOTION

5. It Has Not Been – It *Is*.
   The Signaletic Transformation of Photography   95
   Mette Sandbye

6. The 'Potential Mobilities' of Photography   109
   Debbie Lisle

7. The Cinematograph As an Agent of History   120
   Kamila Kuc

8. What is the Value of a Technological History of Cinema?   133
   Lee Grievson

9. A New/Old Ontology of Film   143
   Rafe McGregor

III Hybrid Photomediations

10. Notes on a Painting of a Painted Photograph — 163
    Ajay Sinha

11. Boredom and Baroque Space — 172
    David Bate

12. Differential Interventions: Images as Operative Tools — 177
    Aud Sissel Hoel and Frank Lindseth

13. Glitch Studies Manifesto — 184
    Rosa Menkman

14. NewFotoScapes: An Interview with Charlotte Cotton — 186
    Jonathan Shaw

15. The Creative Power of Nonhuman Photography — 201
    Joanna Zylinska

IV The Networked Image

16. Benjamin, BitTorrent, Bootlegs: Auratic Piracy Cultures? — 227
    Raúl Rodríguez-Ferrándiz

17. The Gestural Image: The Selfie, Photography Theory and Kinaesthetic Sociability — 251
    Paul Frosh

18. The New Technological Environment of Photography and Shifting Conditions of Embodiment — 268
    Mika Elo

19. Authorship, Collaboration, Computation? Into the Realm of Similar Images — 283
    Katrina Sluis

20. The Horrors of Visuality — 290
    Rob Coley

Notes on Contributors — 313

Photomediations: An Introduction

JOANNA ZYLINSKA

It is perhaps not too much of an overstatement to describe photography as a quintessential practice of life. Indeed, over the last few decades photography has become so ubiquitous that our very sense of existence is shaped by it. In the words of Susan Sontag, 'To live is to be photographed, to have a record of one's life, and therefore to go on with one's life oblivious, or claiming to be oblivious, to the camera's nonstop attentions' (Sontag, 2004). We regularly see ourselves and others represented by the photographic medium, in both its formal and informal guises – from the documentation of our life in its foetal stage via medical imaging, through to the regular recording of our growth and maturation in family, school and passport photographs; the incessant capture of the fleeting moments of our life with phone cameras; and the subsequent construction of our life's 'timeline' on social media. We also make sense of the world around us through seeing it imaged. While photography used to be *something that others* – professionals equipped with large machines that allowed them to capture a better image of the world out there, advertisers trying to sell us chunks of that world, photojournalists dispatched to the world's remote corners that few of us could regularly access – *did*, we can safely say that, in the age of the camera phone and wireless communication, *we are all photographers now*. With 'the lighting, optics, resolution, dynamic range, storage capacity and display of professional digital cameras [being] continuously improved' (*All Our Yesterdays*, 2014: 17), the technological developments rapidly cascade down to everyday consumers.

Yet we are all not *just* photographers today: we have also become distributors, archivists and curators of the light traces immobilised on photo-sensitive surfaces. As Victor Burgin aptly points out, 'the most revolutionary event in the recent history of photography is not the arrival of digital cameras as such, but rather the broadband connection of these cameras to the Internet – in effect turning every photograph on the Web into a potential frame in a boundless film' (2011: 144). One could perhaps go so far as to say that the availability of relatively low-cost storage and networked distribution of digital data has changed the very ontology of the photographic medium. Photographs function less as individual objects or as media content to be looked at and more as data flows to be dipped or cut into occasionally. The intensity and volume of photographic activity today, and the very fact that it is difficult to do *anything* – order food, go on holiday, learn about the Moon, have sex – without having it visualised in one way or another, before, during or *as part of* the experience, gives credence to Sontag's formulation that 'the photographs are us'. 'Andy Warhol's ideal of filming real events in real time – life isn't edited, why should its record be edited? – has become a norm for countless Webcasts, in which people record their day, each in his or her own reality show' (Sontag, 2004).

But, in spite of the embedding of the imaging process in the experience of life on so many different levels, the traditional scholarly and curatorial way of discussing photography still maintains a relatively narrow set of positions and discourses on the topic. The plethora of activities in which photographs are involved as not just objects but also participants of events still tend to be subsumed under one of the two general rubrics: *photography as art* or *photography as social practice*. The first rubric, rooted in the methodology of art history, is encapsulated by numerous histories of photography – from Beaumont Newhall's modernist classic *The History of Photography from 1839 to the Present* (1939) through to Michael Fried's 2008 volume, *Why Photography Matters As Art As Never Before* – presented as stories of the evolution of the medium, enacted by those separate few deemed 'artists'. Photography is seen here as an extension, or even overcoming, of painting. In this view, photographs are positioned as discrete objects that yield themselves to being framed and displayed, individually or in series, on flat surfaces in galleries and other cultural institutions. Photographs positioned as art objects are then analysed in aesthetic and semiotic terms, i.e. in terms of how they affect us and what they mean. Photography functions here as 'the "auristic" artefact..., in which concepts such as "pure vision", "intelligent eye" and "significant form" are privileged' (Gil Glazer, 2010: 8). The value of photographs as singular items is also increasingly tied to the market, with news outlets regularly reporting stories about 'the most expensive photograph ever sold'. Photographs as art objects are therefore always potential commodities, with their singularity and uniqueness validated by the transaction between established auction houses, art galleries, collectors, and, last but not least, artists themselves.

The second rubric under which photography tends to be categorised is the one inspired by French sociologist Pierre Bourdieu's book, *Photography: A Middle-Brow Art* (1990). This more contextual perspective offered by Bourdieu looks not so much at *how* people take and make photographs, as at what they *do with them*: how they store images in family albums; how they join camera clubs; how 'professionals' are different from 'amateurs'; how they all contribute to the emergence of 'popular taste' around photography. The area of photography as professional practice – mainly in the documentary and photojournalistic tradition, but also in fashion and advertising – falls in-between these two traditional rubrics, with the market once again acting as an adjudicator of appropriate categorisation. And thus the work of Henri Cartier-Bresson or Richard Avedon becomes 'art', while many street or fashion photographers who showcase their work for free on public platforms such as Flickr or 500px are seen as hobbyists. Portrait or wedding photography largely remains outside the 'art' designation, with the latter's expectations of 'aura' and 'pure vision'. The outcomes of such professional practice tend to 'conform', instead, 'to a photographic program', to cite Vilém Flusser (2001: 56). Indeed, their success relies precisely on this conformity. The work of wedding or portrait photographers is therefore rarely analysed as 'work' but more as 'labour' (as in the widespread lamentations about the devaluation of the photographic profession, the falling rates for images, etc.). It is principally 'read' in sociological terms and perceived as a tool for capturing and archiving personal memories, and thus, again, as a conduit for social behaviour.

The inadequacy of this rather rigid binary categorisation of photography into art and social practice has been put into question by many. Attempts to open up the narrowly defined category of 'photography as art', and to cast light across the spectrum of various photographic practices, beyond the artist-professional-amateur triangle, have been made from various corners. Geoffrey Batchen, for instance, has called for a new history of photography that 'traces the journey of an image, as well as its origin', 'acknowledges that photographs have multiple manifestations and are objects as well as images', and 'sees beyond Europe and the United States, and is interested in more than the creative efforts of a few white men' (cited in Glazer, 2010: 3). The idea of the photograph's journey raised by Batchen has been taken up by various artists, curators and scholars in their attempts to position photographs as unstable objects, always involved in the process of movement. As curator of the 2011 Paris Photo fair Chantal Pontbriand has put it in the exhibition's catalogue titled *Mutations*, 'The image becomes flexible, polymorph, more than ever temporal, but also corporeal' (Pontbriand, 2001: 13). This altered perception of photography as an unbounded mobile object has also led to the exploration of photography's links with cinema, and to the embracing of the media 'contamination' of the current photographic landscape as an artistic and conceptual opportunity.

One book that deserves a mention is the aptly titled *Photography Changes Everything* published by Aperture in 2012. A unique manifesto for the transformative power of photography put together by curator and writer Marvin Heiferman, it arose out of the Smithsonian Photography Initiative's project during which theorists, artists, scientists, professional photographers and members of the public contributed short postulates on the changing photographic condition. Heiferman's own entry sums up this condition most adequately:

> By its very nature, photography slows time to a standstill in order to corral and flash-freeze information. But just as impressively and importantly, photography is active; it keeps things moving ...
>
> Photographs don't only show us things, they do things. They engage us optically, neurologically, intellectually, emotionally, viscerally, physically. ...
>
> [A]s photography changes everything, it changes itself as well... (Heiferman, 2012: 16-20).

This *Photomediations: A Reader* is part of a larger editorial and curatorial project called *Photomediations: An Open Book* (photomediationsopenbook.net), whose goal is to redesign a coffee-table book as an online experience. The project takes off from these recent development around the technology of photography and around different ways of theorising photography as a diverse practice that not only changes 'everything' but that also undergoes constant change. Yet it is perhaps even more ambitious and daring in its approach than the projects mentioned above. Responding to the inadequacy of the rigid formulations and categories through which photography has been perceived and approached, it proposes instead that it may be time to transform radically, rather than just expand, the very notion of photography. The concept of photomediations is therefore offered as a richer and more potent conceptual alternative. To think in terms of photomediations is not to try and offer just a new history of photography, as attempted by Burgin, Batchen and Ya'ara Gil Glazer, but also a different narrative about the medium, one that remains more attuned to its radically changing ontology. Indeed, the notion of photomediations aims to cut across the traditional classification of photography as suspended between art and social practice in order to capture the dynamism of the photographic medium today, as well as its kinship with other media – and also, with *us as media*. It therefore offers a radically different way of understanding photography.

The framework of photomediations adopts a process- and time-based approach to images by tracing the technological, biological, cultural, social and political flows of data that produce photographic objects. Etymologically, the notion of photomediations brings together the hybrid ontology of 'photomedia' and the fluid dynamism of 'mediation'. Allowing us to sidestep the technicist distinction between analogue and digital photography, as well as – more radically perhaps – that between still and moving image, the concept of photomedia foregrounds instead what is common to various kinds of light-based practices under discussion. As Jai McKenzie argues, 'regardless of technological change, light is a constant defining characteristic of photomedia intrinsically coupled with space and time to form explicit light-based structures and experiences' (2014: 1). For McKenzie, photomedia encapsulate not just photographic cameras but also cinema, video, television, mobile phones, computers and photocopiers. This definition takes cognisance of the fact that, to cite Jonathan

Shaw, over the last decade the photographic apparatus has been 'reunited with its long lost child, the moving image, ... (arguably) ... having given birth to it many years ago' (2014: 4). The concept of mediation, in turn, highlights precisely this intertwined spatial and temporal nature of photography, pointing as it does to a more processual understanding of media that has recently been taken up by scholars and artists alike. In *Life after New Media: Mediation as a Vital Process* Sarah Kember and I make a case for a significant shift in the way we understand so-called 'media'. Rather than focus on analysing discrete media objects, such as the computer, the camera or the iPad, we suggest a richer perspective will open up if we understand media predominantly in terms of processes of mediation, and see them as always already entangled and networked, across various platforms and scales. For Kember and I,

> Mediations does not serve as a translational or transparent layer or intermediary between independently existing entities (say, between the producer and consumer of a film or TV program). It is a complex and hybrid process that is simultaneously economic, social, cultural, psychological, and technical. Mediation, we suggest, is all-encompassing and indivisible. This is why 'we' have never been separate from mediation. Yet our relationality and our entanglement with nonhuman entities continues to intensify with the ever more corporeal, ever more intimate dispersal of media and technologies into our biological and social lives. Broadly put, what we are therefore developing in *Life after New Media* is not just a theory of 'mediation' but also a 'theory of life', whereby mediation becomes a key trope for understanding and articulating our being in, and becoming with, the technological world, our emergence and ways of intra- acting with it, as well as the acts and processes of temporarily stabilizing the world into media, agents, relations, and networks. (Kember and Zylinska, 2012: xv)

Following from the above insight, we could perhaps go so far as to conclude that the photograph as such never just exists on its own. Instead, what emerges are multiple and ongoing processes of photomediation.

Photography can therefore be seen as an active practice of cutting through the flow of mediation, where 'the cut' operates on a number of levels: perceptive, material, technical, and conceptual. In other words, photography can be described as a practice of making cuts in the flow of imagistic data, of stabilising data as images and objects. Performed by human and nonhuman agents alike, with the latter including the almost incessantly working CCTV cameras, Google Street View equipment and satellite telescopes, those cuts participate in the wider process of imaging the world.

In its coupling with movement, the notion of photomediations foregrounds another key aspect of photography: its embeddedness in the flow of time, duration and hence life itself. Seen in this light, photography as part of the process of photomediations presents itself as an inherent part of life in a stronger sense than the one discussed at the beginning of this Introduction: photography does not merely *represent* life but also participates in its active cutting and shaping. To say this is to make an attempt to wrest photography away from its long-standing association with mummification and death, and to show its multifarious and all-encompassing activity – which does include moments of cutting, freeing, stoppage, decay and even demise, but which is not limited by them. Indeed, the conceptual framework of photomediations allows us to move beyond seeing photography as just a tomb, a fossilised version of the past the way modernist theorists of the image such as André Bazin (1960) perceived it. It also allows us to challenge the image of photography as first and foremost a placeholder for the memory of the deceased, the way Roland Barthes defined it in the now classic *Camera Lucida* – a volume that arguably set the melancholy tone for the academic discourse on photography. Yet, in the words of Catalan photographer and writer Joan Fontcuberta, photographs can perhaps be seen more productively as 'exclamations of vitality' (2014: 27).

The recognition of the on-off activity of the photographic process, which carves life into fragments while simultaneously reconnecting them to the imagistic flow, may allow us to conclude not only that there is life in photography, but also that life itself is photographic. As Claire Colebrook puts it, 'All life ... can be considered as a form of perception or "imaging" where there is not one being that apprehends or represents another being, but two vectors of creativity where one potential for differentiation encounters another and from that potential forms a relatively stable tendency or manner' (2010: 31). This idea has its root in the philosopher Henri Bergson's book, *Matter and Memory* (1896), where our experience of the world, which is always a way of sensing the world, comes in the form of images, before it is transformed into concepts. Life is thus always photomediated – or even, we could say, *life is a sequence of photomediations*.

The notion of photomediations has made its way to an online platform called Photomediations Machine (photomediationsmachine.net), set up by myself and Ting Ting Cheng in 2013, which has served as a first practical testing ground for its conceptual and visual working. Taking the inherent openness and entanglement of various media objects on board, Photomediations Machine is a curated online space where the dynamic relations of mediation as performed in photography and other media can be encountered, experienced and engaged. First and foremost, Photomediations Machine serves as an online gallery for unique projects, both recent and historical, that creatively engage with the technological and socio-political dynamism of the photographic medium. The site also features short critical essays on recent developments around photomedia by international writers and artists. Last but not least, Photomediations Machine showcases books and other publications that comment on, or even enact, the current multiple mediations of photography and other media, such as sound, painting, video, or, indeed, the book itself. The site is run on a pro bono basis by a group of academics and artists. The project is non-commercial, non-profit and fully open access. Its machinic affiliation signals that photographic agencies and actions have not always been just human.

Photomediations: An Open Book (of which this Reader is part) is the next step on this experimental journey with and across the photographic medium. Even though Photomediations Machine and *Photomediations: An Open Book* are open platforms, they certainly do not associate openness with an 'anything goes' (or, worse, 'everything is up for grabs') approach. Part of the academic movement of 'radical open access' that promotes open access to knowledge and culture (see Hall, 2008; Adema and Hall, 2011), the platforms advocate informed and responsible curatorial activity. They also recognise the need for singular ethical and political decisions to be made, over and over again, with regard to both the medium and its institutions, such as publishers, galleries, online spaces and intellectual property/copyright, in the current media landscape.

The goal of *Photomediations: A Reader* that you currently have in front of you, in its online version, as an ebook or perhaps as a paper copy, is to participate in this process of experimentation, while also trying to shift the traditional debate on photography beyond many of its established parameters and frameworks. The Reader contains a selection of scholarly and curatorial texts on photography and other media that all explore, but also simultaneously perform and postulate, the vibrant dynamics of photomediations. It consists of four thematic sections. Section I, 'Photography, Optics and Light' tells a history of photography as a story of vision, while the subsequent section, 'The Image in Motion', investigates properties of movement as a process that both brings together and separates the interrelated histories of photography and cinema. Section III, 'Hybrid Photomediations', highlights the diversity of media engagements, in early photographic practice as well as in more recent, and more knowing, experiments with the image-making apparatus. Last but not least, section IV, 'The Networked Image', goes beyond looking at a photograph as a discrete object to consider it as part of the interconnected – and constantly changing – media ecology. *Photomediations: A Reader* is published by Open Humanities Press: an international, scholar-led, not-for-profit open access publishing collective whose mission is to make leading works of contemporary critical thought available worldwide. It is being made available on an open access basis, to anyone with access to the Internet, with print-on-demand paper copies being sold at cost. As part of a broader experiment in open and hybrid publishing – as well as a celebration of the book as a living object – a version of this Reader also exists online in an open 'living' format, which means it can be altered, added to, mashed up, re-versioned and customised.

'Permutation, combinatorics, poetry from a machine; cutting up, taking apart, and putting together again' were, according to media historian Siegfried Zielinski, gestures used by the literary avant-garde in the 1960s 'to creatively attack the bourgeois tradition of the post-war manufacturing of culture' (2013: 58). In the early twenty-first century culture of the supposed image and text deluge, predefined camera programmes and Instagram, an avant-garde gesture can perhaps lie first and foremost in efforts to remap the photographic landscape – and to rewrite its discourses. Rather than pursue the possibility of taking an original photo of a wedding or a unique selfie, we would be better off engaging in the creative activity of photography by trying to arrange different routes through the multi-layered landscape of photomediations. The editorial and curatorial paths proposed in this project are only one possible way of tracing such a new story of photography. They are also an invitation extended to our readers to engage fully with the spirit of this book and to mark their own photomediations routes, well beyond its covers.

Original source and licence

This is a reworked version of the Introduction from the online project, *Photomediations: An Open Book*, http://photomediationsopenbook.net. Licence: CC-BY 4.0.

References

(2014) *All Our Yesterdays. Life through the Lens of Europe's First Photographers (1839 – 1939)*, EuropeanaPhotography exhibition catalogue. Rome: ICCU.

Adema, J. & Hall, G. (2013) 'The Political Nature of the Book: On Artists' Books and Radical Open Access', *New Formations*, Number 78 (Summer): 138-56.

Barthes, R. (1981) *Camera Lucida*. New York: Hill and Wang.

Bazin, A. (1960) 'The Ontology of the Photographic Image', *Film Quarterly*, Vol. 13, No. 4 (Summer): 4-9.

Bergson, H. (1911) *Matter and Memory*. London: George Allen & Unwin Ltd. (First published in 1896.)

Bourdieu, P. (1990) *Photography: A Middle-Brow Art*. Stanford: Stanford University Press.

Burgin, V. (2011) 'Mutating Photography', in *Mutations: Perspectives on Photography* (ed.), C. Pontbriand. Göttingen: Steidl.

Colebrook, C. (2010) *Deleuze and the Meaning of Life*. London and New York: Continuum.

Flusser, V. (2001) *Into the Universe of Technical Images.* Minneapolis: University of Minnesota Press.

Fontcuberta, J. (2014) *Pandora's Camera: Photogr@phy After Photography.* London: Mack.

Fried, M. (2008) *Why Photography Matters as Art as Never Before.* New Haven: Yale University Press.

Gil Glazer, Y. (2010) 'A New Kind of History? The Challenges of Contemporary Histories of Photography', *Journal of Art Historiography,* Number 3 (December): 1-19.

Hall, G. (2008) *Digitize This Book!: The Politics of New Media, or Why We Need Open Access Now.* Minneapolis: University of Minnesota Press.

Heiferman, M. (2012) 'Introduction', in *Photography Changes Everything* (ed.), M. Heiferman. New York: Aperture/Smithsonian.

Kember, S. & Zylinska, J. (2012) *Life after New Media: Mediation as a Vital Process.* Cambridge: MA, MIT Press.

McKenzie, J. (2014) *Light and Photomedia: A New History and Future of the Photographic Image.* London: IB Tauris.

Newhall, B. (1982) *The History of Photography from 1839 to the Present Day,* 5th edition. New York: The Museum of Modern Art. (First published in 1939.)

Pontbriand, C. (2011) 'Introduction: Mutations in Photography', in *Mutations: Perspectives on Photography* (ed.), C. Pontbriand. Göttingen: Steidl.

Shaw, J. (2014) 'Hybridity and Digital Transformations', *NewFotoScapes* (ed.), J. Shaw. Birmingham: The Library of Birmingham.

Sontag, S. (2004) 'Regarding The Torture Of Others', *The New York Times,* May 23, http://www.nytimes.com/2004/05/23/magazine/regarding-the-torture-of-others.html, accessed on January 7, 2015.

Zielinski, S. (2013) [... *After the Media*]. Minneapolis: Univocal.

I Photography, Optics and Light

CHAPTER 1

A New Kind of History? The Challenges of Contemporary Histories of Photography

Ya'ara Gil Glazer

'I want a new kind of history'

Since the late 1970s, when the history of photography became an academic subject, and with increasing interest in photography in the art market, there have been frequent calls by various scholars for a 'new kind of history' of photography. These calls were part of what Rosalind Krauss and Annette Michelson described in a special photography issue of *October* (1978) as a renewed scholarly 'discovery' of the medium, characterized by the 'sense of an epiphany, delayed and redoubled in its power' (Krauss and Michelson, 1978: 3). This rediscovery carried the message that photography and its practices have to be redeemed 'from the cultural limbo to which for a century and a half it had been consigned' (1978: 3).

The calls for a new history of photography suggested that the time has come to substitute Beaumont Newhall's hegemonic modernist classic *The History of Photography from 1839 to the Present* with a new text (1939).[1] Newhall was a librarian and later the first director of photography of the Museum of Modern Art in New York. His work is considered as 'the English-language text that has shaped thinking on the subject more permanently than any other' (Nickel, 2001: 550). Based on the catalogue of his MoMA exhibition *Photography 1839-1937,* 'usually cited as a crucial step in the acceptance of photography as full-fledged museum art' (Phillips, 1992: 17), this book was the predominant photo-history for more than 50 years. It shifted the historiographic focus from the chemical-physical aspect of the medium to its visual aspect.

Similarly, the geographic center of the historiography of photography shifted from Europe to the United States.[2]

Newhall's history has been vigorously criticized in recent decades. It is denounced as based on a formalist methodology that 'forced him to mostly comment on style rather than content', and as focusing 'on genre and the tracing of influences' (Rodriguez, 1982: 485). The critics also argue that his canonization of the *masters of photography*, detached photographic practice from social, political and cultural historical contexts (Nickel, 2001: 553). In the later editions (1949, 1964, 1982), Newhall made significant changes and revisions to his text, though his formalist attitude and selective and authoritarian approach concerning 'masterpieces', 'photographic artists' and photographic genres remained. Nonetheless, as noted by Marie Warner Marien, 'Newhall's aversion to losing the uniqueness of photography in the world of art is a constant underlying value in the text' (Marien, 1986: 5). His emphasis on photographic means, procedures and techniques is characteristic of that concern.

A relatively early event that marked this need for a new history of photography was the series of lectures 'Toward the New History of Photography' organized by the Art Institute of Chicago in 1979. In his lecture for the series, Carl Chiarenza opened with the assumption that 'there will be new histories of photography...' that 'will be critical of past histories...' (Chiarenza, 1979: 35, 41). Contrary to Newhall's approach, Chiarenza's critical vision regarding the future history of photography was that it 'must be part of the history of all picturemaking', i.e. part of a general visual culture.[3]

Another early landmark in the formulation of the need for a new history of photography appears in Andy Grundberg's 'Two Camps Battle over the Nature of the Medium' (1983). In this article for the *New York Times* he defined two distinct 'camps', i.e. two contemporary photographic concepts:

> The lines are drawn between those who think of photography as a relatively new and largely virgin branch of art history, and those who rebel at the very notion of photography being 'estheticized'. The former welcome the medium's elevation to the realm of the museum, the marketplace and traditional art-historical scholarship, while the latter argue that

> photography's 'museumization' ... robs it of its real importance
> – that is, its social meanings. (Grundberg, 1983)

Towards the end of the twentieth-century, the calls for a new history of photography and the debate regarding its character intensified. The 1997 summer issue of *History of Photography*, for instance, was titled 'Why Historiography?' and included articles by young and promising scholars such as Mary Warner Marien, Christine Mehring, and Malcolm Daniel. Its guest editor, Anne McCauley, described the purpose of the issue as a review and reconsideration of the history of photography at the end of the twentieth-century. She suggested the need to move from descriptive writing and 'largely unexplored assumptions' to an integrated history, focused on 'photography's shifting social roles' (McCauley, 1997: 86).

Another project reexamining the theory and historiography of photography is *Photography: Crisis of History,* an anthology of short essays published in 2003, written by an international group of photo-historians, curators, critics and photographers. These authors were asked by scholar and photographer Joan Fontcuberta to 'offer their reflections on the state of the historiographic question in photography' (Fontcuberta, 2003: 14, 17). Their texts, according to Fontcuberta, 'represent different ways of revisiting history, and put forward ideas that will undoubtedly prove very useful in bringing new light to historical studies with a bearing on photography... help[ing] to place us in a position from which to overcome with greater surety that crisis of history in which we find ourselves' (Fontcuberta, 2003: 14). The authors in the anthology, among them Ian Jeffrey, Carmelo Vega, Boris Kossoy and Marie Loup Sougez, referred in various ways to questions such as: 'What are the problems that emerge from his [Newhall's] approach?' (i.e. canonizing certain photographers and photographs and emphasizing 'the history of technique'); 'What are the principal filters – cultural, ideological and political – that have determined the dominant historiographic model?'; Can photography still be studied as an autonomous discipline...?'; 'Is a social history of photography compatible with an aesthetic history, a history of uses with a history of forms?' and 'How are we to produce a "politically correct" history of photography?'

What seems to be an effective summing-up of the need for a new history of photography appeared in Geoffrey Batchen's poem in the

May/June 2002 issue of *Afterimage*, comprised of wishes expressed in the recurrent assertion 'I want a new history [of photography]'. Batchen demands, for instance, a history that 'looks at photography, not just at art photographs', 'breaks free from an evolutionary narrative', 'traces the journey of an image, as well as its origin', 'acknowledges that photographs have multiple manifestations and are objects as well as images', and 'sees beyond Europe and the United States, and is interested in more than the creative efforts of a few white men' (Batchen, 2002: 3).

Shortly before the publication of Batchen's proem, Douglas Nickel made an assessment of photo-history's 'state of research' in the pages of the *Art Bulletin*. Like Grundberg in the early 1980s but with a wider perspective, he concluded that the field is caught between two opposing forces: one that construed photography as high art, with the accompanying aura of prestige, originality and uniqueness; the other arguing for 'photography's social determination' and interdisciplinary character. While the first force is essentially related to the rising power of photography collecting market in the 1970s and intensified during the 1980s and 1990s, and the incorporation of photographs in museum collections at around the same period, the second is the incorporation of photography as an academic field in Art History departments and later in departments such as social and cultural history, anthropology, literature and philosophy. This process was described by Nickel as 'fraught with contradictions' due to the 'dual challenges' of critical theory and the crisis in the field of Art History itself (Nickel, 2001: 554-555).

In this context, Nickel describes how a prominent group of commentators of the 1980s-1990s, who made the history of photography the focus of their research, had revived the ideas of critics such as Walter Benjamin, Roland Barthes and Susan Sontag, from different theoretical perspectives, among them Marxism, feminism and psychoanalysis. Some of them, he argues, had taken a radical political approach to the history of photography, promoting it 'to assume a central position in the larger project of postmodern criticism' (554).[4] He concludes his article commenting that

> The intellectual self-consciousness with which photography's social agency can now be contemplated is the beneficial and necessary end product of two decades of soul-searching on its behalf, but how (or whether) the remains of this process get

reassembled into something vital will be determined largely by the institutional forces that presently control photographic history's fate. (Nickel, 2001: 556)

New histories, new challenges

In response to these calls for a new history of photography, at least six comprehensive academic photo-histories have been published in the United States and Europe between 1984 and 2002. Such volumes serve as essential textbooks for art-history students, and as a general introduction for the interested public. They therefore play a central role in the construction of historical-photographic knowledge. Three of most popular of these histories, according to sales estimates and new editions, are: *A World History of Photography* by Naomi Rosenblum (1984; 4th edition, 2008), *Seizing the Light* by Robert Hirsch (1999; 2nd edition, 2008), and *Photography: A Cultural History*, by Mary Warner Marien (2002; 3rd edition, 2010).[5]

Are these texts really a new kind of history? Almost ten years after Nickel's article, and almost nine years after the publication of the most recent and innovative of these books – Marie Warner Marien's *Photography: A Cultural History* – seems to be an appropriate time to investigate how they comply with the demand for a new history of photography, how they compare with Newhall's history, and how and to what extent they fill the lacunae left by his prototype.[6]

The present article focuses on two sections of these books: the first engages with the Photo-Secession art-photography movement. The second focuses on the Farm Security Administration's documentary photographic project. The Photo-Secession was an American movement of photographers interested in promoting the status of photography as fine art. It was established in New York and was active between 1880 and 1920. The photographic project of the Farm Security Administration (the FSA), was part of the New Deal program for reviving American agriculture throughout the country during the Great Depression of the 1930s. Each of these subjects, according to Newhall, signifies a high point in photographic history.

These sections were selected for two reasons: first because the subjects are familiar to anyone with general knowledge of the history of photography, which makes their analysis both accessible and comprehensible; and second as they represent the problems of photography's manifold character, raising the old but still relevant questions regarding the differences and similarities between documentary practices and art. The discussion of the texts and images representing these two 'poles' in histories of photography testifies to some of the challenges and complexities involved with revising or creating an alternative to Newhall's history.

The sections in the three books will be discussed in relation to Newhall's work, according to the following criteria: the extent and complexity of their historical and photo-historical contexts; the narrative sequence and the approach to canonical photographers; the approach to canonical photographic images; the expansion of the canon and political corrections.[7]

Historical and photo-historical contexts

Rosenblum, Hirsch and Marien's new histories reveal their authors' approach to the importance of historical and photo-historical contexts. While all the new authors discuss photographic issues in a broader historical context, in Rosenblum's and Hirsch's books this context is demarcated by their chapters, which are usually defined stylistically. One of the problems resulting from such categorization is the inconsistencies in the ways by which photographic issues and approaches are discussed. Documentary photographs, for instance, are presented in their books in a much wider historical context than artistic photographs taken at around the same period. The latter seem to have a discrete history of art photography that does not integrate cultural, social, or political historical events, but rather focuses on internal stylistic influences.

Like Newhall's, Naomi Rosenblum's and Robert Hirsch's sections on the Photo-Secession are therefore set in the context of efforts in the USA and in Europe to establish photography as fine art under the heading 'Pictorialism'. The sequence of events – the rejection of mid nineteenth-century artificial painting-like photographs, the efforts to distinguish art photography from amateur photography, the advent of naturalist photography, of camera clubs and of photography salons, and the rise of the

Photo-Secession as a coherent group of pictorial photographers – clearly adheres to Newhall's evolutionary narrative pattern.

Marien, on the other hand, totally deconstructs Newhall's model by eschewing the stylistic categories and examining varying photographic approaches and practices, which operate in parallel within a specific cultural historical framework. In this way, she challenges the traditional contexts in which pictorialist photography and the Photo-Secession are discussed. Though she too refers to the aforementioned sequence of issues and events, she does not emphasize this trend in photography simply as a counter-reaction to painterly photographs or the proliferating amateur photography of the period within the seemingly hermetic world of art photography. Instead, she describes the rise of the pictorialist movement and the increasing significance of photography in everyday modern life in a chapter on 'Photography in the Modern Age'. This chapter includes, for example, sections on social reform photography, science and photography, and war and photography.

While the Photo-Secession is portrayed by Hirsch and by Rosenblum in a way similar to Newhall's – a unique school of art photography within the broader pictorialist movement, headed by Alfred Stieglitz – Marien again rows against the current and insists that Stieglitz's role 'was not unprecedented' (Marien, 2002: 183). While all authors create the impression that the Photo-Secession's journal *Camera Work*, and its exhibition space – gallery '291' (located at 291 Fifth Avenue, New York) were exclusively American phenomena, she describes the Photo-Secession in the context of influential European exhibitions (among them those organized by Stieglitz's mentor H. W. Vogel) and photographic magazines. Just as the Photo-Secession is discussed at length in chapters on art and pictorial photography, references to the FSA photographic project are prominent in reviews of documentary photography in the first half of the twentieth-century in Newhall's text and in the new histories. Newhall opens with a definition of the term 'documentary' and continues with examples of documentary photographers and photographs, beginning in the early years of the twentieth-century, to create an allegedly evolutionary sequence of documentary photography as a genre, almost isolated from a historical context. This is how he describes the FSA photographic project in this sequence, after Lewis Hine, and before Margaret Bourke-White: 'At the same time that filmmakers began to talk about "documentary", here and there photographers were using their cameras in a similar way. In 1935 the United States government turned to these photographers for help in fighting the Depression...' (Newhall, 1982: 238).

There is a marked difference in the new authors' approaches in comparison to Newhall's. Rosenblum, Hirsch and Warner set the FSA photographic project in the context of a more diverse social documentary initiatives and individual photographers. They focus on social documentary and discuss it in relation to various issues such as social change, the social sciences, and ethnographic photography.[8] Unlike Newhall, they also supply a wider social and cultural context to the establishment of the FSA photographic agency and its operation, against the backdrop of the Depression and the New Deal, including the wide distribution and circulation of its images – mainly promoted by the head of the project, Roy Emerson Stryker – as well as viewers' responses to the images. All three authors, for instance, conduct an important discussion regarding the public's ambivalent acceptance of FSA photographs: was this 'real' evidence or 'red propaganda'?

Although providing a broader background to the FSA photographic project, Rosenblum and Hirsch follow Newhall's example, locating it in a chapter on documentary photography (albeit within a section on social documentary). Warner, on the other hand, includes the FSA project in a chapter titled 'New Vision'. Rosenblum employed this term – borrowed from Bertolt Brecht who referred to the period as 'a great lesson for a new vision of the world' – to describe the interaction between modernism and photography in the years between the two World Wars (Brecht, in Frizot, 1998: 457). By setting documentary photography in the context of photographic avant-garde of the 1920s and 1930s, Marien in fact demarcates this branch of photography as no less modernist than the experimental and/or straight photography of the period. This approach, perhaps inspired by the historian Michael Denning in his *Cultural Front*, challenges the traditional split between modernist 'art photography' and documentary photography in the period under discussion.[9]

Nevertheless, while Marien discusses some important formalist aspects of RA/FSA photographs, it is not at the expense of the project's significant social and cultural role, which she emphasizes more than any of the other authors. She is the only one, for example, who suggests that the RA (Resettlement Administration – which later merged with the

FSA), 'was regularly questioned by conservatives who felt that direct, planned government intervention into the economy and the daily lives of citizens was un-American or, worse, crypto-socialist' (Marien, 2002: 281). This is very significant, in light of the perception by late twentieth-century photo-historians of the FSA photographs as mere propaganda for the US government.[10] Warner is also the only author who provides examples of the uses of RA/FSA photographs in popular newspapers and in documentary photo-books. By expanding the visual knowledge of those famous images, she encourages their examination within the contexts in which they were originally produced and circulated during the 1930s and early 1940s. The other authors, like Newhall, present the images as individual examples that do not suggest their numerous cultural manifestations.

Narrative sequence and the canonization of photographers

Newhall's history was attacked as 'developing from one *Master* to another', as 'the key site of analysis becomes the qualities of the individual photograph', rather than the social and cultural contexts in which it was produced and reproduced (Bezencenet, 1982: 485). This approach resembles that of the second best-known museological history of photography after Newhall's, i.e. John Szarkowsky's *Photography until Now* (1989). Like Newhall's, this book is based on an exhibition at MoMA and represents the 'camp' which sees (and constructs) photography as the 'auristic' artefact described by Grundberg and Nickel, in which concepts such as 'pure vision', 'intelligent eye' and 'significant form' are privileged (Hugunin, 1991).

An examination of narrative sequences in the new histories discussed here evokes Newhall's prototype in various ways. The story of the Photo-Secession in Hirsch's book is virtually Alfred Stieglitz's story, opening with the group's establishment by the latter and followed by a citation of his statement concerning its goals, and listing the names of other founders and members. In further sections – 'Decadent Movement and Tonalism', 'Woman Pictorialists', and 'The Pictorial Epoch / The Stieglitz Group', Hirsch describes prominent photographers in the Photo-Secession one by one, with strong emphasis on their affiliation to Stieglitz.

It seems that Hirsch was also influenced by Rosenblum in his sections on pictorialism and the secession group, in particular in his emphasis on women pictorialists, whom Newhall virtually ignores. Nevertheless, her text is much more balanced in regard to background information and detail, and she also corrects Newhall's injustices, including his blurring of Edward Steichen's role in the Photo-Secession:

> The formidable role played by Stieglitz ... has received ample attention, but the active participation of Steichen, who found and installed the exhibition space, designed the cover and publicity for *Camera Work*, and initiated contacts with the French graphic artists whose works eventually formed an important part of Secession exhibits and publications, is less known. (Rosenblum, 1984: 325)

Warner opens her section on the Photo-Secession in a sophisticated way that suggests the complexity and contradictions inherent to the term 'pictorialism'. She cites the prominent photography critic Sadakichi Hartmann's comments on a pictorialist exhibition at the Carnegie Institute in Pittsburgh in 1904, published in *American Amateur*. Hartmann had unfavorably reviewed some of the works in this exhibition, organized, among others, by Stieglitz, as 'overstep[ping] all legitimate boundaries and deliberately mix[ing] up photography with the technical devices of painting and the graphic arts', and calling on the movement's photographers to present reality in a straightforward manner (Marien, 2002: 181).

The term 'straight photography' was later adopted by Newhall to define his favorite 'photographic genre' - primarily represented by Stieglitz's mature works. His chapter on 'Straight Photography' follows the one on 'Pictorial Photography'. However, the distinction between the pictorial and the straight branches of the Photo-Secession made by Hartmann seven years later in *Camera Work* is not mentioned by Marien, a fact that weakens her critique of the movement.[11]

Unlike her narrative of Stieglitz and the Photo-Secession, part of Marien's section on the FSA photographic project, surprisingly retains the pattern of Newhall's narrative sequence, and her account of the FSA photographers is very similar to his. Her writing on Walker Evans, for instance, seems to be a dissonant synthesis of the contextual approach and Newhall's canonical mold. Newhall wrote, for example: 'Walker Evans was one of the first photographers to be hired' and Warner almost literally rewrote his words: 'Among Stryker's first hired was Walker Evans' (Newhall, 1939 238; Marien, 2002: 282). Subsequently, again like Newhall, Warner discusses Dorothea Lange, relatively at length.[12]

The canonization of these two photographers, especially of Evans, is criticized by contemporary photo-historians of the FSA, who argue that such an approach detaches their works from the specific political context in which they were created and presents them as the works of outstanding individual artists. 'We run the risk of developing a "star system" approach to these images', comments Jack F. Hurley: 'We stand back, view the beautiful print on the gallery wall and say, "isn't it wonderful?" It's an Evans' (or Lange, or Lee, or whatever)' (Hurley, 1972: 244).[13] The canonization of some FSA photographers also obscures the contributions of others, among them Marion Post-Wolcott, Jack Delano and Carl Mydans, to name a few.

Rosenblum's profile on FSA photographers appearing at the end of the chapter on documentary photography, separately from the section on the FSA photographic project, is the only one truthful to history in this regard: it begins with a description of the work of Arthur Rothstein, the first photographer hired by Stryker. Stryker met Rothstein when they were students at Columbia University in the early 1930s and called him to join the new and still amorphous project (Hurley, 1972: 244).

Concluding the section on the FSA photographic project, Warner, again like Newhall, mentions other photographers hired by the FSA during the later years of the administration and after its merger with the Office of War Information (OWI.) However, in an obvious effort to provide a politically-correct alternative to his pattern, she focuses on two figures: Gordon Parks, the only black photographer in the FSA/OWI, and Esther Bubley, one of the few women photographers in the FSA/OWI. She also provides details about the later careers of prominent FSA photographers, which again seems to correct Newhall, who was criticized for designing his history according to categories in which such an option would be untenable.

Canonical images

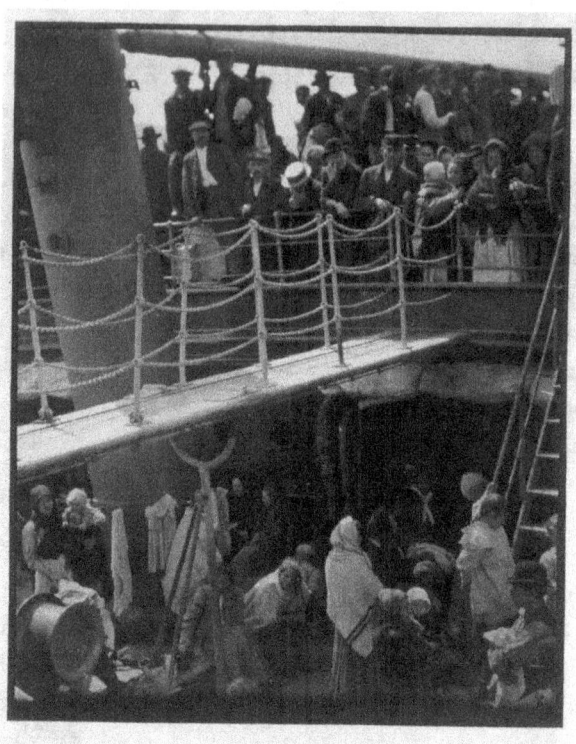

Figure 1.1. Alfred Stieglitz, *The Steerage*, 1907, Photogravure, 15.9x21.6 cm, Museum of Modern Art, New York. Library of Congress, Prints & Photographs Division, The Alfred Stieglitz Collection, Gift of Georgia O'Keeffe [LC-USZCN4-243].

Just as he canonized certain photographers as masters, Newhall also considered their works masterpieces. Both Rosenblum and Hirsch, but the latter in particular, revert to Newhall's model in this regard. Their references to Stieglitz's *The Steerage* (1907) and Dorothea Lange's *Migrant Mother* (1936) are examples of this. Newhall mentions *The Steerage*, a photograph of travelers and re-emigrants from the US to Europe on the first and lower-class decks of the ship *Kaiser Wilhelm II*, as what Stieglitz considered to be his finest work. In his history it is the focal representative of straight photography (appearing on the first double page spread of the chapter 'Straight Photography'), reflecting Stieglitz's preference for 'stick[ing] closely to the basic properties of camera, lens and emulsion' at a time when he 'began to champion the most progressive painting and sculpture, as well as photography' (Newhall, 1939: 167-168). Newhall emphasizes the formal aspect of the image, citing Stieglitz's description of what motivated him to take it:

> A round straw hat, the funnel leaning left, the stairway leaning right, the white drawbridge with its railings made of circular chains; white suspenders crossing the back of a man in the steerage below, round shapes of iron machinery, a mast cutting into the sky, making a triangular shape.... I saw a picture of shapes and underlying that the feeling I had about life. (Stieglitz, in Newhall, 1939: 168).

Rosenblum and Hirsch offer no alternatives to Newhall's formalist reading of *The Steerage*; rather, they reinforce it by emphasizing its affinity with art movements of the period, especially with Cubism. Hirsch actually goes even further than Newhall. While Newhall comments that Stieglitz was flattered by Pablo Picasso's excitement about the picture, and Rosenblum quotes Picasso's statement that he and Stieglitz worked 'in the same avant-garde spirit', he discusses the image, under the heading 'Cubism', as representative of a 'transformation' in Stieglitz's 'aesthetic thinking' under the influence of analytic cubism. Apart from the fact that cubism is a term that fundamentally belongs to the realm of painting (Stieglitz himself, according to Marien, 'praised Picasso's "antiphotographic" work, meaning that it had renounced the simple vanishing-point perspective imposed by the camera'), Hirsch decontextualizes Newhall and Stieglitz's resistance to the assimilation of photography into the realm of painting and its vocabulary, and their efforts for the recognition of photography as a discrete medium. His ignorance of the social content in Stieglitz's photograph is also surprising (Rosenblum, 1984: 405; Hirsch, 1999: 215; Marien, 2002: 189).[14]

Thus Rosenblum and Hirsch maintain the canonical status of the image but fail to discuss contemporary critical references to it. Warner also describes Stieglitz's scene of *The Steerage* but, unlike them, she subsequently echoes Allan Sekula's Marxist-oriented critique in his 'On the Invention of Photographic Meaning' (1975): 'He was looking over the first-class deck to the steerage below, recognizing there not the disheartened immigrants returning to Europe, but a combination of abstract forms....' (Marien, 2002: 185). Nevertheless, Warner's up-to-date and significant reference to Sekula's seminal article is problematic. She mixes history and critique in a way that will most likely confuse the novice reader who is seeking an introduction to the history of photography. By supporting Sekula and presenting opinion as fact, she virtually constructs the readers' perception of the photograph without letting them make their own conclusions, and without even mentioning Sekula's name.[15]

Migrant Mother is the best-known photograph of the FSA project and perhaps of American documentary photography as a whole, an enduring symbol of the Depression.[16] Newhall's description of this image of a mother and children of a poor, migrant agricultural workers' family, taken by Dorothea Lange in Nipomo, California, appears on the first page of his chapter on documentary photography:

> Lange could make a deserted farmhouse, abandoned in acres of machine-plowed land, an eloquent definition of the phrase 'tractored-out', which was on the lips of hundreds of dispossessed farmers. Her photograph of a migrant mother surrounded by her children, huddled in a tent, became the most widely reproduced of all the FSA pictures....
> (Newhall, 1939: 244).

Similarly, Hirsch writes that Lange's FSA photographs 'epitomized the human cost of the Depression' and that *Migrant Mother* was considered by many as the 'quintessential FSA image' (Newhall, 1939: 244; Hirsch, 199: 286).[17] Rosenblum also notes the reputation of the photograph; as in Newhall's history, it is given a full page in her book as a signifier of the FSA photographic project. Warner, on the other hand, comments that: 'Though powerful, *Migrant Mother* is not typical of Lange's work' (Marien, 2002: 285). She is also the only author who presents the image as it frequently appeared in the popular press, thereby shedding light on the circulation of FSA images, and on how urban Americans were exposed to them in the late 1930s and early 1940s. The choice of this version of the image also suggests different possible interpretations of FSA photographs in different texts and contexts.[18]

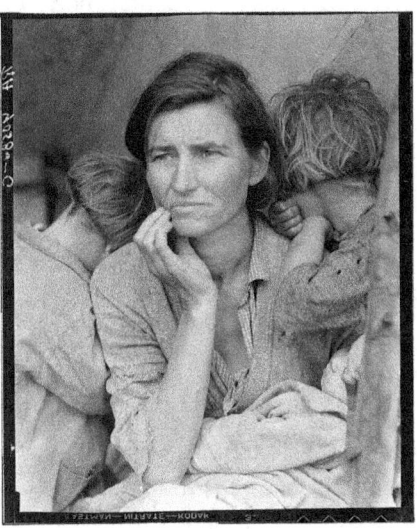

Figure 1.2. Dorothea Lange, *Migrant Mother* (*Destitute pea pickers in California. Mother of seven children. Age thirty-two. Nipomo, California*). 1936, 1 negative: nitrate; 4 x 5 in., Library of Congress [LC-USF34-009058-C].

However, Marien's short summary next to the image, again combining cultural history and critical theory, is confusing. The first part, in which the image is described as recalling 'religious images of the Madonna and Child', seems to echo art and photography historian John Pultz's feminist reading of the image as drawing on 'Renaissance depictions of the Virgin and Child and the secularized versions of these that began to appear in the mid nineteenth century...' This is part of Pultz's analysis of the image as centering 'on the female body ... that is socially constructed through the gaze, and has the quality "to be looked at"' (Pultz, in Wells, 2000: 44).

Such a presentation of the photograph, characteristic of feminist discourse of photography, is again confusing for the reader who expects an introductory textbook that provides a cultural historical framework of photographs. Not only does it shift the focus from the social and cultural historical context in which it was taken, it actually contradicts the media-constructed version of the image chosen by Marien herself, which called on the middle-class public to 'look in her eyes', not as a representation of objectified female body, but as a representative of the most deprived class in American society.[19] A discussion of contemporary readings of the photograph is certainly worthy, but they should be explained as late interpretations, and in a way that acknowledges the image's numerous and varied readings.

Marien's subsequent statement that the image 'also expresses Depression era values' is vague. If these values are implied by the continuation of her above cited sentence: 'the children on either side turn away, symbolically ashamed of their wretchedness' (which also resonate Pultz's writing: 'the two older children turn their heads away from the photographer (out of shame or shyness?)' (Pultz, in Wells, 2000: 44), t1hen such reading also seems decontextualized. The idea of the poor as ashamed or responsible of their situation was characteristic of the late nineteenth-century Social Darwinism but was actually weakened during the Depression. Besides the diluted faith in capitalism due to the economic crisis during that period, the images of the Depression poor played a significant cultural role, constructed by the mass media as the 'deserving poor', representing a tentative national situation that will apparently be overcome soon. Hence, the symbolic figures of the rural poor were connected with the agrarian myth and the ethos of the white pioneers who built America and survived hardship to eventually become successful and prosperous.[20]

> The second part of Warner's discussion of the image determines that the mother's careworn face, her tattered clothes, and the dirty baby near her breast indicate extreme distress, deserving of compassion. Yet her expression hints at a determination to persevere through hard times. (Marien, 2002: 284).

The combination of these oppositions – distress and persevere, or 'tragedy and resistance', according to photography critic John Roberts 'in essence was what the magazine editors were waiting for' (Roberts, in Wells, 2000: 43), namely, a message that aimed to pacify American middle class audience. This combination was also pronounced by Stryker retrospectively, as he described it in 1973 as '*the* picture of the Farm Security Administration ... She has all the suffering of mankind in her but all the perseverance too. A restraint and a strange courage' (Stryker and Wood,

1973: 73). However, Stryker's aim was of course different from that of the popular magazine's editors: he was trying to promote public support for the RA/FSA rehabilitation programmes through images that would arouse both respect and empathy.

For a third time then, and again with no reference to her resources, Warner confuses the reader with an apparent factual characteristics of the image ('the mother's ... face ... indicate[s] extreme distress ... Yet her expression hints at a determination to persevere') instead of discussing its construction (by the mass media versus the FSA, for instance) as such.

Extending the canon and political corrections

As shown earlier, Rosenblum's and Hirsch's approaches to canonical photographs certainly seem like variations on Newhall's book, even though they, and Marien, significantly extended his range. Their extensions also include images of and by representatives of social groups that were under-represented or disregarded by Newhall, among them women, African Americans and Native Americans.

Newhall's list of photographers in his chapters 'Pictorial Photography' and 'Documentary Photography' is almost completely present in the new books, though the authors have expanded this list considerably, both in number and variety. Rosenblum's most notable contribution, for instance, has been to extend the photographic canon beyond the United States and Central and Western Europe. In the chapters under discussion, she adds examples of pictorial and documentary photographers in countries such as Spain, Finland, Czechoslovakia, Romania, Poland, Russia and Japan.

Rosenblum also discusses the important role played by women in the pictorialist movement. This amendment was followed by both Hirsch and Warner. Apart from Gertrude Kasebier – the only pictorialist woman photographer discussed by Newhall – Rosenblum, Hirsch and Warner also present works by Alice Boughton, Anne W. Brigman, Eva Watson-Schutze, Sara C. Sears, Jane Reece and others. They also refer to more women documentarists than Newhall did, including those who worked for New-Deal agencies operating parallel to the FSA, such as Marjory Collins and Martha McMillan.[21]

Commenting that 'women, who were more active in all aspects of photography in the United States, were especially prominent in pictorialism'

(Rosenblum, 1984: 320), Rosenblum's discussion of women pictorialists is a part of the section 'Pictorialism in the United States'. This corrects the imbalance of women photographers in Newhall's history, while Hirsch's and Warner's presentation of the women photographers in a discrete section actually removes it from its historical and local contexts, referring to their work as if it were a 'school' existing separately from pictorialism.

Similarly, political correctness is also apparent concerning the work of black photographers. Warner, as aforementioned, discusses the black FSA photographer Gordon Parks and all three writers discuss works by James van der Zee, who was also neglected in Newhall's book. The new histories also correct a radical lacuna in images of American blacks in Newhall's book (the only African-American image in the last edition of Newhall is that of Paul Robeson by Edward Steichen, taken in 1933). Rosenblum includes images of blacks by Ben Shahn (for the FSA) and by her husband, the Photo League photographer Walter Rosenblum. Warner presents the most detailed story of Photo League's documentation of poor blacks' life in Harlem (and of harassment by the FBI as suspected of subversive communist activity). She also dedicates a number of paragraphs to discussion of black representations in photography in the 1930s, with images by Margaret Bourke-White, Eudora Welty, Carl Mydans, Aaron Siskind and Van der Zee.

Hirsch's most original political addenda are four examples of Native American images in his chapter on documentary photography: 'The Snake Priest, Hopi' by Adam Vroman (1901), 'Bear Bull-Blackfoot' by Edward Curtis (1926) (both these photographers are also discussed by Newhall) 'Class in American History' by Frances Benjamin Johnston (1899), and 'Horace Poolaw, Aerial Photographer, and Gus Palmer, Gunner, MacDill Air Base' by the Native American photographer Horace Poolaw (1944).

It should be noted that despite the significance of the political corrections in the new histories, they rarely involve critical discussions. Warner, for example, refers to historian Deborah Willis' observation that Van der Zee's photographs of middle class blacks 'often suggest that the postwar mass movement of blacks from the south to take factory jobs in the northern cities was a success' – but she does not make it clear that this suggestion was highly deceptive (Marien, 2002: 297). Neither does her description of Gordon Parks' work for the FSA include the racist reception he received from members of the administration's photographic laboratory. He arrived there under a Julius Rosenwald fellowship, without which he would probably never have been accepted to work for the FSA.[22]

One of the few critical discussions of 'correcting images' is done by Hirsch. While Newhall comments, for instance, that 'to Curtis the Indian, as a nation, was the "vanishing race", whose ancient manners, customs, and traditions should be recorded before they disappeared, and this often led him to pose his subjects....', Hirsch suggests that his work was retrospectively 'criticized for its racist attitudes'. He also refers to the unconsciously patronizing stance in Benjamin-Johnston's photograph of 'Class in American History', in which 'viewers observe the stereotypical Native American warrior as a specimen of the old (bad) picturesque wild west' (Newhall, 1939: 136; Hirsch, 1999: 274-275).

A significant though in some cases problematic outcome of the extensions of Newhall's canon is the discussion of the works of certain photographers under different categories, some of which virtually undermine his dictated boundaries between 'pictorialism', 'straight photography' and 'documentation'. Frances Benjamin Johnston, for instance, who was ignored by Newhall, was a prominent ninetieth-century photographer who turned from pictorialism to photojournalism. Her works appear in chapters on documentary photography in both Rosenblum's and Hirsch's book, while in Warner's they appear in 'Photography in the Modern Era' just before those of pictorialist photographers. The text concerning her career concludes the section on women pictorialists.

Other examples are evident in the classifications of works by two significant figures in Newhall's canon: French photographer Eugene Atget, who created an extensive photographic document of Paris; and Curtis, who was previously mentioned, is famous in his romanticized exoticist gaze on Native Americans. Both were active at the turn of the twentieth-century and during its first decades. Atget's works appear in Newhall as representative of straight photography. In Rosenblum they appear in the 'New Technology' chapter, in a section on 'Instantaneous Photographs of Everyday Life'; in Hirsch's chapter 'The New Culture of Light'; and in Warner among documentary works in the 'New Vision' chapter referred to previously.

Curtis's works are discussed in Newhall's 'The Conquest of Action', which more or less parallels Rosenblum's 'New Technology' chapter (in which Atget's works are discussed). In the latter, Curtis's works are discussed in the chapter on early documentation – 'Documentation: Objects and Events, 1839-1890'. In Hirsch's book, Curtis is also referred to as a documentarian, in a section titled 'Ethnological Approaches' of the chapter 'Social Documents', while in Warner's they appear in the chapter on 'Photography in the Modern Age' in the section on 'Anthropological Pictorialism'.

Conclusion and a remark concerning Newhall

The challenges concerning contemporary histories of photography are answered to varying degrees and in different ways by the new histories written by Rosenblum, Hirsch and Marien. Compared with Newhall's *History of Photography from 1839 to the Present*, the authors of the new books provide broader cultural and social historical contexts and discuss broader aspects of the medium. They are less canonical, less West-oriented, and include images of and by minorities and discriminated-against social groups.

However, none of these authors have re-shuffled the cards. Substantially, their work derives from Newhall's model, and Hirsch's seems to be the most obvious example of this. His history, like Rosenblum's and Marien's, expands Newhall's model and canon, provides a wider historical background and incorporates some original ideas and innovations. For the most part, however, it seems like an updated Newhall.

Rosenblum's and Marien's histories are much more contextual. They both emphasize the background and content of photographs rather than the careers of the photographers, and they both extend the scope of photographic history to non-Western areas. Warner's approach is much more radical. She makes the most extensive revisions to Newhall's narrative, including sophisticated (even if sometimes problematic) references to issues of contemporary critical theories of photography.

A fundamental difficulty encountered by all authors of the new histories is that of formulating a cohesive methodology to account for different approaches and different aspects of photography. The example of 'art' versus 'documentary' (i.e. documentary not initially intended as art) discussed in this article is evidence of this. In Rosenblum's and in Hirsch's books, the social and cultural context in which the FSA

A New Kind of History? The Challenges of Contemporary Histories of Photography   41

photographic project is discussed is disproportionate to that of the Photo-Secession. Furthermore, while Warner sets both topics within a wide cultural-historical framework, her history still bears Newhall's imprint, particularly regarding the inconsistent canonization of some photographers. Discussions of the works of 'documentary' photographers in sections on art photography, and on 'artistic' photography in chapters on documentary photography, are symptoms of this difficulty. However, it is not only the limitations of Newhall's model that have given rise to these structural and methodological problems. They are also largely inherent to any historiography or theory of photography, as Barthes suggested in *Camera Lucida*:

> From the first step, that of classification (we must surely classify, verify by samples, if we want to constitute a corpus), photography evades us. The various distributions we impose upon it are in fact either empirical (Professionals / Amateurs), or rhetorical (Landscapes / Objects / Portraits / Nudes), or else aesthetic (realism / pictorialism), in any case external to the object, without relation to its essence ... We might say that photography is unclassifiable. (Barthes, 1981: 5).

It is worth noting, however, that while all the new authors indirectly react to Newhall's classic, their explicit references to it and to him are surprisingly minimal. Rosenblum and Hirsch at least refer to his book as 'the best-known general history that has appeared in the twentieth-century' and as the text that 'defined the modernist approach' to photography. Conversely, Warner uses Newhall's name in two marginal contexts only (Rosenblum, 1984: 9; Hirsch, 1999: 344; Marien, 2002: 298-9; 391).[23] This is disturbing because all three histories – though innovative in many ways and responsive to most of the criteria summed up by Batchen – are largely founded on Newhall's seminal work.

Post-conclusion: photography as art in the new histories

Batchen ends his proem with the question 'What kind of history do you want?'. The fact that classifying photographic approaches, practices and practitioners, products and expressions is such a complex undertaking, enables recognizing the agenda behind the new histories' attempts to answer Batchen's question. A common denominator among the three texts is evident: all the authors' discussions of photography in the ninetieth-century and the first half of the twentieth-century present a relatively balanced picture of different trends in photography, but the chapters concerning the 1950s and 1960s, and, more radically, the 1970s to the present, are essentially focused on art photography (i.e. photographs for the museum or gallery wall – to use Michael Fried's definition) by photographers whose intention is primarily artistic. In Rosenblum's book almost 85% and in Hirsch's almost 100% of the post-1970 images can be classified as art. Warner's final chapter 'Convergences: 1975-Present' comprises more than 90% art.[24]

Has photographic expression since the 1970s been essentially artistic? The answer is a categorical 'No'. There are many photographic expressions in contemporary culture that are not art. Photojournalism, advertisement and fashion photography, digital news photographs (sometimes by executors or victims of an event) and the proliferation of amateur photography on the web are some examples.[25] Newhall's history was attacked as an 'art history of photography' (Gasser, 1992: 57). Examination of Rosenblum's and Hirsch's books indicates that even though they offer a wider historical context than Newhall, they had a singular problem in removing their classifications from his traditional categorization. Moreover, although Warner's approach appears to be the most self-aware and compound alternative to this approach, when it comes to contemporary photography she also seems to be rather ambivalent regarding the 'divorce' from Newhall's prototype and from 'categories previously constituted by art and its history', to cite Rosalind Krauss (Krauss, 1986: 150). This is not an illegitimate tendency, but it is an undeclared one, that makes these books' structures and methodologies incoherent and misleading.

Original source and licence

Journal of Art Historiography (Number 3 December 2010): 1-19. © Ya'ara Gil Glazer. Permission to republish granted.

References

Barthes, R. (1981) *Camera Lucida: Reflections on Photography.* New York: Hill and Wang.

Batchen, G. (2002) 'Proem', *Afterimage*, vol. 29, 6 (May/June).

Bertrand, A. (1997) 'Beaumont Newhall's "Photography 1839-1937" – Making History', *History of Photography*, vol. 21: 2 (Summer).

Bezencenet, S. (1982) 'What is a History of Photography?', *Creative Camera*, vol. 208 (April 1982).

Chiarenza, C. (1979) 'Notes Toward an Integrated History of Picturemaking', *Afterimage* (Summer).

Cooney, T. A. (1995) *Balancing Acts: American Thought and Culture in the 1930s.* New York: Twayne Publishers.

Denning, M. (1996) *The Cultural Front.* New York: Verso Press.

Fleischhauer, C. & Brannan, B. W. (eds) (1988) *Documenting America, 1935-1943.* Berkeley: University of California Press.

Fontcuberta, J. (ed.) (2003) *Photography: Crisis of History.* Barcelona: Actar.

Gasser, M. (1992) 'Histories of Photography 1839-1939', *History of Photography*, vol. 16 (Spring): 50-60.

Grundberg, A. (1983) 'Two Camps Battle over the Nature of the Medium', *The New-York Times*, August 14, http://www.nytimes.com/1983/08/14/arts/photography-view-two-camps-battle-over-the-nature-of-the-medium.html .

Hirsch, R. (1999) *Seizing the Light: A History of Photography.* New York: McGraw-Hill Higher Education. (Second edition's title has been changed to *Seizing the Light: A Social History of Photography*).

Hugunin, J. R. (1990/1991) 'A Critical Contest' (a revision on an essay originally published in *Views*, Fall 1990 / Winter 1991.)

Hurley, F. J. (1972) *Portrait of a Decade: Roy Stryker and the Development of Documentary Photography in the Thirties.* Baton Rouge: Louisiana State University Press.

Hurley, J. F. (1993) 'The Farm Security Administration File: In and Out of Context', *History of Photography* 17.3 (Autumn): 244-252.

Krauss, R. (1986) 'Photography's Discursive Spaces', in *The Originality of the Avant-garde and Other Modernist Myths.* Cambridge, MA: MIT Press.

Krauss, R. & Michelson, A. (1978) Photography: A Special Issue. *October*, vol. 5, (Summer).

McCauley, A. (1997) 'Writing Photography's History before Newhall', *History of Photography*, vol. 21: 2 (Summer): 87-101.

Natanson, N. (1992) *The Black Image in the New Deal*. Knoxville: University of Tennessee Press.

Newhall, B. (1982) *The History of Photography from 1839 to the Present Day*. New York: The Museum of Modern Art. (First published 1939.)

Nickel, D. R. (2001) 'History of Photography: the State of Research', *The Art Bulletin*, 83: 3 (September).

Phillips, C. (1992) 'The Judgment Seat of Photography', in *The Contest of Meaning: Critical Histories of Photography* (ed.), R. Bolton. Cambridge MA: MIT Press.

Rodriguez, J. (1994) 'History Man', *British Journal of Photography*, vol. 141 (January).

Rosenblum, N. (1984) *A World History of Photography*. New York: Abbeville Press.

Stryker, R. & Wood, N. (1973) *In this Proud Land*. Greenwich: New York Graphic Society.

Warner Marien, M. (1986) 'What Shall We Tell the Children? Photography and its Text (Books)', *Afterimage* vol. 13 (April).

Warner Marien, M. (1995) 'Photography is Another Kind of Bird', *Afterimage*, vol. 23 (September/October).

Warner Marien, M. (2002) *Photography: A Cultural History*. New York: Harry N. Abrams Publishers.

Wells, L. (2000) *Photography: A Critical Introduction*. London: Routledge.

Notes

1. The book was first titled *Photography: A Short Critical History*.
2. For a detailed survey of the history of photography before Newhall see McCauley, 1997 and Gasser, 1992.
3. Chiarenza's article was published in the summer issue of *Afterimage*, 1979.

A New Kind of History? The Challenges of Contemporary Histories of Photography   45

4   Among these writers he mentions Rosalind Krauss, Allan Sekula, Sally Stein, Victor Burgin, Christopher Phillips and John Tagg. While their work was largely in reaction to the medium's 'apotheosis as a museum object', Nickel defines it as a 'negative, iconoclastic critique' by authors who 'neglected to counter its negative critique adequately with any positive program of study or foundational theory of their own, or even attempt to define for the field coherent limits and scope' (Nickel, 2001: 555).

5   Rosenblum, 1984; Hirsch, 1999; Marien, 2002. All three books appear in Amazon and Barnes and Nobles websites as the bestselling comprehensive academic history of photography books (keywords: 'history of photography'; sort by: best selling.) In Amazon they appear after Newhall's fifth edition (1982; latest print: 2010), while in Barnes and Noble Newhall's book is the least popular among the four. The order of popularity is, in Amazon: Hirsch's, Rosenblum's, Marien's; in Barnes and Noble: Rosenblum's, Hirsch's, Marien's. Non-English-language history of photography books such as *A History of Photography* (Jean Claude Lemagny and Andre Rouille, New York: Cambridge University Press) and *A New History of Photography* (Michele Frizot, Koln: Konemann) have been published in only one edition in English, in 1987 and 1998 respectively.

6   Marien herself was one of those who pointed to a need for a new history of photography, in two articles from 1986 and 1995.

7   Newhall's 1982 edition (latest reprint: 2010) is the latest and most up-to-date. Its publication date is the closest to the new histories' publication dates, and therefore it was chosen to be compared with them.

8   Rosenblum, Hirsch and Marien mention photographers and groups of photographers in the US, in Northern and Eastern Europe, among them Jacob Riis, Lewis Hine, Berenice Abbott, the 'New York photo league', Bill Brandt, Humphrey Spender, Helmar Lerski, August Sander, and Roman Vishniac. Rosenblum also gives some instances of Japanese documentary photographers such as Kuwabara Kineo and Horino Masao. Hirsch gives some instances of biased photographic documentations of Native Americans. Marien also presents photojournalism from 1939-1945 war in this chapter, while the other authors present such images in a chapter on photojournalism.

9   Denning defines 'documentary aesthetic' as a 'central modernist innovation' (Denning, 1996: 118).

10 For an extended critical discussion of this issue, see Hurley, 1993.

11 This distinction in which Hartmann described the painterly branch of the movement as demises, served Newhall's interest. It is actually cited by the latter, who also saw the first branch as opposed to the nature of photography.

46 Ya'ara Gil Glazer

However, as noted by Alison Bertrand, some photographs noted by Newhall as 'straight' were actually 'pictorially' manipulated. See Bertrand, 1997: 341.

12 After Lange, Newhall discusses Ben Shahn, while Marien discusses Arthur Rothstein.

13 Beverly W. Brannan and Carl Fleischhauer also comment that since FSA photographs were 'rediscovered' in the 1960s and 1970s, 'the books in which [they] appeared usually identified them only by the name of the artist and a brief title... one image to a page, each one framed in white ...' They conclude that 'both the passage of time and this style of publication have isolated the photographs, obscuring the circumstances of their creation'. See Fleischhauer and Brannan, 1988: 7. 14   In fact, the only photographic experiments that can be entitled 'cubist' are Alvin Langdon Coburn's experimental 'Vortographs', which are fundamentally different from Stieglitz's work.

15 Sekula is mentioned by Marien in another context, in a section on contemporary theory of photography titled 'Thinking photography' in the final chapter of the book (423).

16 This prevailing title of the photograph was actually coined by Newhall in his history. The original title given to it by Lange was *Destitute pea pickers in California. Mother of seven children. Age thirty-two. Nipomo, California. 1936* (Library of Congress, LC-USF34-009058-C).

17 However, the latter, who also comments that this image overshadowed Lange's other important works, offers no single visual or verbal example of these important works, unlike the other new authors.

18 The instance given by Warner is a clipping from *Midweek pictorial* 17 Oct 1936: 23. Library of Congress LC-USZ62-117092. http://www.loc.gov/pictures/item/96518456/.

19 In fact, the FSA image that is perhaps the second most renowned parent-and-children image is Rothstein's photograph of a father and his children fleeing a dust storm. *Farmer and sons walking in the face of a dust storm. Cimarron County, Oklahoma, 1936* (LC-USF34- 004052): http://www.loc.gov/pictures/collection/fsa/item/fsa1998018983/PP/.

20 For further reading on poor agricultural workers as representing 'citizens of the kind who built America' see Cooney, 1995: 187.

21 Of the three authors, Rosenblum presents the most examples of women photographers. In 1994 she published *A History of Women Photographers* (Abbeville Press).

A New Kind of History? The Challenges of Contemporary Histories of Photography   47

22   Nicolas Natanson cites photographer Esther Bubley's description of the hostility Parks had suffered from members of the technical team of the FSA photography laboratory. See Natanson, 1992: 62.

23   Warner's case is maybe the most surprising since already in 1986 she published a comprehensive article on Newhall's history ('What Shall We Tell the Children?').

24   These images appear in Rosenblum's chapters 11 and 12: 'Photography since 1950: The straight image' and 'Photography since 1950: Manipulations and color', in Hirsch's chapters 16, 17 and 18: 'New frontiers: Expanding boundaries', 'Changing realities' and 'Thinking about photography', and in Warner's chapters 6 and 7: 'Through the lens of culture (1945-1975)' and 'Convergences (1975-present)'. In Newhall's 1982 edition there are four images dated 1970 and later. They are all art. The other images in the final chapter, titled 'New Directions', are also art photographs.

25   It is worth mentioning in this regard Carl Chiarenza's words from 1979 on Aaron Scharf's book *Art and Photography* (1968): 'as Scharf approached the last chapter of his book photography seemed to emerge slowly as art rather than as the something other that it was at the beginning of the book' (Chiarenza, 1979: 37).

CHAPTER 2

Painting with Light: Beyond the Limits of the Photograph

Melissa Miles

For the Polish-born artist, Josef Stanislaus Ostoja-Kotkowski, the colour and dynamism of light was a long-term fascination. After migrating to Australia in 1949, Ostoja-Kotkowski was captivated by the many possibilities of light and sought to represent them in various aspects of his practice. Ostoja-Kotkowski is perhaps best known for his electronic art, but he also worked in theatre design, filmmaking, painting, photography, kinetic sculpture and laser art. In pursuit of the fugitive qualities of light, Ostoja-Kotkowski crossed the boundaries of diverse mediums.

The vibrant, dazzling light that Ostoja-Kotkowski experienced while working at the Leigh Creek Coalfields and as a house painter in Central Australia during the mid-1950s captured his imagination, and he often spoke of his frustration that traditional artistic media could not fully convey the sensation that he recalled:

> The terrific iridescence you can get behind the eyes in Central Australia forces you to think of the source of light – whether it's beam, lantern or sun – and to think of it as the most impressive, most flexible and richest tool imaginable for an artist, the life-giving source. You come across phenomena which seem to wipe everything else off – something like the auroroa... Why couldn't a painting change its shape, form and color?... It seemed to me that you could achieve this by using light as a tool and that the closest thing to the source of light we know and can handle confidently is electronics. (Thomas, 1976: 183-4)

Among Ostoja-Kotkowski's various efforts to use electronics to represent the fluidity of light was a fascinating technique that he developed in the late 1950s. Using an old television set with a picture that was specially modified, Ostoja-Kotkowski made a series of luminous abstract photographs. Described by Ostoja-Kotkowski as 'electronic paintings', these works have remained largely neglected in histories of Australian art and photography and were panned by contemporary art critics. However, as they raise a series of compelling issues about the limits of artistic agency and medium specificity that anticipated many of the concerns of the current 'post-medium' age, it is timely that Ostoja-Kotkowski's 'Electronic Paintings' be reconsidered.

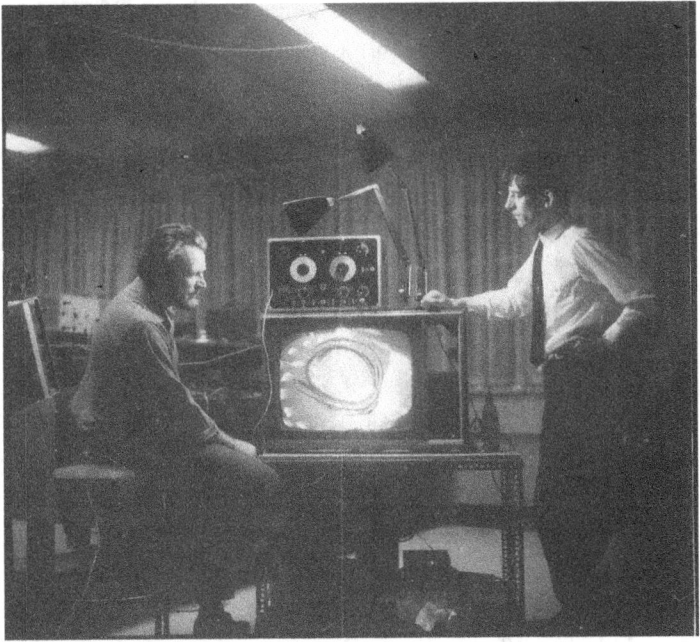

Figure 2.1. J. S. Ostoja-Kotkowski at Hendon, South Australia. SLSA: PRG919/4/130.

The process of making Ostoja-Kotkowski's electronic paintings was complex. He began experimenting with an old television set during the late 1950s, and soon found that he could produce abstract forms and patterns by introducing extra contrast and throwing the picture out of alignment and synchronisation (figure 2.1). With the assistance of Dr Angus Nicholson, the electronics engineer Malcolm Kay and the Philips Electronic Workshops at the Australian Research Laboratories at Hendon, South Australia, Ostoja-Kotkowski refined this process. The normal synchronising circuit of the cathode ray gun was disconnected from the television and a specially developed control panel helped to guide the random patterns that appeared on the screen (Ostoja-Kotkowski, 1968: 5). These patterns, which could be derived from either broadcast television programs or from square wave and sine wave generators, were manipulated by magnetic fields. Ostoja-Kotkowski explains this technical process as follows:

> A permanent magnet, or more conveniently a DC electromagnet can be used to bend parts of the picture while an AC electromagnet supplied with a current at picture repetition frequency (frame frequency) can be used to form swirls and folds, the nature of the shape depending on the phase angle between the magnetic field and the picture repetition frequency. (1964)

Rather than being a screen for viewing images, the television was accordingly transformed into a source of light for creating abstract patterns, which were captured with the use of a camera. The resultant 'Electronic Paintings' were the product of both chance and the artist's skill in manipulating the random components that form the patterns. Ostoja-Kotkowski's ultimate goal was to develop a computer for electronic painting in which this manual operation would become redundant and the artist's mental image would be transformed into an electronic painting 'through the direct linking of thought-waves with the technical unit' (Ostoja-Kotkowski, PRG919/4/1) (figure 2.2).

Although that second stage of the project was not realised, Ostoja-Kotkowski's experiments at Hendon enabled him to use the television as a controlled light source with which to create a range of expressionistic, abstract photographs. The glowing, swirling forms suggest rays of light radiating from a hidden source and fracturing through prisms. A total of 120 of these photographs were made at this time, and 44 were selected for Ostoja-Kotkowski's solo exhibition at the Argus Gallery in Melbourne in June 1964.

Ostoja-Kotkowski's photographs were enlarged up to 30 x 30 inches for this exhibition, and printed in black-and-white (figures 2.3 and 2.4). The choice of black-and-white printing, the exhibition catalogue reveals, was based on financial considerations rather than aesthetic ones (Ostoja-Kotkowski, 1964). Ostoja-Kotkowski (1975) later experimented with colour television images projected on a large screen while working at the Marconi Experimental Laboratories in Chelmsford, England, but his 'Electronic Paintings' shown at the Argus Gallery were to remain limited to the tonal possibilities of black-and-white photography due to the cost of colour printing at that time.

Ostoja-Kotkowski (1968: 5) was nonetheless careful not to refer to these works as photographs, and instead described them as 'electronic paintings' made with a brush of light and a television screen as a canvas. Comparable conceptions of photography as painting or drawing with light are as old as the medium itself, and famously found form in Julia Margaret Cameron's photograph, *Cupid's Pencil of Light* (1870), and Oskar Rejlander's *Infant Photography* (1856), which both feature an infant, photography, drawing or painting with light. Diverging somewhat from these earlier notions of photography as painting with light, Ostoja-Kotkowski maintained that his own electronic painting occurred not with the camera but with the electronic means of the television set – the camera was merely a transparent recording device with which to fix the moving electronic image.

Despite Ostoja-Kotkowski's insistence upon referring to these black-and-white photographs as electronic paintings rather than photographs, their material connection to photography was difficult to deny. The celebrated modernist photographer Wolfgang Sievers did much of Ostoja-Kotkowski's printing in his Collins Street photography studio in Melbourne. A letter from Sievers to Ostoja-Kotkowski, dated 23 May 1964, or four weeks prior to Ostoja-Kotkowski's Argus exhibition, suggests that it is likely that Sievers printed Ostoja-Kotkowski's 'Electronic Paintings'. The modes of printing discussed in the letter and the subsequent installation of the 'Electronic Paintings' at the Argus Gallery indicate that Ostoja-Kotkowski was struggling to overcome the material limits of photography. Sievers's letter refers to mounting prints on pine board

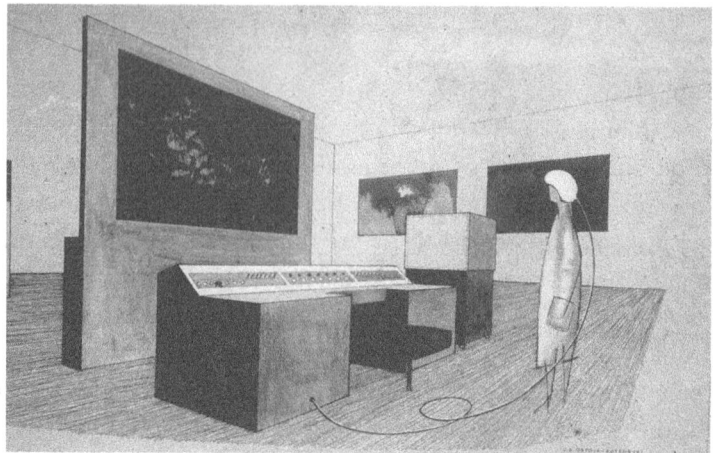

Figure 2.2. J. S. Ostoja-Kotkowski. *Sketches for EP Development*, c. 1963. SLSA: PRG919/47/205.

and the use of a variety of printing papers, including Argenta Photolinen, which had the effect of mimicking the appearance of paintings. The framing and installation of the photographs also deviated from contemporary conventions in photography framing. Some of these photographs were installed in the gallery at a diagonal, some were mounted on board without a frame, and others were framed to resemble paintings with a surrounding mount, timber frame and no glass. With titles such as *Trance, Nymphex, Mantissa* and *Mask*, Ostoja-Kotkowski's 'Electronic Paintings' were further wrested from the referential domain of photography and placed in a more evocative, other-worldly context of illusion and abstraction. However, despite all of his efforts, Ostoja-Kotkowski later reflected with frustration that 'no matter how I exhibited these results, they were going to be called photography and I wanted to know how to make a painting' (Thomas, 1976: 184).

Ostoja-Kotkowski was trained as a painter and commented after embracing electronic media that he had not changed his ideas about painting, just updated his tools: 'The idea of electronic images is a step towards developing a means of electronic painting which sooner or later will come to be practised as much as the orthodox portrayal of an idea on canvas or board by means of pigments, wax, oil, p.v.a., etc.' (1964). Arguing that painters are behind the times in 'fiddling with paint and brushes', he insisted that art should reflect the technological developments of the day.

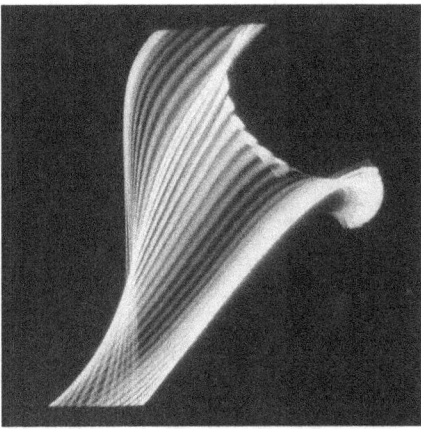

Figure 2.3. J. S. Ostoja-Kotkowski, *Electronic Painting*, 1965. SLSA: PRG919/4/350.

Ostoja-Kotkowski's preference for the term 'electronic painting' over photograph must not be seen as a desire to distance himself from photography in general. Ostoja-Kotkowski was a very active and highly

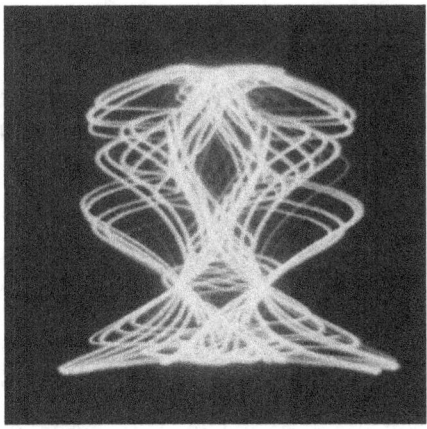

Figure 2.4. J. S. Ostoja-Kotkowski. *Electronic Painting*, 1965. SLSA: PRG919/4/341.

respected member of Australian and international photography communities. As well as receiving awards from the Australian Photographic Society, publishing regularly in photography journals and presenting lectures at national photography conventions, Ostoja-Kotkowski was given the honour of being named 'Excellence FIAP (EFIAP)' of the *Fédération Internationale De L'Art Photographique* in Berne, Switzerland in 1967 for his contributions to photography. Ostoja-Kotkowski may have embraced photography in other aspects of his practice, but he continually stressed that his electronic paintings were paintings and not photographs.

Yet critics of the Argus Gallery exhibition were unwilling to follow Ostoja-Kotkowski's lead and embrace these works as a new form of painting with light and electronics. The artist often bitterly described how Melbourne critics considered the show worthless and a waste of time and money. He regularly argued that these critics were behind the times and lacked vision: 'Everything with them has to be traditional. Unless you sit down with an easel, a paint brush and oils, to them it is not art. They cannot understand that in this age we have to branch out into new methods. To paint this world of space, surely we have to use electronics' (Batman, 1965: 23). In an interview with Robert Scarfe in 1971, Ostoja-Kotkowski reflects on this dismissive reception as a major setback in his career:

> That was my first exhibition and I didn't sell a single exhibit, and it was a tremendous financial blow to me, and it took a good two to three years to recover from it. That was just thanks to someone who doesn't know enough about it. There was only one critic who helped me in Melbourne – the rest were just against it, and this is very bad. (Scarfe, 1971: 9)

An analysis of the reviews of Ostoja-Kotkowski's 1964 Argus Gallery exhibition suggests that critics had trouble approaching the work because it challenged prevailing assumptions about the limits of the medium. The renowned Melbourne art critic, Bernard Smith (1964: 5), asserted that Ostoja-Kotkowski's 'Electronic Paintings' were 'not painting' and described them ambivalently as 'moving patterns of light of an impersonal clinical beauty'. Alan McCulloch (1964) of the *Herald* similarly wrote that it is a 'ghastly prospect' that electronic images could be considered a substitute for painting, but conceded that the experiments were technologically worthwhile. While McCulloch asserted that Ostoja-Kotkowski's 'Electronic Paintings' were not paintings, he also argued that they were not photographs: 'The images look like black and white photographs of the abstract constructions of the Russians, Gabo and Pevsner. They are not however. Photography plays a part, but the images are made electronically' (1964: 23). Australian photography historians, who have consistently excluded Ostoja-Kotkowski's work from narratives of Australian photography, also seem to have accepted this argument that Ostoja-Kotkowski's works are not photographs. Neither paintings nor conventional photographs, these works have slipped between the gaps of both media and history.

Adrian Rawlins (1965: 42) provides a clue to the absence of Ostoja-Kotkowski's work from the history of Australian photography when he argues that although his electronic paintings look like photographs and are produced through photographic processes, they are ultimately not photographs because they reveal no tangible connection to 'things'. 'It isn't a photograph', writes Rawlins, 'because it is not *of* anything'. Rawlins (1965: 43) likens Ostoja-Kotkowski's works to Man Ray's rayographs, but ultimately differentiates them because of 'the organic nature of Ostoja-Kotkowski's motifs'. Whereas the referent is clearly visible in many of Man Ray's rayographs, Ostoja-Kotkowski's electronic paintings 'give no hint of their means of production'.

This connection between photography, its means of production and its object was integral to notions of medium specificity during the mid-twentieth century, which delimited the critical reception of Ostoja-Kotkowski's work. Despite the 'essentialist connotations' (Doane, 2007: 129) of the term, medium specificity must be understood as a historically explicit idea that changes over time. During the mid-twentieth century, medium specificity was closely bound to the formalist modernism espoused by critics such as Clement Greenberg and Beaumont Newhall, and placed emphasis on the material or technical means of creative expression. To Greenberg (1966), abstract expressionist painting represented the ultimate exemplar of modernist painting because, rather than claiming to offer a three-dimensional view of the world, it limited painting to the core qualities of paint applied to a two-dimensional plane.

Newhall's concerns for photography's unique characteristics were linked to the promotion of straight, un-manipulated photography. In the 1949 edition of his book, *The History of Photography,* Newhall is critical of photographic abstraction and questions whether the more abstract works of László Moholy-Nagy and Man Ray can be seen as photographs at all:

> The vision which led to these applications of the photographic technique is quite separate from the vision of those who seek to interpret with the camera the world of nature and man. Viewing these photograms and solarized prints and distorted negatives, we are constantly reminded not of photographs, but of paintings. (1949: 211)

Although Newhall gave a more thorough account of Moholy-Nagy and Man Ray's photographic abstractions in the revised and enlarged 1964 edition of this book, his initial concerns point to the way in which abstract photographs unsettle assumptions about the very definitions of photography. Implicit in Newhall's identification of abstract photographs with painting is a desire to bolster the status of photographs as unmediated images of the 'real' world.

Although Newhall later modified his approach to abstract photography, comparable notions of medium specificity persisted in the writings of John Szarkowski, the influential photography curator at the Museum of Modern Art in New York. Published in 1966, two years after Ostoja-Kotkowski's first exhibition of 'Electronic Paintings', Szarkowski's book *The Photographer's Eye* reiterated some of Newhall's thinking and sought to define photography's specificity with reference to ideas of composition, authorship, influence and originality. According to Szarkowski (Petruck, 1979: 206), the diverse photographs collected in his book share the common vocabulary of this independent medium: 'these pictures are unmistakably photographs. The vision they share belongs to no school or aesthetic theory, but to *photography itself* [emphasis added]'. Such notions of medium specificity problematically leave no room for works such as Ostoja-Kotkowski's 'Electronic Paintings', which were accordingly received in negative terms as 'not photographs' or 'not painting'.

The assumption that photographs must be 'of' something is underpinned by the belief that light's primary function in photography is to reveal and fix presence. Light is shed on an object from a place beyond its material and discursive limits, and then acts as a bridge connecting the object and the photosensitive emulsion. As a kind of fugitive printmaker, light inscribes the image into the photosensitive surface while ultimately having no visible presence in itself. It is pertinent that Ostoja-Kotkowski employs these same, fugitive qualities of light to exceed the limits of the medium. If medium specificity speaks consciously to the constraints and possibilities of a given medium, as Mary Ann Doane (2007: 131) argues, then Ostoja-Kotkowski's desire to embrace the immateriality of light through electronics marks an attempt to transcend these constraints. Ostoja-Kotkowski uses light to exceed the boundaries of his practice's material support, whether it be painting's brushes and paints, or photography's indexical connection to its object. However, light's ultimate transparency and its dependence on other objects and materials to be made visible ensured that Ostoja-Kotkowski's success in this endeavour was to remain provisional.

Ostoja-Kotkowski was not alone in his interest in light's transgressive possibilities for art. His exhibition of 'Electronic Paintings' coincided with the production and exhibition of other light-, colour- and technology-focused practices that similarly challenged notions of medium specificity. Frank Hinder's *Luminal Kinetics* were made in 1967–8, and Ludwig Hirshfeld-Mack's *Colour-Light Plays*, originally produced at the Bauhaus during the 1920s, were reconstructed for presentation in Australia in 1964. Although these works suggest that there was a wider interest in extending the possibilities of the medium through an engagement with colour and light, like Ostoja-Kotkowski, Hinder complained about the reception of his work. State galleries may have collected his luminal kinetics, but Hinder regrets that the work was not displayed because it was considered 'too much trouble' (McNamara, 2008: 13).

To many of his critics, Ostoja-Kotkowski's use of light and electronics to cross the boundaries between media resulted in a loss of the artist's presence, his emotion or 'the soul' in his art. Neil Jillett takes a humorous approach to this issue when he comments in *The Age* that 'The works to be exhibited by Mr. Ostoja-Kotkowski at the Argus Gallery are so electronically avant garde that we can expect some of Melbourne's best-known computers at the opening sherry party on Monday night' (1964). The implication that Ostoja-Kotkowski's electronic work speaks to machines more effectively than to humans recalls some of the anxieties surrounding photography when it first emerged in the nineteenth century. Marcus Aurelius Root's denigration of amateur photography as 'mere *mechanism*' during the mid-nineteenth century can be understood as a reaction against the conception of photography as 'light-writing' and 'sun-painting'. These photographic metaphors effectively subordinate the role of the photographer as a creative agent to the productive and generative qualities of light, and position the photographer as a mere operator of a mechanical device – the camera (Green-Lewsis, 1996: 37–64; Edwards, 2002: 113–8). Similarly, to many of Ostoja-Kotkowski's critics the use of machines and the apparent absence of signs of the artist's touch in the finished work, meant that artwork produced with electronics emphasised the mechanical over distinctly human characteristics like a soul and emotion.

Writing in *Meanjin* in 1966, Earle Hackett (1966: 494–5) comments on the lack of emotion in Ostoja-Kotkowski's 'Electronic Paintings', noting that there was no place 'for sudden irrational gestures with their overtones of emotion.' Elwyn Lynn (1966: 16) likewise complained that 'one feels (if feeling comes into it) only retinally, not emotionally involved'. The painter, James Gleason (1966: 78), is scathing in his review of one of Ostoja-Kotkowski's op-art exhibitions presented two years after the Argus exhibition: 'These works are as perfectly finished and as immaculate as things tooled by machinery instead of being shaped by fallible human muscle and tendon. Instead of emotion, there is clinical exactitude'. Speaking more generally about Ostoja-Kotkowski's work as op art, Gleason writes:

> It is entirely sexless and as morally aseptic as a theorem… I have no doubt that some of the discoveries of Op-art could be used as a subtle form of torture. In the hands of an inventive artist-inquisitor it could become a cruel weapon. A word like beauty has no meaning in this context. Here we have art being used like a drug to produce certain physical effects. (1966: 78)

Ostoja-Kotkowski was very conscious of these concerns about emotion in electronics. In personal notes for a lecture, dated September 1963, he describes his initial worries about electronic painting: 'The similarity [to painting] is obviously there, but I felt that the mechanical implications were too strong to allow to express the human feelings necessary to make a photograph a work of art' (PRG919/1/35). In an article written several years later, titled 'Prometheus unbound', Ostoja-Kotkowski reveals how he came to grips with this apparent absence of human feeling in electronic art. After referring to one of his critics, Ostoja-Kotkowski (1978: 6) writes: 'Giving light a form is basically no different from giving paint a form, or piano a sound form – it depends entirely on the artist, his ability, his quality to handle the brush, the keyboard, or whatever medium he has to express his SOUL'. Ultimately, to Ostoja-Kotkowski, the adoption of electronic painting did not amount to the mechanisation of creative, artistic processes. Electronic painting relied upon training similar to that required for traditional painting, and he commented that only artists were capable of painting electronically. In 'The medium is not the message' Ostoja-Kotkowski (1971: 24) remarked upon the need to shift focus away from the medium and towards the work's meaning: 'It is always the final statement of an artist that is important – not the tools he used to realise his idea'.

Although Ostoja-Kotkowski seeks to challenge the limits of medium specificity, in a formalist sense, his work may be better understood in light of Raymond Williams's more inclusive interpretation of medium specificity. Published in Williams's 1977 book *Marxism and Literature*, this approach to the medium places more emphasis upon the social and cultural context in which media are practised than on their distinct materials and technologies. Understanding Ostoja-Kotkowski's work as contextually embedded shifts the focus of his electronic paintings towards the ways in which his technologies speak to the social and cultural language of their day. Adrian Rawlins alludes to the importance of taking a broader contextual approach in his own account of 'Electronic Paintings', written in 1965:

> Ostoja-Kotkowski does not seek to smear art with science... but to free the imagination from the impediment of means. [His electronic drawings] give no hint of their means of production. But their very form, because of its means of production, is perfectly attuned to the space age... By moving into a polychromatic world parallel to the polychromatic world of movies and industrial design, Stanislaus Ostoja-Kotkowski begins to explore a new synthesis of art and technology which is perfectly in tune with today – and tomorrow. (Quoted in Jones, 2008: 207)

It is not simply the material conditions of a work or its technical means of production that constitute the media of photography, painting and electronic art. Following Williams, these media can be considered the product of a convergence of materials, conventions and ideas that are brought together for different purposes. Using light, the most elusive of substances, as his medium *and* his subject, Ostoja-Kotkowski draws on the technologies available to him to underscore what photography might have in common with painting, or even sound and set design, and to show how those commonalities might lead to new ways of overcoming the limitations of mediums.

The notion that we live today in a 'post-medium' era, popularised by Rosalind Krauss (2000: 56), among others, belies the ways in which an earlier generation of artists sought to create what Krauss refers to as a 'different specificity' for art. In Ostoja-Kotkowski's practice, this specificity was not bound by materials or processes, but was evident in his approach to art itself as an expression of individual experience and subjectivity. Ostoja-Kotkowski has much in common with Krauss's more recent promotion of a different specificity, which purports that the most successful post-medium art reflects its own practice in relation to the past, and acknowledges the medium specific practices that are being replaced, modified or combined in a self-conscious exploration of the very idea of art. Ostoja-Kotkowski's practice similarly remained self-aware, as his various lectures and publications attest, while being grounded consistently in a larger desire to expand the possibilities of art production and reception.

Ostoja-Kotkowski was never afraid to write an angry letter in response to a bad review and was fond of reminding people that he had the last laugh. Despite the disastrous critical reception of his 'Electronic Paintings' at the 1964 Argus exhibition, a month after the exhibition closed he was commissioned to make a film based on the principles of electronic painting. The film later won an Australian Film Institute silver award at the Melbourne Film Festival. 'The fact that many people failed to recognise my work set me back financially, and the panning I received from the critics was frustrating', he said in 1968. 'But I know sooner or later this form of art will become commonplace, and the critics will have to accept it' (Day, 1966). Traversing the ground between photography, painting and electronic image-making, Ostoja-Kotkowski's cross-disciplinary works of light are imbued with a tension that can tell us much about the ways in which expectations of the medium historically promoted certain possibilities for meaning while delimiting others. However, most importantly, an analysis of these works and their modes of reception reveals how such limits can be overcome to generate much dynamic and inclusive approaches to the role of the medium in art and art history.

Original source and licence

This paper was presented at the Impact 7 conference, Monash University, 20-27.09.2011. See Melissa Miles, 'Painting with Light: Josef Stanislaus Ostoja-Kotkowski and the Limits of the Photographic Print', in Luke Morgan (ed.), *Intersections and Counterpoints: Proceedings of Impact 7*, an International Multi-Disciplinary Printmaking Conference, Clayton: Monash University Publishing, 2012. © Melissa Miles. Permission to republish granted.

References

Batman (1965) 'A Mural for 100 years', *The Bulletin*: 23.

Day, M. (1966) 'Op Art Comes to Melbourne', *Kalori Art Magazine* (February): 6-9.

Doane, M. A. (2007) 'The Indexical and the Concept of Medium Specificity', *Differences: A Journal of Feminist Cultural Studies* 18 (1): 128–152.

Edwards, S. (2002) 'The Dialectics of Skill in Talbot's Dream World', *History of Photography* 26 (2): 113–118.

Gleason, J. (1966) 'The Clinical Artist-Scientist', *Sun-Herald* (September 25): 78.

Green-Lewis, J. (1996) *Framing the Victorians: Photography and the Culture of Realism*. Ithaca and London: Cornell University Press.

Greenberg, C. (1966) 'Modernist Painting', in *New Art: A Critical Anthology* (ed.), G. Battack. New York: Dutton.

Hackett, E. (1966) 'Electronic Painting: The "Images" of Ostoja-Kotkowski', *Meanjin Quarterly* 25 (4): 494–5.

Jillett, N. (1964) 'Search for Musicians'. *The Age* (June 27).

Jones, S. (2008) 'Animating Geometry: Drawing with Light', in *Modern Times: The untold story of modernism in Australia* (eds), A. Stephen, A. McNamara. Carlton: The Miegunyah Press in association with Powerhouse Publishing.

Krauss, R. (2000) *A Voyage on the North Sea: Art in the Age of the Post-medium Condition*. London: Thames & Hudson.

Lynn, E. (1966) 'Beholder's Eye', *The Bulletin*: 16.

McCulloch, A. (1964) 'Electronics... and Painting', *Herald* (July 1): 23.

McNamara, A. (2008) 'The Bauhaus in Australia: Interdisciplinary Confluences in Modernist Practice', in *Modern Times: The Story of Modernism in Australia* (eds), A. Stephen, P. Goad, A. McNamara. Carlton: The Miegunyah Press in association with Powerhouse Publishing.

Newhall, B. (1949) *The History of Photography from 1839 to the Present Day*. New York: Museum of Modern Art.

Ostoja-Kotkowski, J. S. (1964) *Electronic Paintings*. Melbourne: Argus Gallery.

Ostoja-Kotkowski, J. S. (1968) 'Art and Technology', *ASEA Bulletin* 3 (4): 5–7.

Ostoja-Kotkowski, J. S. (1971) 'The Medium is not the Message', *Hemisphere* 15 (12): 18–24.

Ostoja-Kotkowski, J. S. (1975) 'Audio-kinetic Art with Laser Beams and Electronic Systems', *Leonardo* 8 (2): 142–144.

Ostoja-Kotkowski, J. S. (1978), 'Prometheus Unbound', *Tabs* 36 (3): 3–6.

Rawlins, A. (1965) 'Beyond Painting', *Announcer*: 42-3.

Scarfe, R. (1971) 'Kotkowski', *The Griffin* (March 10): 8-9.

Smith, B. (1964) 'Display emphasises drawing's value', *The Age* (July 1): 5.

Szarkowski, J. (1979) 'Introduction to the *Photographer's Eye*', in *The Camera Viewed: Writings on Twentieth Century Photography* (ed.), P. Petruck. New York: Dutton.

Thomas, L. (1976) *The Most Noble Art of Them All: The Selected Writings of Laurie Thomas*. Brisbane: University of Queensland Press.

Documents and Manuscripts

Ostoja-Kotkowski J. S. 'Electronic painting', handwritten notes, Ostoja-Kotkowski Archive. State Library of South Australia. Archival number PRG919/47/216.

Ostoja-Kotkowski J. S. Undated personal letter, Ostoja-Kotkowski Kotkowski Archive, State Library of South Australia. 'Album relating to electronic records in the 1960s'. Archival number PRG919/4/1.

Ostoja-Kotkowski, J. S. (1963) Untitled typed lecture with handwritten date. September.

Ostoja-Kotkowski Archive, State Library of South Australia, Archival Number PRG919/1/35.

Ostoja-Kotkowski, J. S. Untitled interview, audio recording, Ostoja-Kotkowski Archive, State Library of South Australia, '1964 interview about electronic music and painting' (16 minutes)'. Archival number PRG919/3/62.

Sadka, D. (1967) 'ABC Sound and Image, ABC Talk – Perth Festival of the Arts', February: 2. Stanislaus Ostoja-Kotkowski Albums, The University of Melbourne, Special Collections.

Sievers, W. (1964) 'Letter to Ostoja-Kotkowski', 23 May. Ostoja-Kotkowski Archive, State Library of South Australia. Archival Number PRG919/1/242.

CHAPTER 3

Why Burn a Photograph?
A Film by Hollis Frampton

Alexander García Düttmann

Why burn a photograph? Why put it on a hotplate and let the paper slowly be consumed by heat? Why allow the image to go up in smoke so that perhaps another image must be printed before I can look at it again? Why engulf a photograph in flames and make it smolder until there is nothing left but a sort of crater in the middle, a temporary parenthesis, a respite, or a pit, for nostalgia? Why start with an image, a one-dimensional surface, and end up with cinders, a protruding grey landscape, a dark sculptural object, or a dirty bulky lump, that crack when touched and dissolve into thin air? Why move from 'contemplative distance' (Moore, 2006: 60) to 'tactile immediacy'?

Burning a photograph is different from tearing it apart. If I tear it apart, no matter how small the bits and pieces that will be left in the end, my disposition is such that to some extent I act blindly. I am so actively involved in what I do that I can hardly witness the photograph disappear. I make it disappear and I see it disappear but I do not witness its disappearing. I am part of the critical mass needed for the act to come about and be performed. The difference between burning and tearing up a photograph is the difference between making something disappear and letting it disappear, between use and mention, between a strange craft and art, between staying at home and having bitter thoughts about a girl who laughed at me outrageously and going to the cinema, or to an art gallery. Of course the letting will always involve some making, if only because the pressurized liquid gas in a lighter needs to be ignited or because the photograph needs to be placed on the hotplate. Conversely, the making will always involve some letting, if only because I can pause as I tear up the photograph and decide whether the bits and pieces are small enough by now or require further downsizing. In the so-called digital age, the closest one tends to come to the physical experience of tearing up a photograph is the dissection of a credit card after its validity has expired, or after it has been used fraudulently by a third, unknown party. One just hopes that the plastic fragments will be as tiny as they need be to disallow an evil person from deciphering the encrypted information and emptying one's bank account swiftly.

There is something matter-of-fact about burning a photograph by placing it on a hotplate, something distanced and distancing, something that lacks the direct implication of the one who puts his hands to the plow, as it were, and tears up the photographic paper on which an image has been printed. A photograph burning is a spectacle for a witness who remains outside, on the margins, or in the wings. How often have we seen a film with a scene where someone strikes a match, holds a letter, an incriminating document, or a photograph, close to the flame, and then throws the burning paper into a fireproof receptacle while he watches it disintegrate! How often have we seen celluloid burned by a projector, accidentally or as a filmic device! And yet to place a photograph on a hotplate and see it disappear could be regarded as a melodramatic gesture as much as tearing it apart. The staging magnifies the fire, transforms it into a conflagration, into a public representation with flames like succulents; the act of tearing a photograph apart, on the other hand, has a minimizing, personalizing, or privatizing effect, no matter how many people actually look at the staged fire or participate in the manual shredding.

Torn photographs, it should be remembered, feature in Hollis Frampton's *Poetic Justice*, the second installment of his Hapax-Legomena films. In Frampton's *(nostalgia)*, made in 1971 as the first installment in the series, thirteen photographs are placed on a hotplate and filmed from above. Steadily, the paper turns into carbon. The images become more and more unrecognizable as the S of the searing electric coils begins to leave its imprints on the paper. *(nostalgia)* has been called a 'structural film'. Regardless of how helpful or even pertinent the term may be, the talk of 'structural film' points to the rigor of the fixed camera and the precision of the staging, to the predetermination achieved by the formal set-up, as if Frampton had tried to keep the melodramatic impact at bay by making what happens in the image and on the screen as objective and as anonymous as possible. What happens is out of reach. The spectator never catches sight of the instant when the photograph is placed on the hotplate, and each sequence appears to be of equal, or similar, length, with each repetition of a sequence anticipating the next repetition. The uncontrolled subjective gesture or act, the excess that cannot be accounted for, have been excluded, it would seem, in favor of the cold black-and-white ideality of the natural process of combustion.

A voice tells the spectator details about the different photographs. Yet it does so in advance, ahead of the information provided to the eyes. The voice keeps referring to the photograph that the spectator will see only once the photograph he sees at the moment of listening will have been reduced to ashes, will have performed the burning's little song and dance and will have entered the film, will have been metamorphosed into cinematography without leaving anything behind but dissolving flakes. 'Temporality is everything', as Rachel Moore puts it (2006: 58), a source of fatigue and a source of excitement. It hollows itself out. Only one photograph, the photograph of an artist's lab, or a darkroom, is not described, or commented upon, and remains outside the series, a 'hapax legomenon' in the visual and aural realm, just as only one comment, the one that comes last, remains outside the series as well, for the photograph which it describes is never seen and perhaps cannot be seen. Is symmetry restored to frame the asymmetry of sound and image? If so, this symmetry is an open symmetry. The spectator feels that the series could have begun before the film starts and end after the film stops. In the film, photographs are alluded to that are not exhibited on the hotplate. A black screen separates each take, the regularity of its insertion triggering a sort of mute metronomic beat. The film features an aerial prologue, a sound rehearsal that can be heard but not seen. It includes a sentence that is never repeated, though it would seem to belong to the actual text: 'These are recollections of a dozen still photographs I made several years ago'. If the spectator is not too fatigued and confused by the procedure that keeps disrupting the correspondence between the senses, or between the senses and sense, and if the spectator is still able to listen to the voice and remember what it has said when the next photograph is fed to the cold sun of the hotplate, to the light from which it originated, if, as unlikely as it may appear, the spectator masters Frampton's future perfect and engages in a mental activity, in a conceptual exercise of reflective coordination that protects his ears and his eyes against the aesthetics, or the beauty, of a pure image and a pure sound, he may come up with a list of reasons why a photograph might be burnt. Does the burning of a photograph, the play of visibility and invisibility, of chronological repetition, that is doubled by the play of sight and sound, of repeated non-coincidence, alert the spectator to the 'doubling presence of death' (Foucault, 1963: 77) without which one could not see anything, as Foucault maintains in his early study of Raymond Roussel? In a space and time without death, everything would be absolutely visible and invisible at the same time.

In the case of the photograph of Carl Andre, the artist confesses to seeing less and less of him in recent times, less than he would like to see him anyway, while there are other people, he says, of whom he sees more than he cares to see, more than his eyes can take, as it were. Hence burning a photograph can be a reminder that we don't see what we ought to be seeing, the friends we ought to be frequenting, or that we have become trapped in a condition of distraction. The spectator who has watched the film before, or who ponders it after a first viewing, knows that Pascal is named towards the end of the film, though it is hard to make sense of this reference in the context in which it appears. As the spectator sees a photograph that Frampton made for *Vogue* magazine, the voice tells of a photograph that shows a man in an orchard. It is a photograph Frampton has found, not one he produced himself. The voice says: 'On the other hand, were photography of greater antiquity, then this image might date from the time of, let us say, Pascal; and I suppose he would have understood it quite differently'. Obviously, this is also a joke, a joke about how to look at a photograph and what to see in a photograph, a joke about what we see and what we do not see when we look at a photograph. 'Divertissement', or entertainment, the attitude towards others and the world that Pascal batters in his *Pensées*, derives etymologically from the Latin verb 'divertere', which means to separate, to turn away, to divert. One is entertained when one's attention is taken away from something and directed at something else. 'Distraction' comes from Latin 'distrahere,' to draw asunder or apart. Each time one wishes to be entertained, one seeks distraction. For Pascal, the distraction of 'divertissement' always lies in a movement that tends towards the outside and, in a sense, towards itself since it tends not towards a goal to be attained but towards the turmoil and uproar that reign outside, out there. Man, trying to escape a confrontation with his own condition, his own misery, looks for turmoil and uproar, for constant movement, exposing himself to the trouble caused by 'a thousand accidents, which make afflictions unavoidable' (Pascal, 1977: 17). Even friendship, Pascal stresses, can be part of the distraction caused by 'divertissement'. He believes that few friendships would survive if one of the two friends knew what the other one says about him in his absence, speaking 'sincerely and without passion' (502). One wants friends to be flattered by them, not to discover the 'depth of one's heart' and to see oneself 'as one is'. One wants friends to be able to rely on one's ears: 'If one consults the ear only, it is because one lacks heart' (356). However, on one occasion Pascal also notes: 'These people lack heart. One would not want them to be one's friends' (383). Does the blocked continuity, the structural discontinuity that causes sound and image to divert and diverge, or that tears apart spoken comment and seen photograph, draw attention to the ambivalent role both the ear and the eye can play? For if, as Pascal stresses, finite human beings prove unable to see the infinite nothingness from which they stem and the infinite into which they are thrown, the infinitude of creation that swallows them, some such beings are still able to contemplate others with the 'eyes of faith' (210).

Yet Frampton's anamnestic comments on the somewhat surreal photograph of Andre's handsome boyish face, which appears in a small picture frame next to a metronome whose large needle the sculptor's hand either puts in motion or prevents from moving, also end with the ambiguous words: 'I despised this photograph for several years. But I could never bring myself to destroy a negative so incriminating'. The photograph is destroyed in lieu of the negative, as if the negative were indestructible and could only be destroyed symbolically, by way of destroying a printed image; or as if the photograph always maintained itself in reserve and thereby proved its indestructibility, not on account of its quality, of the artist's achievement, but on account of its negativity, its incriminating character. Does it incriminate the artist because it reminds him of his distraction or because it reminds him of his failure as a photographer? To know as an artist that one has produced such an image, such a negative is so unbearable that one cannot even go near it, let alone look at it. All one can do is use it, print yet another photograph and burn it yet again. Once the artist has ceased to distract himself, once he has discarded all the habitual excuses, such as his youth, his inexperience, his other, more convincing work, his need to pay for the child's schooling, his reliance on the art world to subsist, he realizes that what he makes turns out to be beyond his reach, whether in the case of a truly successful work of art, a work of art that truly works, as a whole or in some of its parts, or in the case of a truly incriminating artwork. A truly incriminating work is a work of art that keeps accusing the artist, judging and blaming him for having burdened the world with his so-called art, with something that will never allow itself to be incinerated, that will escape the iconoclast's grasp, because it has already branded or burnt an indelible mark in the artist's memory, causing him sleepless nights of never-ending insomnia. Frampton must have asked himself whether the artist Hollis Frampton, the artist Hapax Legomena, who replaced Frampton when the artist had grown out of one of his former selves, the artist Carl Andre and virtually all the other artists of all times, would ever forget the bullshit he had devised, whether any holocaust would ever be so purifying as to undo the negative once and for all, or whether any future metamorphosis, any resurrection in the future, would allow him to cease being a criminal. One of the first things that the voice tells us, the substitute voice, the voice of Michael Snow reading flatly, clumsily, casually, and perhaps in a manly tone a text of personal 'recollections', of souvenirs or postcards from the past written by a subject formerly known as Hollis Frampton, is that the portrait of Carl Andre the spectator has not seen yet is the first still photograph Frampton ever made 'with the direct intention of making art'.

Hence photographs can be burnt as a painful reminder of a distraction that threatens to render a life meaningless and as an equally painful reminder of the difficulty of destruction in art. Is it indeed possible to delete the traces and vestiges of art meant as art, of pretentious artiness, of the frame that is not structural but ornamental? The double pain, real or ironic, bestows the meaning of a ritual upon the formal set-up of (*nostalgia*). Burning, when painful, means sacrificing, offering the friend's image to atone for one's betrayal of friendship, and to acknowledge the intractable negativity of bad art that one is incapable of abolishing. But since the two reasons mentioned are also incompatible with each other, at least to the extent that the artist must hold his friend dear to burn his image and remind himself of his distraction, and that at the same time the image he is burning is the one he must look at again and again in anger because he so much wants to, and cannot, destroy the negative, a certain irony permeates this cinematographic ritual. As a consequence, what we see is what we see and yet also proves to hover undecidably between different meanings. What if irony were Hollis Frampton's melodrama?

If one continues scrutinizing (*nostalgia*) for other reasons that might justify the burning of a photograph, bearing in mind that a photograph might be placed on a hotplate and burnt for no other reason than as an appealing visual device, a device fit for a film that reflects on itself as an experimental medium, one will find that Frampton keeps resorting to a moral register of friendship and an artistic register of debunking, and that he often does so in a humorous manner that makes light of the seriousness suggested by morality and art. Some of the more whimsical comments come across as if made up for the occasion, though, given how idiosyncratic friends and artists can be, they may contain perfectly true anecdotes. About an unnamed married friend who has not been his friend 'for nearly ten years', Frampton tells the spectator: 'We became estranged on account of an obscure embarrassment that involved a third party, and three dozen eggs'. About his friend James Rosenquist, with whom he seldom meets because he and James both live far apart from each other, he states: 'I cannot recall one moment spent in his company that I didn't completely enjoy'. About Michael Snow's reaction to a photograph he took of him and a poster he conceived for one of his shows, he observes: 'I recall that we worked half a day for two or three exposures. I believe that Snow was pleased with the photograph itself, as I was. But he disliked the poster intensely. He said I had chosen a typeface that looked like an invitation to a church social. I regret to say that he was right. But it was too late. There was nothing to do about it. The whole business still troubles me. I wish I could apologize to him'. About a self-portrait, he remarks: 'There are eleven more photographs on the roll of film, all of comparable grandeur. Some of them exhibit my features in more sensitive or imposing moods'. And Frampton adds: 'I take some comfort in realizing that my entire physical body has been replaced more than once since it made this portrait of its face'. About an initial series of photographs that captured the window of a cabinetmaker's shop on West Broadway, he notes: 'I rejected it for reasons to do with its tastefulness and illusion of deep space'. About photographs of 'junk and rubble' taken in the spring of 1961 'in imitation of action painting' and then shown to a neighbor who was a painter interested in 'Old Masters,' he says: 'My neighbor saw my new work, and he was not especially pleased'. About a likeness of Frank Stella that shows him blowing smoke rings, he asserts: 'Looking at the photograph recently, it reminded me, unaccountably, of a photograph of another artist squirting water out of his mouth, which is undoubtedly art. Blowing smoke rings seems more of a craft. Ordinarily, only opera singers make art with their mouths'. When examining the photograph of the interior of a bank on Wall Street, made with the intention of imitating Lartigue's sense of mystery 'without, however, attempting to comprehend his wit', he bluntly declares: 'My eye for mystery is defective'. When considering a photograph of Larry Poons on a mattress, made in a state of ecstatic happiness unrelated to the image itself and the result of a single exposure, he tells the spectator: 'Months later, the photograph was published. I was working in a color-film laboratory at the time. My boss saw the photograph, and I nearly lost my job. I decided to stop doing this sort of thing'. Sometimes the object chosen for a photograph appears to be rather odd, as if the artiness had merged into the choice of object: 'I set up my camera above an empty darkroom tray, opened a number 2 can of Franco-American Spaghetti, and poured it out'. But hey, such spaghetti did in fact exist until recently – 'Franco-American' is not a pun on America doing art but merely a brand name of the Campbell Soup Company. At other times, Frampton proposes an interpretation of one of his images that ridicules the expectations that informed beholders might have of photography as an art. Is he also ridiculing the image itself? He claims, for example, that his photograph of two adjacent toilet cubicles amounts to an 'imitation of a painted renaissance crucifixion'. After identifying a 'bowl with its lid raised' as an iconic portrait of St. Mary Magdalene, he concludes his interpretation with the following sentence: 'I'm not completely certain of the iconographic significance of the light bulbs, but the haloes that surround them are more than suggestive'.

So what is it, then, that Frampton holds in reserve for his last comment, the one that refers to an image we never see, an impossible image? Sadly, it is a disappointment. The image is said to depict the open door of a truck that has turned into an alley, into a 'dark tunnel with the cross-street beyond brightly lit'. As Frampton develops the negative, he becomes aware of a detail, something reflected in the rear-view mirror attached to the truck's door. It is a reflection of a reflection of the almost invisible cross street caused by the window of a factory. Time and again, the photographer enlarges the image so as to recognize what it is that this small section of his image reveals. He keeps failing. 'Nevertheless, what I believe I see recorded in that speck of film, fills me with such fear, such utter dread and loathing, that I think I shall never dare to make another photograph again. Here it is! Look at it! Do you see what I see?' Commentators have written about the allusion to Antonioni's *Blow-Up*, although, when asked about such an allusion, Frampton did not confirm it. They have also speculated on whether or not, if one lets oneself be guided by the logic of (*nostalgia*) rather than the topological lay-out of Manhattan's streets, the photographed reflection of a reflection could be a double reflection of the photographed darkroom that the spectator sees in the beginning (Moore, 2006: 28) and that, in the film, is not preceded by a comment. The darkroom would come to symbolize, or encapsulate, a photographer's career, but also the incrimination of the artist whose relationship to his own photographs is at best ambiguous. Be it as it may, the final envoy, the last address or consignment that sends the spectator off into darkness, is too reminiscent of the photograph of Carl Andre, of the collapse of its manifest intention of artistry into a debacle of artiness. Frampton's comment presents itself so much as the last possible comment on photography and art that it proves as incriminatory as the photographs he dismisses for confounding art with the will to art. The artist makes too much of an effort and, unable to end the fucking film, falls short of his achievement. Or perhaps he looks back when he reaches the end, loathes the whole endeavor, everything he has accomplished so far, and decides to sink the project, ruin (*nostalgia*) for the spectator who has patiently watched the film up to the point where the last comment leaves him alone with his own blindness, free and constrained to imagine whatever he wishes to imagine, maybe an 'infinite film' (Frampton, 2008: 36) that is always the same and always different, like the takes and the ashes in (*nostalgia*), for no photograph burns in the same manner as another photograph. Photographs must not even be burnt as the very fact of burning them may already betray an excess of seriousness, some melodrama.

The question 'why burn a photograph?' reveals itself to be a question about seriousness in life and art. It reveals itself to be a question about that which an artist can bring about, something that will then, strangely, remain out of his reach, incriminating him, returning to him without allowing itself to be touched, something beyond participation and for this reason forever given, something forever given without ever becoming available. Frampton's answer to the question 'why burn a photograph?' encourages the spectator of (*nostalgia*) not to let go of seriousness, to envisage its relevance from the limit of what may easily be dismissed as an exaggeration, namely the fatality of a self-incrimination rooted in life and art and hence indistinguishable from an incrimination that stems from the other, that renews itself incessantly and constantly reopens a burning wound in the mind, all the more ungraspable the more it originates in a comportment or in the creation of an artwork that could have been different. Yet in life and in art, such seriousness also requires some of the flippancy, the irreverence, with which Frampton treats his photographs and his film, but also the subjects of his photographs and their art. Retain the flippancy only and you get an adolescent's enjoyment and entertainment. Retain the seriousness only and you get pious artiness and self-righteousness. Why burn a photograph? For no good reason. Or to testify, in life and in art, to the tension that traverses and exposes seriousness and that allows it to be seriousness in the first place. It is a tension generated when the out-of-reach is reached. To reach the out-of-reach is a paradox and thus it imposes two irreconcilable and yet equally necessary forms of behavior, necessary for each form of behavior to be what it aspires to be, seriousness and flippancy. Is Frampton, the moment he stops burning photographs and, regrettably, botches the end of his film, too serious or too flippant?

Original source and licence

'Left' issue (issue 8) of the online journal *World Picture*, summer 2013; http://www.worldpicturejournal.com/WP_8/Duttmann.html. © *World Picture* journal. Permission to republish granted.

References

Foucault, M. (1963) *Raymond Roussel*. Paris: Gallimard.

Frampton, H. (2008) 'For a Metahistory of Film: Commonplace Notes and Hypotheses', *Photography and Cinema*, D. Campany. London: Reaktion Books.

Moore, R. (2006) *Hollis Frampton: (nostalgia)*. London: Afterall Books.

Pascal, B. (1977) *Pensées* (ed.), M. Le Guern. Paris: Gallimard.

CHAPTER 4

Processing Color in Astronomical Imagery

KIMBERLY K. ARCAND, MEGAN WATZKE, TRAVIS RECTOR,
ZOLTAN G. LEVAY, JOSEPH DEPASQUALE, OLIVIA SMARR

1. Image as translation

Astronomy is largely funded by taxpayer dollars, and because the nature of the scientific process includes the dissemination of results – in the form of proof or a 'public report' (Miller, 2004: 279) – many in the professional community believe in the responsibility of releasing meaningful results to the public (Frankel, 2004: 418). Quite often, the images produced from astronomical data are a great asset in doing this; they provide a principal source of information that forms public conceptions about space (Snider, 2011). One can draw a parallel from Felice Frankel's work in creating visually appealing images of materials science and the importance of producing 'wonderful and accessible images' to effectively communicate science (Frankel, 2004: 418).

With advancements in detector technology, many astronomical images created today sample data from wavelengths outside those of human vision. These data must be translated, through the use of processing, adding color and artifact removal, smoothing and/or cropping into human-viewable images. The choices involved in deciding how best to represent or translate such data underscore the idea that 'what we encounter in the media is mediated' (Mellor, 2009: 205).

There is, however, a lack of robust studies to understand how people – particularly non-experts – perceive these images and the information they attempt to convey. The extent to which the choices – including those surrounding color – made during image creation affect viewer perception, comprehension, and trust is only beginning to be more closely examined. For example, the influence of images in news reports has not been extensively studied (Jarman et al., 2011: 4). Are there rules when it comes to presenting something visually that cannot be seen with the human eye? Is there an inherent amount of manipulation through the choice of color in this process of creating astronomical images? Or is it simply providing a proxy so that we can experience something (that is, views of the universe) that otherwise may not be available to us?

The intent behind the manipulation of astronomical data for the creation of public images is important. The choices made by the scientist must not, of course, change the overall interpretation (Rossner and Yamada, 2004: 11). The assumption made here is that the intent is to add value and information, make the presentation of the data aesthetically pleasing, make the information accessible, and/or make the material understandable. Images can, after all, be both informational and beautiful (Frankel, 2004: 418). Color plays a vital role in these goals.

But to manipulate an image responsibly, the scientist or science image processor must also understand the perspectives of non-experts and be willing to embrace openness and transparency in their work to foster trust with the public (Irwin, 2009: 7). We argue that non-experts may not necessarily perceive colors in the same way that the scientific community does. In fact, until recently, there has been little scholarly research into the differences in perception of color between lay audiences compared with professional scientists, in particular, astronomers and astrophysicists. In this paper, we describe the current state of affairs in the creation of astronomical images using color, raise some of the issues in doing so, and outline some of our efforts to address these questions using research-based methodologies.

1.1 Historical notes, and image as truth

Photographs, though made by human hands using machinery humans have invented, have been perceived as being free of human bias (Schwartz, 2003: 28). Photographs have also been considered as 'records of the real' (Rothstein, 2010). Photography's veracity, though once seen as an inherently true vehicle of a snapshot in time, has seemingly decreased since the purported 'reintroduction of the human hand' (Schwartz, 2003: 30) through the ability to manipulate images quickly and efficiently with digital imaging software such as Adobe Photoshop. There is, understandably, a negative connotation to manipulating photos, so much so that 'to photoshop' has become a pejorative verb.

Since image manipulation is more convenient and accessible today, it is perhaps more in the public consciousness than it was with analog (film) processing. However, such control over an image's appearance has been around since the beginnings of photography. Aside from deceptive or entertaining uses of altering photographs, a skilled darkroom technician can evoke detail and tonality from the negative that is not apparent in a 'straight' print, using techniques including altering exposure and development (contrast), dodging, burning, intensification, toning, etc. Ansel Adams, for example, was well known for his ability to adjust his processing from exposure through printing, even though many non-experts would likely consider his photos to be faithful representations of well-known landscapes (Adams and Baker, 1995).

The correspondence between photographs of scenes and how the eye sees those same scenes still affirms the general truth of photographic images today. The question of 'is this what it really looks like' is commonly heard from the non-experts who look at astronomical images.[11] How does the color mapping being used to create those astronomical images play into this assumed truth? To explore this further, one needs to understand the origins of the astronomical image from the first telescopes.

2. Creation of the astronomical image

The history of astronomical imaging arguably began in 1609 when Italian astronomer Galileo Galilei, with his new astronomical telescope,[2] observed craters on the surface of Earth's Moon (figure 4.1a) and discovered four lunar bodies orbiting Jupiter. He then transcribed them into drawn format and published his findings in 1610.[3]

Astronomical imaging has been evolving ever since with the development of increasingly sophisticated technology. For example, during the 20th century, astronomers began making three-color composite images using filters on film. (Filters in this case refer to ways to limit the amount of light in each image. For example, some filters enable the astronomers to look at the light emitted by only hydrogen atoms, or in other instances, in the higher energies detected by the telescopes.) Making three-color astronomical images involves stacking three different images of the same field of view of different slices of light, typically assigning red, green, and blue as the colors for each layer.

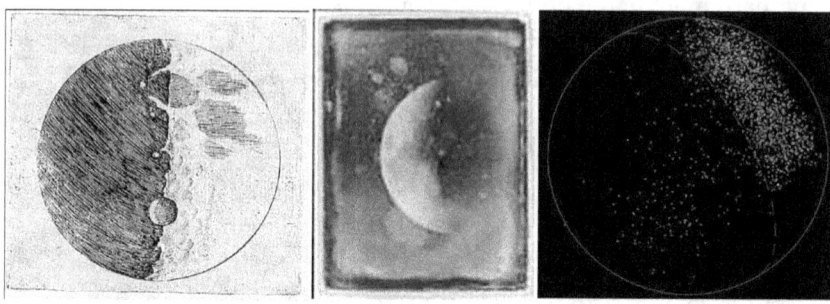

Figure 4.1a (left). Galileo's transcription of our Moon's surface from *Sidereus Nuncius* in the 17th century. (Credit: Wikimedia Commons.) Figure 4.1b (middle). One of the oldest surviving daguerreotype images of the Moon, from 1852, taken by John Adams Whipple (Credit: Harvard/Wikimedia Commons http://commons.wikimedia.org/wiki/File:1852_Moon_byJAWhipple_Harvard.png). Figure 4.1c (right). The Moon in X-ray light, taken in 2001 by the Chandra X-ray Observatory. (Credit: NASA/CXC/SAO)

During the second half of the 20th century, there were major advances for astronomical telescopes on the ground with larger and more sophisticated mirrors being constructed (DeVorkin, 1993). This period also saw the dawn of the Space Age (Portree, 1998), of which astronomers were eager to take advantage (for example, Tucker and Tucker, 2001: 28). By being able to launch telescopes into space, astronomers could build detectors and other instruments that were sensitive to ultraviolet, X-ray, and other types of light that are absorbed by the Earth's atmosphere. Given these new technologies, and specifically since the launch of NASA's Hubble Space Telescope, the period since the 1990s is considered a 'new era' for astronomy (Benson, 2009: 322). There are now many space-based telescopes and observatories on the ground available to look at a wide range of different types of light from the cosmos. Astronomical data from such modern telescopes are no longer captured on film. They are instead natively digital and arrive from the telescope in a form that generally requires processing in order to create an image.

This boon in astronomical data also means that today we find popular media flush with astronomical images. But the transition in science image communication from hand-drawn observation to emerging photomechanical techniques in astrophotography and the most advanced space-based optics today reflects a shift in the purported subjectivity of the scientist when producing these images as vehicles of visualizing his or her data. Mechanically produced images were assumed to eliminate the 'meddling' mediation of the human hand – an instrument having no will, desires, or morals of its own (Daston and Galison, 1992: 83). But as the next section notes, complete objectivity and neutrality in the interpretation of scientific data into the pictorial form is not feasible, nor is it desired. The science embedded in the image often informs the human choices for the color composite.

2.1 *The processing pipeline*

2.1.1 *Translation from 1's and 0's into pixels*

As mentioned previously, modern astronomical images – whether from an optical telescope like the Hubble Space Telescope or one that looks at X-rays like the Chandra X-ray Observatory – are inherently digital. When a satellite, for example, observes an object in space, its camera records the exposure of light-sensitive electronics to photons. These exposure recordings then come down to Earth from the spacecraft via a network in the form of 1's and 0's. Scientific software then translates that data into an event table that contains the position and, in some cases, certain information for the time and energy, of each photon that struck the detector during the observation. The data is further processed with software to form the visual representation of the object as pixels (Rector, 2007: 599).

2.1.2 *Mapping color*

Color plays an important role in human perception and culture, and also has some meaning in the realm of science. The spectrum of light that can be detected with the human eye can be broken into various colors from red to green to violet. In astronomy, these colors are applied to wavelengths of light far beyond the range humans can see. Using telescopes in space and those on the ground, astronomers can now 'see' from radio waves to gamma rays, across the full range of the electromagnetic spectrum (see figure 4.2).

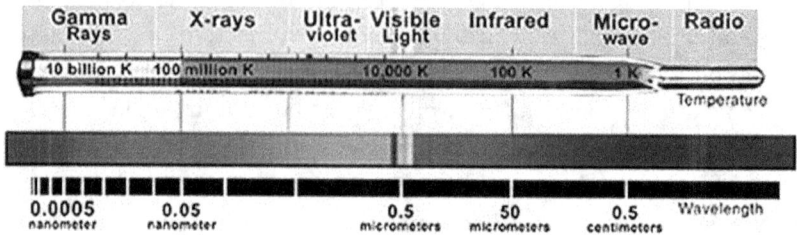

Figure 4.2. Electromagnetic radiation comes in a range of energies, known as the electromagnetic spectrum. The spectrum consists of radiation such as gamma rays, X-rays, ultraviolet, visible, infrared, and radio. (Illustration: NASA/CXC/SAO)

The data that are received by telescopes originates as variations of brightness with no inherent color. Color must then be added to the image. To do this, scientists or science image processors put together a color map that 'translates' portions of the data to various colors that can be seen with the human eye.

Here we take this opportunity to raise the issue of false color. The term *false color* is often used to describe astronomy images whose colors represent measured intensities outside the visible portion of the electromagnetic spectrum.[4] But a false color image is not wrong or phony as the term might imply (Hurt, 2010). It is a selection of colors chosen to represent a characteristic of the image (intensity, energy, or chemical composition, for example). False color images are not actually 'false in any sense of the word, but only a matter of different visual codes' (Snider, 2011: 9). The colors used are representative of the physical processes underlying the objects in the image.[5] Alternatively, a scientist or image processor may want to be able to differentiate between low, medium, and high energy, assigning red, green, and blue (RGB) in a 'chromatic order' (Wyatt, 2010: 35) from low to high energy as it does in a rainbow.

This use of RGB for low, medium, and high energies can be applied to wavelengths that fall outside human vision. For this first example, we look at the black hole at the center of the Milky Way, known as Sagittarius A* (figure 4.3a) as observed by the Chandra X-ray Observatory. In this image, the X-rays near the black hole (seen as the bright white structure in the center) and greater surrounding area are shown in three colors: red

(2-3.3 keV), green (3.3-4.7 keV), and blue (4.7-8 keV).[6] All of these X-ray wavelengths are invisible to the human eye but can be seen in relation to one another through an application of color.

As we mentioned earlier, some astronomical images are colored to highlight certain scientific features in the data. For example, an image of supernova remnant G292 (figure 4.3b) shows colors that were selected to highlight the emission from particular elements such as oxygen (yellow and orange), neon (red), magnesium (green), and silicon and sulfur (blue).[7] Again, this is an image made from X-ray light. Each color represents the specific wavelengths of light that each element gives off or is absorbed in this environment. Compare figures 4.3b and 4.3c; the colors added in 4.3b provide additional insight into physical characteristics of the X-ray gas in this supernova remnant that could not be gleaned from the black and white image.

In both cases, the choice of color is contributing to the informational quotient of the image because the colors reflect the processes inherent in these objects. When color maps are combined, they yield 'new insights into the nature of the objects' (Villard, 2010). However, since the selection of wavelengths and decisions on color are not standardized, it may be confusing to non-experts and lead to perceptions of phoniness in the images.

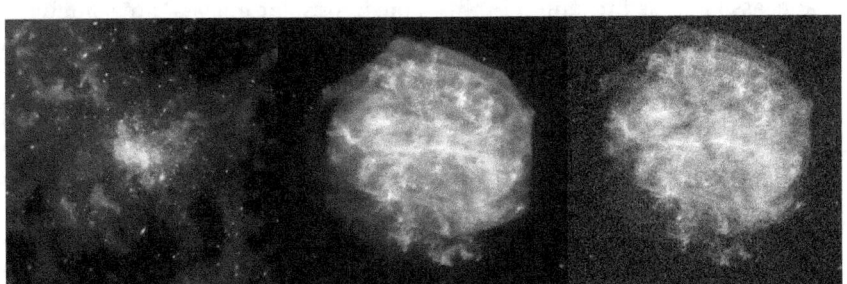

Figure 4.3a (left) Sagittarius A* in X-ray light. Figure 4.3b (middle) Supernova remnant G292 in X-ray light. Figure 4.3c (right) Raw, unprocessed broadband X-ray image of supernova remnant G292. (Credit: NASA/CXC/SAO)

How does all of this relate to the ethical issues of color representation? For one, it exemplifies the idea that scientists and their collaborators make use of interpretation, selection, judgment, and artistry (Daston and Galison, 1992: 98) when deciding how to represent specific scientific data. To put it another way, both scientific and aesthetic choices are being made when an image is created. Modern astronomical images function as 'an illustration of the physical properties of interest rather than as a direct portrayal of reality as defined by human vision' (Rector, 2005: 197; see also Rector, 2007). The next section of this paper examines the various degrees of manipulation possible in the color mapping of astronomical images and whether those decisions might be perceived as ethical by non-experts.

3. Other colorful examples

3.1 A recognizable object seen differently

While perhaps not considered by the greater public to be an astronomical object, the Sun, of course, is our closest star. The most common view of our Sun is that as seen from the ground: an unchanging yellow disk. Images from NASA's Solar Dynamics Observatory (SDO) reveal the Sun (figure 4.4a) in a much different way. Using detectors that observe in 13 distinct wavelengths from X-ray to ultraviolet, the space-based SDO captures curving and erupting prominences, and the features in the images trace magnetic field structure. The hottest areas appear almost white while the darker areas indicate cooler temperatures on our local star. The colors assigned as presented in this tableau of solar images[8] are somewhat arbitrary in hue and saturation. However, when colors are combined to create a multiwavelength view of the Sun, colors are chosen in an RGB ordering according to temperature. In the single wavelength views, these images seem to 'flaunt' their color (Wyatt, 2010: 35), almost purposefully making the familiar unfamiliar. Is this more acceptable because the Sun is an easily recognized object by most citizens of our planet? It could be that because the color is so unexpected, it immediately functions as a visual cue that the color is not being presented as reality but rather as a layer of information for the viewer. Similarly, this might be part of the reason why brightly false-colored radar maps on the nightly news are acceptable (figure 4.4b). Foreign colors on recognized objects have less of a claim to veracity. Their point is, perhaps, clearer to the viewer. If one observes, however, that images 'are not self-explanatory' but rather that they 'need to be interpreted, and the human task of interpretation is often a [big] obstacle' (Gladwell, 2004: 2), then there is still a risk of non-experts misunderstanding the purpose of color, even on a recognizable object that is not being understood as 'true'. This is particularly the case when no explanation of the color table is offered with the images. The satellite imagery for weather forecasts still utilizes color for a specific purpose – indicating variations in temperature or precipitation, for example – and either it is accompanied with a color legend or with verbal or textual narration. Any solar images would also benefit from clear, descriptive information to explicitly relate the purpose of the color.

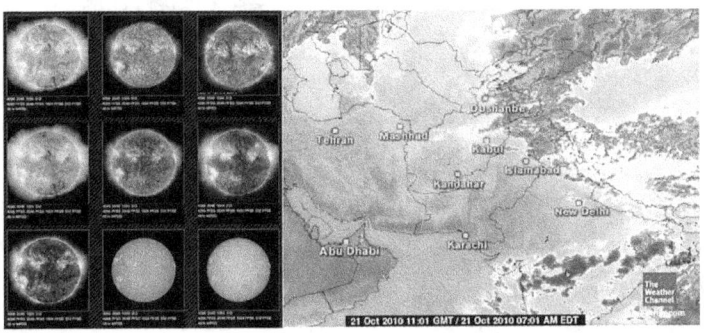

Figure 4.4a (left) Multi-bandpass images of the Sun. (Courtesy of NASA/SDO and the AIA, EVE, and HMI science teams.). Figure 4.4b (right) Satellite imagery of Asia. (Credit: The Weather Channel)

In another sense, the recognizable object can be something that grounds an unfamiliar and exotic process to a shared experience or common conception through the use of the visual metaphor (Frankel, 2002: 254). For example, figures 4.5a and 4.5b present a 2010 Chandra X-ray Observatory press release that shows a multiwavelength view of the massive galaxy M87. The galaxy harbors a super massive black hole at its center, producing massive jets of energetic particles, creating shockwaves that ripple throughout the galaxy. This process was compared with images and video of the Icelandic volcano Eyjafjallajokull, which erupted in 2010 and showed analogous shockwaves to those seen in M87. The color choice for the galaxy image added to the analogy with warm and cool hues providing contrast to the shockwaves in a similar way as was seen in the volcano imagery.

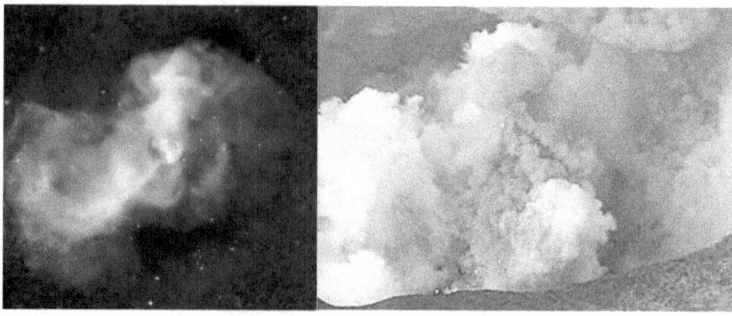

Figure 4.5a (left) M87 in X-ray (blue) and radio (red) light. Figure 4.5b (right) Icelandic volcano Eyjafjallajokull. (Credit: NASA/CXC/SAO; Volcano image: Omar Ragnarsson)

3.2 *Cultural norms and misconceptions*

NGC 4696 is a large elliptical galaxy in the Centaurus Galaxy Cluster, about 150 million light years from Earth. This composite image that was released to the public (figure 4.6a) shows a vast cloud of hot gas (X-ray = red) surrounding high-energy bubbles (radio = blue) on either side of the bright white area around the supermassive black hole.[9]

Astronomers and other experts in this area understand that the color blue physically represents higher temperatures than red does. (Blue stars, for example, can burn at temperatures that are tens of thousands of degrees higher than red stars.)

However, most non-experts consider red to be hotter than blue. In a study done on this particular image of NGC 4696, 71.4% of the non-scientist study participants thought red was hotter than blue (Smith et al., 2010). To get across the point that this image is an immensely hot cloud of gas, the image processors inverted the more traditional, physically aligned color scheme and colored the highest-energy/hotter-temperature features red (figure 4.6a). Figure 4.6b shows the color mapping that is more typical of astronomical images, where the band passes are in chromatic order (red, green, and blue are mapped from low to medium to high energies, respectively). The use of color here might be viewed as perpetuating a misconception. One could question if it is the responsibility of the scientist to correct or disabuse common notions, such as that red is hotter than blue. The primarily red image seems to convey – in a cultural language – the extreme heat of this object better, even though its color mapping

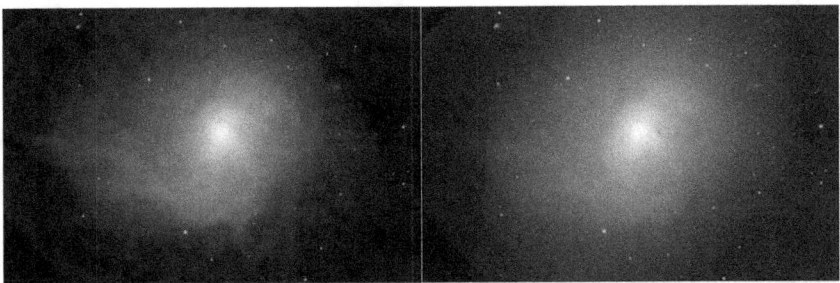

Figure 4.6a. Alternating colors: red (Figure 4.6a, left) and blue (Figure 4.6b, right) color-coded versions of galaxy NGC 4696 in X-ray, infrared, and radio light. (Credit: NASA/CXC/SAO)

might be considered by the scientific community to be non-standard. The responsibility may in fact fall to both scientists and the public to develop a mutually consistent visual literacy, a framework from which to view and understand these images (Trumbo, 1999).

Is it the case that one must 'be true to the real nature of science, not to an idealized preconception' of that science (Ruse, 1996: 304)? Or can one also 'acknowledge the realities of human nature' and make choices for the greater good – that is, choices that reflect the greater number of people who would then understand that image in a more meaningful way (Ruse, 1996: 304)? Aligning these images to cultural norms (regarding the perception of color, at least) might make the image and the science more trustworthy and relatable for the non-expert. Though it may seem counterintuitive not to explicitly follow the highest degree of 'truth' represented in the data of a scientific image, the benefits of following cultural norms could outweigh the risks – particularly when the reasoning behind the choice is properly explained.

4. Discussion: color and construction

The examples above are just a small sample of the different ways astronomical data can be presented. The images are constructed from actual data. They look different due to the subjective choices of the scientist and science image processors – including choices of color. As Trumbo notes, 'these seemingly simple considerations determine what the viewer encounters and ultimately contribute to what the viewer understands'

(Trumbo, 2000: 387). How is it possible to maintain (or obtain) public trust in colored science images such as these?

Perhaps the way to do this is two-fold: through transparency and a more active provision of information. If non-experts can develop a visual literacy through access to the choices made – and to the information on why these choices need to be made in the first place – then it may be possible to decrease any feelings of the public being misled (at best) or deceived (at worst). Opportunities to provide viewers with a more complete narrative of the choices being made might include systematically posting raw (unmanipulated), black and white versions of the data that the scientist first analyzes. It could also be helpful to provide more opportunities for non-experts to see behind any *'Wizard of Oz'* curtain directly and be able to manipulate astronomy images themselves using free and open-source software, such as some observatories are starting to do.[10]

Some steps are being taken to address these questions through analytical research. In 2008, the Aesthetics and Astronomy[11] (A&A) project at the Smithsonian Astrophysical Observatory was formed to help better understand and clarify how non-experts perceive astronomical images. The goal of this project is to help provide scientists and science communicators with a more informed consensus on the perspectives of non-experts and help make these questions become less of an ethical issue. The A&A program consists of experts from a variety of fields including astrophysicists, education and public outreach professionals, and aesthetics experts from the field of psychology. By conducting both online and focus group-based studies, the A&A has begun to tackle the issues of color in astronomical images.

A project such as A&A represents an important step in better understanding how people of various backgrounds consume and relate to scientific images. The visual products of science are embedded with a sense of authority of the science itself. The color images are created to represent and visualize the science, but they are seldom actually used to do the science. There are rigorous techniques used by researchers to analyze their data. In other words, the scientific results are not subjective in the way the color images are. This authority is 'enhanced by the traditional unidirectional model of science communication to the public' (Greenberg, 2004: 83). This is likely even more of the case when the process by which the image was produced is very complex – and with many choices having been made by the scientist – so much so that non-experts become less likely 'to engage critically with it' (Greenberg, 2004: 83). That authority then, when unquestioned, can become more powerful. By not spelling out the various enhancements for the greater good, astronomy professionals risk embodying that lack of questioning as to how an image was made and how those decisions affected the final product. One of the goals of the scientist or science communicator is to help facilitate engagement with the audience in a 'dialogic, "two-way" or "bottom-up" approach – sciences on one side, in a more symmetrical relationship with publics on the other – where openness and transparency are valued' (Holliman, Jensen, 2009: 37). One objective in creating images should be making the images and the science they embody accessible to the non-experts to which they are being presented.

5. Summary and conclusion

Modern telescopes and the availability (online and otherwise) of the many resulting images have helped make astronomical imagery visible. People can experience a deep personal reaction to astronomical images (Arcand & Watzke, 2011), and some of that emotion may be influenced by the choice of color. Enhancing astronomical images with color adds to the information quotient of the image and enhances the aesthetic appeal. This aestheticism appeals to a pre-existing 'sensibility' within the viewer and can elicit an emotional response that 'entrances' or otherwise seduces the viewer (Hall, 1996: 28). These images are also of highly 'exotic and inaccessible' (Hall, 1996: 20) processes and phenomena that make the pictorial representation of the data as well as visual metaphors important and useful. Taken in context with the text of a science article, these images 'are not simply adjuncts to the written word; they are integral to the process of meaning making' (Jarman et al., 2011: 4).

In order to help establish or maintain public trust in the representation of such scientific data, it is imperative that additional transparency is provided by the image creator to reveal details on how the images were made, including the choices of colors for each image and why those colors were chosen. If the greater public perceives an image to have been 'faked' or otherwise believes the use of false color has no purpose but to mislead, then this undermines the credibility of the science that is being conveyed.

Likewise, it is incumbent upon the public to develop and embrace a visual literacy to enable a critical reading of these images (Trumbo, 2000; Jarman et al., 2011). This issue of accountability and full disclosure is important to reconcile the perceived 'truth' in an image derived from manipulated data.

Though color to the scientist might not be the most important factor of the research result, color to the non-expert is perceived as having importance. It is the way our minds function every day in a cultural context, from the red traffic light telling a driver to stop to the yellow tinge of a baby's skin being a clue to jaundice or a green hue in the sky warning of bad weather. These colored pixels have power, and they convey meaning. These visual representations of data tell a story and say that the 'role of the image in the communication of science is an increasingly complex one' (Trumbo, 2000:380).

In summation, for astronomy it is not feasible to have a rigidly standardized treatment of color due to the inherent complexity of the data and the many types of data being used. However, it should be possible to convey the imagery with such transparency that the aesthetic appeal is maximized while assuring the greater public that scientific integrity has been maintained, and subjectivity made plain, to aid in their interpretation and critical reading of the visual representation. Effectively communicating the science of the universe continues to be challenging, yet offers significant rewards for expert and non-expert alike.

Acknowledgements

This material is partially based upon work supported by the National Aeronautics and Space Administration under contract NAS8-03060. Portions of this paper have been presented at Brown University (2010, 2011). Portions have also been used in an online exhibit (http://chandra.si.edu/art/color/colorspace.html) and article (http://www.huffingtonpost.com/megan-watzke/cosmic-microwave-background_b_3045048.html). Special thanks to Dr. Sheila Bonde and Dr. Paul Firenze of Brown University, Dr. Peter Edmonds of SAO, and Dr. Lisa Smith of University of Otago, New Zealand for input.

Original source and licence

Studies in Media and Communication Vol. 1, No. 2; December 2013; ISSN 2325-8071; E-ISSN 2325-808X. Published by Redfame, publishing URL: http://smc.redfame.com. Licence: CC BY 3.0.

References

Adams, A., & Baker, R. (1995) *The Print (Ansel Adams Photography, Book 3)*. London: Little, Brown.

Arcand, K. K., & Watzke, M. (2011) 'Creating Public Science with the *From Earth to the Universe* Project', *Science Communication,* 33, 3 (September), http://dx.doi.org/10.1177/1075547011417895.

Benson, M. (2009) *Far Out: A Space-Time Chronicle*. New York: Abrams.

Brunner, R. J., Djorgovski, S. G., Prince, T. A., & Szalay, A. S. (2001) 'Massive Datasets in Astronomy', *Invited Review for the Handbook of Massive Datasets* (eds), J. Abello, P. Pardalos, and M. Resende, arXiv:astro-ph/0106481.

Hall, B. S. (1996) 'The Didactic and the Elegant', in *Picturing Knowledge: Historical and Philosophical Problems Concerning the Use of Art in Science* (ed.), B. S. Baigrie. Toronto: University of Toronto Press.

Christensen, L. L., Hurt, R. L., & Fosbury, R. (2008) *Hidden Universe*. Berlin: Wiley-VCH.

Daston, L., & Galison, P. (1992) 'The Image of Objectivity', *Representations* (No. 40), *Special Issue: Seeing Science*: 81-128.

DeVorkin, D. H. (1993) *Science With A Vengeance: How the Military Created the US Space Sciences After World War II*. New York: Springer; corrected edition.

Frankel, F. (2004) 'The Power of the "Pretty Picture"', *Nature Materials,* 3: 417-419, http://dx.doi.org/10.1038/nmat1166.

Frankel, F. (2002) *Envisioning Science: The Design and Craft of the Scientific Image*. Cambridge: MIT Press.

Gladwell, M. (2004) 'The Picture Problem: Mammography, Air Power, and the Limits of Looking', *The New Yorker* (December 13), Annals of Technology.

Greenberg, J. (2004) 'Creating the "Pillars": Multiple Meanings of a Hubble Image', *Public Understanding of Science*, 13: 83-95, http://dx.doi.org/10.1177/0963662504042693.

Hurt, R. (2010). *Phony Colors? Or Just Misunderstood?* Retrieved from http://www.spitzer.caltech.edu/explore/blog/112-Phony-Colors-Or-Just-Misunderstood-.

Irwin, A. (2009) 'Moving Forwards or in Circles? Science Communication and Scientific Governance in an Age of Innovation', in *Investigating Science Communication in the Information Age* (eds), R. Holliman, E. Whitelegg, E. Scanlon, S. Smidt & J. Thomas. Oxford: Oxford University Press, 3-17.

Jarman, R., McClune, B., Pyle, E., & Braband, G. (2011) 'The Critical Reading of the Images Associated with Science-Related News Reports: Establishing a Knowledge, Skills, and Attitudes Framework', *International Journal of Science Education, Part B*. http://dx.doi.org/10.1080/21548455.2011.559961.

Mellor, F. (2009) 'Image-music-text of Popular Science', in *Investigating Science Communication in the Information Age* (eds), R. Holliman, E. Whitelegg, E. Scanlon, S. Smidt & J. Thomas. Oxford: Oxford University Press, 205-220.

Miller, J. D. (2004) 'Public Understanding of, and Attitudes Toward, Scientific Research: What We Know and What We Need to Know', *Public Understanding of Science*, 13: 273-294. http://dx.doi.org/10.1177/0963662504044908.

Portree, D. S. F. (1998) *NASA's Origins and the Dawn of the Space Age*, Issue 10 of Monographs in Aerospace History. NASA History Division, Office of Policy and Plans, NASA Headquarters.

Rector, T., Levay, Z. G., Frattare, L. M., English, J., & Pu'uohau-Pummill, K. (2007) 'Image-Processing Techniques for the Creation of Presentation-Quality Astronomical Images', *The Astronomical Journal* 133: 598-611. http://dx.doi.org/10.1086/510117.

Rector, T., Levay, Z. G., Frattare, L. M., English, J., & Pu'uohau-Pummill, K. (2005) 'Philosophy for the Creation of Astronomical Images', *Communicating Astronomy with the Public 2005 Conference Proceedings*: 194-204.

Rossner, M., & Yamada, K. M. (2004) 'What's in a Picture?: The Temptations of Image Manipulation', *Journal of Cell Biology* 166: 11-15. http://dx.doi.org/10.1083/jcb.200406019.

Rothstein, E. (2010) 'Marveling at Wonders Out of This World'. *New York Times, Exhibition Review,* Retrieved from http://www.nytimes.com/2010/07/29/arts/design/29museum.html.

Ruse, M. (1996) 'Adaptive Landscapes', in *Picturing Knowledge: Historical and Philosophical Problems Concerning the Use of Art in Science* (ed.), B. S. Baigrie. Toronto: University of Toronto Press.

Schwartz, D. (2003) 'Professional Oversight: Policing the Credibility of Photojournalism', in *Image Ethics in the Digital Age* (eds), L. Gross, J. S. Katz, J. Ruby. Minneapolis: University of Minnesota Press, 27-51.

Smith, L. F., Smith, J. K., Arcand, K. K, Smith, R. K., Bookbinder, J., & Keach, K. (2010) 'Aesthetics and Astronomy: Studying the Public's Perception and Understanding of Non-traditional Imagery from Space', *Science Communication Journal* Vol. 33, No. 2: 201-238. http://arxiv.org/abs/1009.0772.

Snider, E. (2011) 'The Eye of Hubble: Framing Astronomical Images', *FRAME: A Journal Of Visual And Material Culture* 1: 3-21. http://www.framejournal.org/view-article/9#_ftnref.

Trumbo, J. (1999) 'Visual Literacy and Science Communication', *Science Communication* 20: 409-425. http://dx.doi.org/10.1177/1075547099020004004.

Trumbo, J. (2000) 'Essay: Seeing Science: Research Opportunities in the Visual Communication of Science', *Science Communication* 20: 379-391. http://dx.doi.org/10.1177/1075547000021004004.

Tucker, W., & Tucker, K. (2001) *Revealing the Universe: The Making of the Chandra X-ray Observatory*. Cambridge: Harvard University Press.

Villard, R. (2010) 'Living in a Technicolor Universe', retrieved from http://news.discovery.com/space/astronomy/technicolor-universethis-week-astronomers-released-an-arresting-color-picture-of-a-pair-of-colliding-galaxies-combined-from.htm.

Wyatt, R. (2010) 'Visualising Astronomy: Let the Sun Shine In', *Communicating Astronomy with the Public*, 8: 34-35.

Notes

1   For example, as noted during a focus group at the Smithsonian Astrophysical Observatory for the Aesthetics & Astronomy research project, December 2010.

2   Note that Thomas Harriot's telescope preceded Galileo's as the first astronomical telescope, though Galileo's findings are considered to be more significant. See Edgerton Jr, S. Y. (1984) 'Galileo, Florentine "Disegno," and the "Strange Spottednesse" of the Moon', *Art Journal*, Vol. 44 (3): 225-232.

3   Galileo's drawings of the moon allowed him to argue that the lunar surface was filled with mountains and valleys. This was in direct contradiction with Aristotelian doctrine stating that all celestial bodies were perfectly smooth. See Whitaker, E. A. (1978) 'Galileo's Lunar Observations and the Dating of the Composition of "Sidereus Nuncius"', *Journal for the History of Astronomy*, 9: 155-169.

4   See also http://chandra.si.edu/photo/openFITS/overview.html by Chandra EPO Group at SAO (DePasquale, Arcand, Watzke et al., 2009).

5   It might be desirable to replace the term false color with representative color to help remove some of the negativity that the inclusion of false helps summon (Christensen et al., 2008: 20).

6   Where keV equals kilo-electron volts, a unit of energy being observed.

7   See 'Chandra Images and False Color', ed. Chandra EPO Group at SAO (Arcand, Watzke et al., 2005), http://chandra.si.edu/photo/false_color.html.

8   Images from http://sdo.gsfc.nasa.gov/data/ (November, 2011).

9   For more on this object see http://chandra.si.edu/photo/2006/bhcen/. Chandra EPO Group at SAO (Edmonds, Watzke, Arcand et al., 2006).

10 Examples of publicly-oriented open-FITS programs are at http://chandra.si.edu/photo/openFITS/, http://www.spacetelescope.org/projects/fits_liberator/datasets_archives/.

11 http://astroart.cfa.harvard.edu/

II The Image in Motion

CHAPTER 5

It Has Not Been – It Is.
The Signaletic Transformation of Photography

METTE SANDBYE

In 2011, the use and distribution of private photographs on websites such as Facebook, Picasa, and Flickr was as extensive as never before. Millions of photographs of private and apparently insignificant everyday moments and situations were being uploaded daily.[1] Also, in that year, Swiss-American UK-based artist and composer Christian Marclay (born 1955) won the exclusive Venice Biennial Golden Lion Grand Prize for his film *The Clock* from 2010. It is a 24-hour-long film that painstakingly assembles sampled sequences from a massive number of movies to take the viewer through a full day. At the same time, the film is synchronized to real time: that is, to the time in which it actually plays. In this article, I intend to show a connection between several seemingly disparate elements: Marclay's film and a film by another artist, David Claerbout (born in 1969); the general development of digital amateur photography; and 'the paradigm of the signal', as Bodil Marie Thomsen calls one of the major recent developments within electronic and digital media. I intend to show how we can grasp and use this concept of 'the signaletic' with regard to the medium of photography in order to describe and to theorize the new use of digital photography. Departing from *The Clock*, but analyzing another art work more in depth, namely Belgian artist David Claerbout's video *Sections of a Happy Moment* (2007), I will show how contemporary artworks can give insight into what happens with photography in the light of its recent and very radical digital changes. I will argue that concepts such as presence, performance, and even aesthetic involvement are much more relevant than realism, nostalgia, and the freezing of time to describe what goes on in the new digital photography. Inspired by the concept of 'the signaletic', I will propose a new understanding of photography as a social device related to everyday life, to communication, to presence, and to the blurring of boundaries between fiction and reality, the body, and the outside world.

Photography and Web 2.0

> Maybe what's happening now to photography was always its destiny and fate. But it's not the end of photography. It's rather the end of photography *as we know it*. To understand this change, we need *a new media ecology*.[2]

When digital photography became widespread in the mid-1990s, people started to predict the 'death of photography', referring especially to its realism and non-manipulated objectivity, but analog photography has always been manipulated to a certain degree. Instead, I will propose that the real change when it comes to the conception and use of photography came much later, namely with the Internet, the advent of Web 2.0 and its focus on user-generated content. Especially, vernacular photography has changed dramatically in less than a decade, to such an extent that we can now talk about analog 'old photography' and digital 'new photography'. When we use these terms it is important to underline that the concept of the 'new' is very much related to the *use* of photography, which has changed dramatically with the advent of the Internet. Photography is not any more what it was when both the general public and the following development of a theory of photography during the twentieth century connected the medium with realism, objectivity, indexicality, and a melancholic freezing of the past, preserving it for eternity. Although the 'old' photography – as articulated by the early phenomenological photography theories of André Bazin and Roland Barthes – confirmed 'what-has been' (Barthes, 1981) and fulfilled a 'mummification desire' to embalm time (Bazin, 1980), the new digital practices on the Internet show 'what-is-going on', i.e. *presence*.

When I look at almost any of the millions of publicly accessible private photography albums available, for instance, on Picasa or Facebook,

I am struck by at least two major differences from traditional analog photography albums: first, a specific situation is often depicted in many almost identical images, with sometimes up to several hundred of them being stored in albums as an archival database. This presentation is, of course, due to the fact that taking as many photographs as you want of a given situation is free, whereas before you had to pay for the development of each analog photograph and thus became more cautious about how many you actually took. But the technological development has opened up the possibility of using the still camera in a more 'filmic' way, using exposure times of several seconds. In that way, you can take photographs that unfold in time without them becoming a film – and many people do indeed use that possibility. These stored photographs thereby enhance the feeling of *experiencing* a moment rather than embalming it. Second, and this, of course, relates to the same technological development, the subject of the image is often much more apparently insignificant than with 'old photography': a flower, a cat, a half-eaten meal, 50 images of two kids playing in a swimming pool, and 30 images of a cloud crossing the sky. I would propose that these images are presented in public on a global scale in order to communicate the feeling of being present with an audience, known or unknown.

Today photography is predominantly *a social, everyday activity* rather than a memory-embalming one, creating presence, relational situations, and communication as well as new affective involvements between bodies and the new photographic, media-convergent technologies, such as the mobile phone. Look at people taking photos in the streets during spectacular events as well as in their daily lives: the camera(-phone) is often held at a distance, with the outstretched arm functioning as a bodily extension, whereby we 'touch' the world, and the assessment of the photograph immediately following the shooting situation is part of a social act. In light of this epistemological change, the medium of photography demands a reformulation, one that photographic historians and theoreticians have had problems articulating. Increasingly, everyday amateur photography will be regarded as a performative practice connected to 'presence', as opposed to the storing of 'precious' memories for eternity, which is how it has hitherto been conceptualized.

In 2001, the first mobile phone camera was put on the market, but it only took off in 2004, the same year that the web platform Flickr was launched. Photography is a central part of these new digital communities in Web 2.0. Photography is converging not only with the Internet but also with mobile phones. In 2004, 246 million camera phones (mobile phones with digital cameras) were sold worldwide – nearly four times the amount of the sales of digital cameras. And mobile phone commercials increasingly highlight the camera. While 'analog photography' was directed at a *future* audience (because it took time to have the film roll developed and the images printed), pictures taken by camera phones can be seen immediately by people at-a-distance who are in possession of mobiles equipped with an MMS or email service. In the United Kingdom, where around one in two mobiles were camera phones in 2007, '448,962,359 MMS picture messages were sent in 2007, the equivalent of 19 million traditional (24 exposure) rolls of camera film'.[3] The affordances of digital photography potentially make photographic images both instantaneous and mobile.

'New' photography

Within the past 5-7 years, the material base of photography has been revolutionized to such an extent that we can talk about 'new photography', the digital. The future of the medium seems inextricably linked to mobile phones and to the Internet and, to a much lesser degree, to paper images, albums, and traditional cameras. All this indicates that digital photography is a complex technological network in the *making* rather than a single fixed technology. We therefore also need to rethink the theory of photography. Although photography scholars used to theorize photography as a distinct technology with a 'life of its own', photography has now converged with the omnipresent technologies of the Internet and mobile phones. We cannot theorize or research amateur photography in particular without including such media. At the same time, this convergence of new media and the proliferation of amateur photography does not mean the end of photography, as many proclaimed with the advent of digital photography around 1990, but the end – or at least the radical change – of photography 'as we know it', as Martin Lister states in the quote above. These developments represent a radical moment, a paradigm shift, in the understanding and conception of photography. Instead of terms such as index, referent, nostalgia, melancholic freezing, and mummification desire, we need a new conceptual framework to fully grasp and acknowledge the change of the medium of photography with digital cameras, Web 2.0, and mobile phones: a new media ecology, as Lister calls it. Here, the concept of 'the signaletic' as developed in Bodil Marie Stavning Thomsen's article, 'Signaletic, Haptic and Real-time Material' (2012), seems highly applicable to the medium of photography.

While much (earlier) writing on digital photography either focussed on the dualism truth/analog vs. construction/digital or resembled technological determinism by only considering technical affordances, today we must realize that technologies cannot be separated from embodied practices, from *doings*. The specific affordances of technologies shape, but do not determine, whether and how they can be used and made sense of in practice. This also means that digital photographs can be many different 'things', according to how they are made meaningful and performed in specific contexts. Photography must be understood as, at the same time, a social practice, a networked technology, a material object, and an image. Both the phenomenological version of photography as a *memento mori* and the sociological (Bourdieu) and constructivist approach (represented especially by the Anglo-American school of Discourse Criticism, with scholars such as John Tagg, Allan Sekula, and Martha Rosler) must be supplemented by an analytical approach that includes the practices, the affect, as well as the performative self-construction, and the creation of 'presence', sociability, and community that is embodied in everyday digital photography.

It is most remarkable that one of the most widely read anthologies on photography, *The Photography Reader*, opens with the question 'What is a photograph?' (Wells, 2003: 1) and that methodology books and readers on visual culture almost exclusively discuss the methods to analyze photographs that already exist as signs to be deciphered – as if they were texts. One of the more recent general overviews of the state of the theory of photography is James Elkins's *Photography Theory* (2007). In this book, the main theoretical foci are (still) the questions of indexicality, truth, and referentiality, that is, the question of what photography *is*. It is highly problematic that photography *as a practice* has been so relatively little discussed in academic photography literature. Technology cannot be separated from the question of performative practice. The performative aspects of photography are obvious not only when people take photographs, staging and posing, but also when editing their photographs, putting them in frames and albums, on blogs, and on websites. An important aspect of photography as performance is to articulate and transmit a feeling of *presence*.

Clocks and moments

I will now return to the question of how a work of art can assume the function of articulating sensations and new emotional, as well as conceptual, paradigms and epistemologies in other ways than descriptive and/or analytical terms, i.e. how a work of art can provide us with the insights that academic literature on photography is lacking. There are many explanations behind the allure of Christian Marclay's 2011 Golden Lion-winning film *The Clock*. First of all, the cinematic experience of floating in a comfortable sofa in a dark cinema room in the middle of the hot, buzzy, and very fatiguing adventure that is the Venice Biennial, experiencing a seemingly unending row of clips with famous actors from famous Hollywood films, was fantastic. In that sense, the film can be seen as a tribute to the classic Hollywood film and the film experience *per se*. *The Clock*, which lasts 24 hours, is constructed out of moments in cinema when time is expressed or when a character interacts with a clock, or just a particular time of day, where a clock appears in a specific film. It is about how time gets lived *in* movies and portrayed back to us. You could even argue that we learn to live out time partly by having seen how it plays out in film. Among the thousands of clips collected and sampled by the artist during several years, the film includes clips from such diverse films as *High Noon*, starring Gary Cooper; *Titanic*, with Leonardo DiCaprio; *Easy Rider*, with Peter Fonda; and the Arnold Schwarzenegger action movie *Eraser*. It is, of course, not a real-time movie but rather a simulation of the experience of time passing. At the same time, as the film thematizes time and our constant dependence on and interaction with clocks, it transfers a bodily experience of the passing of time in itself directly to the audience, since the film is synchronized to the real time of the actual screening of it. The film itself thus functions as a clock. So when it was 1.15 PM in the film, it was 1.15 PM in Venice. The film manages to depict the passing of time at the same time as the bodily feeling of *being in* time, in a very original way. In 1907, the French philosopher Henri Bergson wrote *Creative Evolution*, in which he articulated a phenomenological experience of time being divided between the rational, cosmological, measurable time and the sensed, psychologically and personally experienced time, *la durée*: an opposition that has been a focal point for phenomenology during the twentieth century. I would suggest that Marclay's film simultaneously includes both aspects of time, and in that sense, it points toward an alternative way of understanding the relationship between time and visual media.

But, let me turn to another film that condenses this experience to the medium of photography and thereby brings us even further in the search for an understanding of the new media ecology of photography: *Sections of a Happy Moment* (2007) by Belgian artist David Claerbout.[4] It is a 25-minute-long video consisting of b/w still images of the same constructed family photograph 'decisive moment'. In the silent and therefore non-dialogue film we meet an Asian-looking family consisting of what appears to be six family members in the courtyard of a nondescript high rise estate. A little boy has just thrown a ball in the air to a girl that seems to be his sister, who raises her arms to catch the ball. We watch the two children and the other four family members, two men and two women, probably parents and grandparents, all smiling and looking up in the air at the ball. There seem to be three generations gathered in this 'happy moment'. The situation could be seen in any 'classical' family photograph, but here it is depicted in hundreds of photographs. The video is a visually complex depiction of that very moment depicted simultaneously, with at least 15 cameras from many different angles and mounted into one sequence lasting 25 minutes in perception time but less than a second in depicted time.

Apart from the six figures placed in the middle of the courtyard, five other people can be seen: an old man carrying a plastic bag has stopped to watch the scenery. He is situated a few meters away from the group, contemplating them with an empathetic smile. Two teenage girls are crossing the square, turning their backs on the group, thereby not seeing the ball in the air or the other persons. They seem to be lost in their own conversation, and they are moving out of the 'situation frame'. Lastly, an elderly couple is caught in the act of sitting down on plastic chairs outside one of the entrances to the high rise building. The fact that they are in the midst of sitting down enhances the photographic momentariness of the situation. Judging from the clothes of the figures it seems to be summer, and since they are all casting long shadows, it is probably late afternoon. The film is in black and white. First of all, this choice removes the attention from the narrative and raises the effect of a moment being sculpted in time, one could say. Second, it raises the contrast between the smiling people and the modernist concrete and almost inhuman architecture that surrounds them. Incidentally, the film seems to articulate a critical attitude toward the ideas behind classical modernist, mass produced architecture.[5] This is also underlined in a sculpture of naked human figures, made in a modernist, vitalistic, almost abstract style that was seen in the middle of the twentieth century, which appears in this high rise building 'plaza' as a piece of dead material, contrasting with the lively family group.

The film consists of hundreds of different still images of the same moment, each shown between 5 and 13 seconds, and accompanied by a simple, contemplative composition for one piano. The artist had placed at least 15 cameras in and all around the scenario, which is depicted from many different angles and focus points: as extreme close-ups focusing on the facial expression or bodily gesture, as full-frames depicting all 11 figures in one shot, via a frog's or bird's eye perspective, etc. Some of the shots are taken from a high perspective inside the buildings. Invoking the gaze of a sniper looking out, but half covered behind a curtain or a glass wall, some of these images add a slightly uncanny feeling to the film: the family is being watched.

Database time images

As viewers we experience an ongoing moment without beginning and end; one could call it a radical performance of the momentality, intensity, and presence of time itself. It certainly is a family photograph that we see, but we do not relate it to an indexical, nostalgic freezing of the past and a specific memorable moment but much more to a performance of a photographic presence that we experience with our own body over 25 minutes. The 'digitality' of the images makes some of them look slightly 'paintbrushed' or softened, especially the ones where a cropped or zoomed detail fills most of the screen and where we thus focus on, for instance, the girl's ponytail or the little boy's necklace. The black-and-white film appears as a haptic surface where you can sense the materiality of time in itself, as a sculpture of time sculpted out of the very moment via the many cameras used by Claerbout and his crew. The images in the film are not related to narration, but are rather used as signifiers of pure time in order to make the audience 'sense' time.

In interviews, the artist has mentioned that he has been inspired by the 'time philosophy' of Henri Bergson, especially as it is echoed in Deleuze's film books and his notion of the 'time-image' (Deleuze, 1986, 1989). And you can remark that the film is an artistic articulation of the Bergsonian *la durée*, the psychologically imagined as well as bodily felt duration of time as opposed to the experience of time cut up in rationally divided frames of minutes and seconds. Actually, the rational time, the clock time, is exactly the subject of Marclay's film, but synchronizing the filmic time with the perception time, he manages to show how the clock time is bodily experienced as a psychological '*durée*' just as much as Clearbout's extended moment. So, at first glance, Marclay's film seems to represent rational time, whereas Claerbout's demonstrates psychological time. But my point is that each of them does both, thereby inviting us to re-articulate the relationship between time and photography in favor of a more presence-oriented conception of time in relation to photography. In different ways, and through film as well as still photography, both films are magical contemplations of time itself and of the possibility of photograph-based media to articulate time. Thomsen quotes Maurizio Lazzarato's 'video philosophy' in order to use his description of the 'haptic' video image to describe 'the signaletic image' as 'A place, a movement space for time as such. It is no longer quite simply about an image that is going to be seen but about an image in which you interfere, with which you work (a time of events)' (2012: non-pag.). Likewise, these two artworks become not only representations of people and situations but also places for contemplation of time as presence.

Both *The Clock* and *Sections of a Happy Moment* could in principle have been made with traditional analog technology, but it is the 'signaletic' qualities of digital media that provide them with both the practical tools and the very idea behind the works. One could argue that a 'digital epistemology' was needed in order to 'think' these works. They explore 'the database logic of new media', to use a phrase from Lev Manovich (2001); that is, they collect an immense amount of filmic/photographic database material, which is digitally stored and composed with an archival, repetitive, circular, or 'flat' logic, rather than structured by a traditional, progressive narrative. Manovich writes:

> After the novel, and subsequently cinema privileged narrative as the key form of cultural expression of the modern age, the computer age introduces its correlate – database. Many new media objects do not tell stories; they don't have beginning or end; in fact, they don't have any development, thematically, formally or otherwise which would organize their elements into a sequence. Instead, they are collections of individual items, where every item has the same significance as any other. (2001: 194)

In Web 2.0, we can encounter 200 almost identical images of two boys playing in a swimming pool on their mother's private Picasa website,[6] and many private photography websites are structured as such database collections without a beginning or an end. Manovich calls the database the new symbolic form of the computer age: 'A new way to structure our experience of ourselves and the world' (2001: 194), and he analyzes various artworks articulating the 'poetics of the database'. *The Clock* and *Sections of a Happy Moment* are not constructed around a traditional narrative, but as collections of almost similar or only slightly differing data 'objects'. It is the transmission of the signal of timeliness in itself that is the message in Marclay's and Claerbout's works. As Saint Augustine famously stated in his *Confessions* (year 398): 'What is time? If one asks me, I know. If I wish to explain to someone who asks, I no longer know'. Both artworks give form to duration, a form that needs to be experienced over time. 'Time' is not being depicted as 'sign', it is happening here and now – as 'signal'. 'Time' is not the subject matter as much as it is a constitutive matter to be bodily experienced. They manage to make 'time' felt, via the photographic freezing and at the same time the prolonging of time in Clearbout's work and the physical effect of the passing of time in Marclay's filmic work. As Claerbout has put it: 'In my work I think of the digital as a platform in which past, present, and future are not distinguishable from one another and instead coexist happily'.[7] The notion of 'the signaletic' is related to the transmission of real-time signals in digital, global media such as surveillance cameras, for instance. In that sense, the two artworks described are not 'signaletic', nor is the above mentioned database of private family photographs. But, it is my argument that they nevertheless philosophically and aesthetically articulate aspects of 'the signaletic' that we can use to enhance our understanding of contemporary digital photography, as it is used, for instance, in private Web 2.0 photograph albums.

Photography as signaletic presence

Digital collections of photographs, for instance, on Flickr and Picasa, can be seen as such archival databases filled with often very similar images. Showing us the signaletic database logic of photography especially, Claerbout proposes a new understanding of photography that throws light on these Web 2.0 practices. *Sections of a Happy Moment* thus helps us formulate an epistemologically new conception of photography as process, presence, and bodily 'affect'. Having formulated this new theory of photography, we will also be able to look back into the history of the medium and highlight the everyday, social, performative, as well as material aspects of photography, which have hitherto been neglected.

I realize that we are just starting to see how the digital production, perception, and use of photography will develop in new and truly ubiquitous ways that we cannot dream of even today and that this development in the near future will have important implications for our very understanding of the thing or phenomenon we call 'photography'. Works like *The Clock* and *Sections of a Happy Memory* are still extremely difficult and time-consuming to produce, but soon technological improvements will allow anyone with a computer to compile thousands of clips, as done by Marclay, or photograph the same moment from a hundred different angles the way Claerbout did. Therefore, we will see artists pushing technology even further in the years to come, articulating in this way new philosophical aspects of technology. However, as classifications such as Jay David Bolter and Richard Grusin's 'remediation' (1999) have demonstrated, the conceptualization of a new medium is often based on what precedes it. Thus, the digital photograph albums that we meet in Web 2.0 are to a large extent still constructed and perceived as the traditional analog precursor. Simultaneously, as they remediate older forms, new media inventions or practices can also shed light on some older practices. So the new use of photography we experience with Web 2.0, which, I argue, is conceptualized in *Sections of a Happy Moment*, can actually highlight the aspects of the medium that were always already there: the conception of photography as a primarily social, participatory, and performative phenomenon. More philosophically put, it might change our conception of what authenticity and identity mean in relation to photography.[8]

To return to my introduction, the way photography is used and presented in social networks like Picasa, Facebook, and Flickr differs from the function of photography as espoused by Barthes and Bazin. Susan Murray has described sites such as Flickr as follows:

> On these sites, photography has become less about the special or rarefied moments of domestic/family living (for such things as holidays, gatherings, baby photos) and more about an immediate, rather fleeting display of one's discovery of the small and mundane (such as bottles, cupcakes, trees, debris, and architectural elements). In this way, photography is no longer just the embalmer of time that André Bazin once spoke of, but rather a more alive, immediate, and often transitory, practice/form. (2008: 151)

According to Søren Mørk Petersen, Flickr is really about articulating an aesthetics of the everyday and the ephemeral. Like Murray, he stresses the presence character of images and photo sharing on Flickr. His fieldwork demonstrates how people take photographs with their cell phones and upload them directly in order to get a quick and 'fresh' comment by other 'Flickrs' and that this element – closely related to pervasive computing within everyday life – is the primary function of Flickr. It thereby contradicts Barthes' and Bazin's phenomenological connection of photography to death: 'when it registers the banal and mundane aspects of everyday life and not least when it is shared, it becomes a practice closer to life than death' (Peterson, 2008: 146). 'The practice of mob logging, everyday photography, and photo sharing express a desire to retain the experience and sensation of presence and the affective character of everydayness. Uploading becomes a practice that can negotiate the different sensations of presence and the present' (Petersen, 2008: 154).

In summary, I have described two new 'signaletic' databased photograph practices. One, the ubiquitous presence of everyday Web 2.0 photography from mobile phones to social network sites, is extremely widespread but not yet comprehensively theorized. The other practice, as seen in the two video works, is a self- and media-reflexive 'niche product' of the same technological as well as epistemological development, of the database logic as symbolic form. Artists such as Marclay and Claerbout can be said to react to the new media developments; and by exploiting them they are enhancing our understanding of the nature of the media. By bringing attention to their presentation of the photographic construction of *presence*, I hope to have inspired readers to theorize 'photography' differently and to develop a new media ecology, which is now still in an embryonic state.

Original source and licence

Journal of Aesthetics & Culture, Vol. 4, 2012 http://www.aestheticsandculture.net/index.php/jac/article/view/18159. Licence: CC-BY NC 3.0 This is a slightly edited version of the original.

References

Barthes, R. (1981) *Camera Lucida: Reflections on Photography*. New York: Hill and Wang.

Bazin, A. (1980 [1945]) 'The Ontology of the Photographic Image', in Alan Trachtenberg (ed.), *Classic Essays on Photography*. New Haven: Leete's Island Books, 237-44.

Bolter, J. D. & Grusin, R. (1999) *Remediation: Understanding New Media*. Cambridge: MIT Press.

Deleuze, G. (1986) *Cinema 1: The Movement-Image*. Minneapolis: University of Minnesota Press.

Deleuze, G. (1989) *Cinema 2: The Time-Image*. Minneapolis: University of Minnesota Press.

Elkins, J. (ed.) (2007) *Photography Theory*. London: Routledge.

Lazzarato, M. (2002) *Videophilosophie. Zeitwahrnehmung in Postfordismus*. Berlin: b_books.

Manovich, L. (2001) *The Language of New Media*. Cambridge: MIT Press.

Murray, S. (2008) 'Digital Images, Photo-Sharing, and our Shifting Notions of Everyday Aesthetics', *Journal of Visual Culture* 7: 147-63.

Petersen, S. M. (2008) 'Common Banality: The Affective Character of Photo Sharing, Everyday Life and Produsage Cultures' (PhD diss., IT University).

Pinney, C. (1997)*Camera Indica*. Chicago: University of Chicago Press.

Thomsen, B. M. Stavning (2012) 'Signaletic, Haptic and Real-time Material', *Journal of Aesthetics & Culture, Vol. 4*, http://www.aestheticsandculture.net/index.php/jac/article/view/18148

Wells, L. (ed.) (2003) *The Photography Reader*. London: Routledge.

Notes

1. According to Facebook (February 2010), 2.5 billion photographs are uploaded each month.

2. Media and Photography Professor Martin Lister at the conference 'Private Eyes', Copenhagen University, November 2009.

3. http://www.themda.org

4. Claerbout was also shown at the Venice Biennial 2011, at Palazzo Grassi, with his *The Algiers' Sections of a Happy Moment* (2008), which is a further development of the concept from *Sections of a Happy Moment* (2007).

5. A more in-depth analysis of this critical stance would be most interesting in a thematic reading of the film, but lies outside the scope of this article.

6. http://picasaweb.google.com/hstebby47 (accessed November 20, 2011).

7. Artinfo, http://www.artinfo.com/news/story/31145/ori-gersht-puts-five-questions-to-david-claerbout/ (accessed May 1, 2009).

8. For instance, as in Christopher Pinney's (1997) studies of Indian studio photography, where a heavy amount of staging and image manipulation such as handcoloring is perceived as an authentification tool. His fieldwork in these Indian villages has implications for our traditional Western conceptual connection between concepts such as authenticity, truth, indexicality, and non-manipulation.

CHAPTER 6

The 'Potential Mobilities' of Photography

DEBBIE LISLE

In the summer of 1944, American Sergeant Paul Dorsey was hired by the Naval Aviation Photography Unit (NAPU) to capture 'the Marines' bitter struggle against their determined foe' in the Pacific islands (Philips, 1981: 43). Dorsey had been a photographer and photojournalist before enlisting in the Marines, and was thus well placed to fulfil the NAPU's remit of creating positive images of American forces in the Pacific. Under the editorial and professional guidance of Edward Steichen, NAPU photographers like Dorsey provided epic images of battle (especially from the air and sea), and also showed American forces at ease – sunbathing, swimming, drinking and relaxing together (Bachner, 2007). Steichen – by now a lieutenant commander – oversaw the entire NAPU project by developing, choosing and editing the images, and also providing captions for their reproduction in popular newspapers and magazines such as LIFE. Under his guidance, selected NAPU images were displayed at the famous Power in the Pacific exhibition at the Museum of Modern Art in New York at the end of the war, and distributed in the popular U.S. Navy War Photographs memorial book, which sold over 6 million copies in 1945.

While the original NAPU photographers (Steichen himself, Charles Kerlee, Horace Bristol, Wayne Miller, Charles Fenno Jacobs, Victor Jorgensen and Dwight Long) had been at work in the Pacific since the summer of 1942, Dorsey was hired specifically to document the advance of American Marines through the Marianas and Volcano Islands. In line with the NAPU's remit, Dorsey provided a number of famous rear view shots of combat action on Guam, Saipan and Iwo Jima. However, there are a number of his photographs that do not fit easily within that vision of war – images of wounded Marines and dead Japanese soldiers, as well as shots of abject Japanese POWs with their heads bowed and faces averted. It is this last group of enemy images that proves the most interesting, for not only do they trouble NAPU's explicit propaganda framework, they also challenge our traditional assumption that photography is an inert form of representation.

It is not hard to imagine that photographs of abject Japanese POWs reinforced feelings of triumph, conquest and justice that circulated in America's post-war victory culture. Indeed, images of emaciated and incarcerated Japanese soldiers provided the perfect contrast to the hyper-masculine, hard-bodied, beefcake figures that populated the NAPU photographs and symbolized American power in the Pacific. However, once Japan was rehabilitated into a powerful American ally, and the decision to drop the atomic bomb was questioned once again in America's Culture Wars of the 1980s and 90s, it was no longer acceptable to feel triumphant in the face of Japanese abjection and suffering. Instead, these images helped foster a new kind of belated patriotism – and a new global disposition – in which Americans generated their own magnanimity by expressing pity, compassion and sympathy for victims of their previous foreign policy decisions (Lisle, 2007: 234).

While that patriotic interpretive framework tells us much about how dominant formations of American identity are secured by the production – especially the visual production – of enemy others, it cannot account for images or viewer interpretations that exceed, unwork, or disrupt war's foundational logics of friend/enemy and perpetrator/victim. I focus on Dorsey because he offers one such 'deviant' image (figure 6.1).

This photograph was taken by Dorsey on Guam in July 1944, and its caption tells us that the Japanese prisoner 'waits to be questioned by intelligence officers' (Philips, 1981: 189). As the POW looks into Dorsey's camera lens (and therefore at us, the viewers), he is subject to the collective gaze of the American marines situated behind him, and presumably others that lay out of the frame, behind Dorsey. What is fascinating about this particular image is the prisoner's refusal to obey the trope of abjection so readily assumed by other Japanese POWs documented in the NAPU archive and in other popular war-time imagery. Indeed, when I first encountered this image I immediately framed the POW's return gaze as defiant – a challenging, bold, and forceful reply to American aggression in the Pacific. The problem, of course, was that this resistant gaze soon became reductive; that is, by replicating war's foundational logics of difference it effaced a number of other dispositions at work in the photograph. What I find compelling about the POW's return gaze is its refusal to be contained within the available subject positions of either 'abject POW' or 'defiant resistor'. Indeed, this unruliness is what keeps me coming back to Dorsey's image, for it teaches us that photography itself always exceeds the conventional assumption that it is a static form of visual representation.

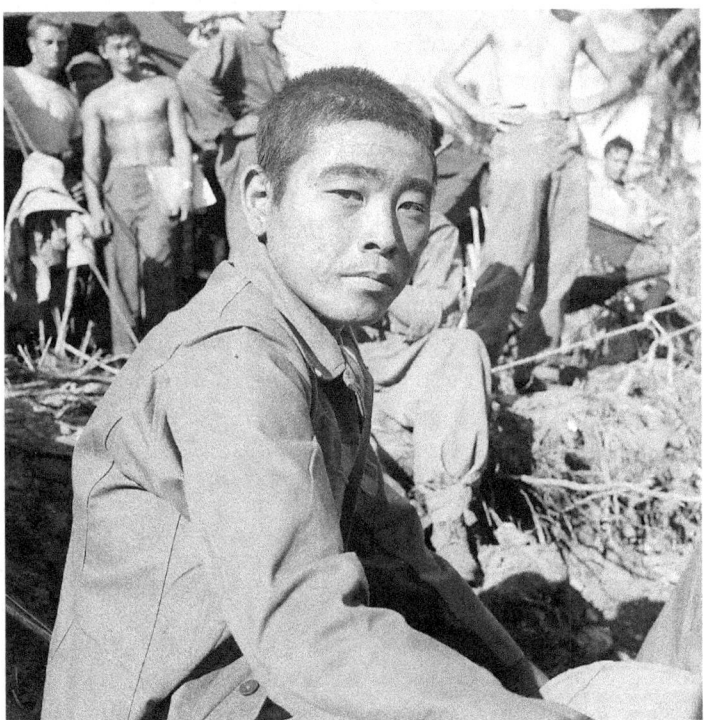

Figure 6.1. Paul Dorsey's photograph of the Japanese POW is # 80-G-475166 in the NAPU archive and is reproduced here courtesy of the United States National Archives.

Photography, animation, movement

The connections between movement, stillness and photography have two important starting points. The first, and more general, is Walter Benjamin's concept of the dialectic image in which the past and the present come together 'in a flash' and constitute what he calls 'dialectics at a standstill' (Benjamin, 1999: 463). Unlike Theodor Adorno, who lamented Benjamin's Medusa-like tendency to turn the world to stone, I read Benjamin's concept of standstill – of stillness in general – as something fizzing and pulsating with 'political electricity' (Adorno, 1997: 227-42; Buck-Morss, 1997: 219). This is to deny our most basic assumption about photography: that it is an inert visual form that freezes and captures discrete moments in time and space. My central argument is that photography's assumed stillness is always constituted by a number of potential and actual mobilities that continually suture and re-suture viewing subjects and images into one another.

Developing Benjamin's idea of the past and present coming together 'in a flash', Roland Barthes provides the second starting point with his notion of the *punctum* of photography: 'this element which rises from the scene, shoots out of it like an arrow, and pierces me' (Barthes, 2000: 25). Conventional understandings of the punctum frame it as a static moment – so powerful that it *freezes* the viewer, *stops* them in their tracks, and *captures* their attention. My point is that the affective punch of the photograph is not a frozen moment at all; rather, the punctum – like the dialectic image – is fizzing with political electricity. Therefore, to suggest that a viewing subject is arrested in the moment of perception – that they are somehow captured by a photograph's meaning – is to mistakenly understand the act of looking as a static behaviour.

I want to use Dorsey's image of the POW to push these theoretical starting points and explore the mobile dispositions that are generated when a viewing subject encounters a photograph. What most interests me about Dorsey's photograph is the level of animation it produces. The POW's return gaze is actually rather blank: it is unclear whether he is angry, weary, bored, insane or none of the above. But it is the viewing subject's anxiety at such ambivalence – such unknowability – that provokes a powerful desire to name it. The visceral sensations and emotional responses provoked in viewers (Are we taken aback? Do we sympathize with the POW? Are we equally blank?) very quickly become settled interpretations, for example, 'his defiant gaze resists American power'. What I want to do is explore the pre-interpretive moment when images like Dorsey's reach out and grab us – for it is in that moment that photography's 'political electricity' reveals itself most clearly.

Production, signification, interpretation

The mobility inherent in the photograph has an important antecedent at the level of production. Since the Brownie camera was introduced in WWI, photographers have carried their mode of representation with them – in Dorsey's case, his portable camera was carried with him as he travelled with the Marines through the Pacific (Philips, 1981: 29). It is the photographer's itinerary – his or her movement prior to clicking the camera's shutter – that shapes and determines a photograph's content. More to the point, the action of clicking the camera's shutter is never an isolated moment; rather, it is punctured by all of the previous clicks and moments leading up to it – especially on a long photographic assignment like Dorsey's – and contains within it all of the subsequent clicks and moments that potentially come after it. In this sense, the photographer's click recalls Benjamin: it is a 'charged force field of past and present' (Buck-Morss, 1997: 219). That complicated temporality is also manifested in the photographer's contact sheet (or, more recently, computer file), which operates as a visual travelogue of discrete moments that bleed into one another.

The mobility inherent in photography extends itself into the level of signification; that is, the arrangements of signs depicted within the frame of each discrete image. Critic Gilberto Perez gives us a clue to this mobility in his comments about Eugène Atget's famous 'painterly' photographs of Paris:

> A photograph begins with the mobility, or at least potential mobility, of the world's materials, of the things reproduced from reality, and turns that into a still image. More readily than in a painting, we see things in a photograph, even statues, as being on the point of movement, for these things belong to the world of flux from which the image has been extracted. (Perez, 1983: 328).

I agree that the origin point of a photograph is potential mobility, but that mobility is never completely vanquished when it is turned into a still image. For me, photographs – no matter what they depict – are always saturated with the 'potential mobility of the world's materials', and in this sense they are never still. Indeed, the world of flux out of which the image is extracted *includes* the image itself, and in that sense, an image can never be isolated from the world it is derived from. If we follow Perez and characterize the world as one of flux, but then insist that the photograph can never be extracted from that world, it follows that the photograph, too, is characterized by fluctuation and change – in short, by mobility. The point, here, is to read a photograph counter-intuitively – not as an arrest of movement or a freezing of time, but as a collection of signs that is always potentially mobile. This is what Roland Barthes was hinting at when he suggested that a photograph is 'a mad image, chafed by reality': any photograph is haunted by absence because the depicted object is no longer present, but it is also full of certainty that the depicted object *did* exist at a previous time and place (Barthes, 2000: 113-15). This is precisely Benjamin's point as well, that 'what has been comes together with the now' (Benjamin, 1999: 463). Following on from Barthes and Benjamin, I want to argue that photographs don't freeze a moment in time, but instead set in motion a continual journey between feelings of absence in the present (i.e. 'it is not there') and present imaginings of the past (i.e. 'but it has indeed been').

As Barthes' notion of the punctum reveals, the most powerful register at which photography's inherent mobility operates is in the sensations, responses and feelings provoked in viewers. This is why we say that a photograph has the capacity to *move* us: the best images take us from one emotional state (e.g. passive, curious, bored) and carry us into another (e.g. shocked, sad, amused). It is this emotional terrain of our responses to photography that both Roland Barthes and Susan Sontag have explored in depth. Why are we moved by some images and not others? Are documentary or artistic photographs more likely to reach out and prick us? What is the most appropriate or ethical response to pictures of another's suffering?

Sontag suggests a different connection between photography and mobility in that it enables a particular *touristification* of the world; that is, cameras help 'convert the world into a department store or museum-without-walls in which every subject is depreciated into an article of consumption, promoted to an item for aesthetic appreciation' (Sontag, 1971: 110). While Sontag's political economy of photography (with its Frankfurt School echo) continues to be explored by anthropologists and scholars in Tourism Studies, I want to argue that it offers a particularly reductive account of photography's potential mobilities. While Sontag does address photography's constitutive and rather complex relationship with reality, she still conceives of photographs themselves as static and inert representations. Indeed, what she wrestled with in *On Photography* was the 'insolent, poignant stasis of each photograph', and the photograph's capacity to make reality 'stand still' (Sontag, 1971: 111-12; 163). The problem with such a view is that it limits our account of interpretation; in short, it suggests that viewers either accept a photograph's static message (and are thus moved), or reject it (and remain unmoved). But the moving, here, is the sole prerogative of the viewer: there is no sense in which the photograph and its contents are *themselves* mobile. I want to argue that the relationships established in the act of looking between viewing subjects and the objects contained within an image are much more complex and varied than Sontag's framework suggests.

Photography's affective mobility

To reveal the mobilities underscoring photography's affective punch, we must redistribute its more familiar power relations through W. J. T. Mitchell's important question: *what do pictures want?* Such a question subverts our usual approach to photographs (i.e. what do *we* want from photographs?) by redeploying the privileged agency of the viewer into the image itself. In other words, it is the *image* that demands something of the viewer rather than the other way around. What it demands, of course, is a response. Certainly this is an emotional response, for even being bored by a photograph is a response of sorts. But an emotional response is also an affective response, which means that the punch carried by a photograph is as physical as it is metaphorical or visual. Indeed, it is precisely in the act of perception, where the emotional and the affective fuse, that photography's assumed stillness is powerfully subverted.

If Mitchell animates the picture by affording it some of the viewer's agency, then Gilles Deleuze goes one step further by exploring what happens to agency in the act of perception. For Deleuze, a work of art – for our purposes, a photograph – is not an inert or still document, but rather a 'block of sensations' (Deleuze, 2003; Deleuze & Guattari, 1994 and Bogue, 2003). It is not a finished object produced by an autonomous artist or beheld in its entirety by an autonomous viewer; rather, it is a combination of percepts (initial perceptions) and affects (physical intensities) that passes through all subjects at the point of visual perception. This kind of relational encounter with an image not only deconstructs Modernity's foundational distinction between the subject and the object, it also opens up an affective connection between all subjects engaged in the act of looking; in this case, the photographer, the subjects and objects within the photograph and the viewer.

From Deleuze, we know that perception is characterized by common physical responses in all subjects: the movement of the optic nerve, the dilation of the pupil, the squint of the eyelid, the craning of the neck to see up close. However small, however imperceptible, these physical sensations are all still movements; indeed, they are movements repeated by all seeing subjects. My point is that these imperceptible modes of attention are consistently engaged in the act of viewing photographs. What this suggests is that taking account of the affective level of perception changes our traditional understandings of interpretation; indeed, even if a photograph fails to move us emotionally, it certainly moves us physically, though we may not be conscious of it.

Drawing from Mitchell and Deleuze, then, we can say that a photograph's 'insolent, poignant stasis' makes no sense. A photograph is constantly animated not just by the potentials inherent in its enframed subjects and objects, but more importantly, in the acts of perception undertaken by viewers. Certainly some photographs move us emotionally – to tears, to laughter, to rage – and indeed, this emotional terrain is where Barthes and Sontag offer important insights. My point is that *all* photographs, no matter what they depict, move us physically through the act of perception. If we take Mitchell's question seriously and extend agency to the photograph, then it is in the affective register that we can discern a more relational encounter between subjects and objects because both are in a constant state of mobility.

Ambivalence and paralysis

How might Mitchell's question apply to Dorsey's photograph? What does this image want from us? What does it demand from our acts of looking? The dispersed account of agency put forward by Mitchell suggests that the act of looking can never be contained within the subject; indeed, what is produced in each act of looking is some kind of subject-object-world assemblage in which each component is characterised by its potential and actual mobilities. With respect to Dorsey's image, then, the multiple lines of sight at work in the photograph indicate multiple – and mobile – relationalities. Primarily, there is the relationship between the viewer – any potential viewer – and the photograph. If we follow Mitchell's line of questioning, however, we need to ask how the photograph itself shapes the emotive and affective experience of visual interpretation – how the photograph's demand is transmitted to the viewer.

Firstly, this demand is channelled through Dorsey's line of sight that extends through his camera's viewfinder and into the formal elements of the photograph: the focused POW in the foreground, the blurred figures in the background, the light and shade on the subjects' clothing and skin, the battle scarred terrain, and the position of these elements within the viewfinder's frame. As viewers we cannot see Dorsey, but his presence fills – and indeed constitutes – the photograph. Secondly, the photograph's demand is channelled through the POW's line of sight that extends to Dorsey (who is both photographer and marine Sergeant), and potentially through his camera to imagined viewers. It is precisely the return gaze of the POW that packs such an affective punch – not because of what it *means*, but rather because of how it makes us *feel* emotionally and physically. While a conventional account would understand this affective punch as shocking, stopping or capturing the viewer, I want to argue it does the opposite – it suddenly reveals the fizzing, vibrant mobilities that transmit the picture to us, and us to the picture.

There are, I think, important lessons for us in Dorsey's photograph. It is a powerful antecedent to Judith Butler's exploration of the Abu Ghraib images, and her repetition of Sontag's question of 'whether the tortured can and do look back, and what do they see when they look at us' (Butler, 2007: 966). The POW's gaze provides an answer to the first part of this question – they certainly do look back. But as to what they see when they look back at us, that question can only be answered if we redistribute both agency and mobility into the photograph to empower and mobilize the tortured, the abject, and the objectified. That leaves us with Sontag's much more vexing question of what we do *after* we look at photographs. As Butler explains, Sontag has denounced the photograph 'precisely because it enrages without directing the rage, and so excites our moral sentiments at the same time that it confirms our political paralysis' (Butler, 2007: 966). This sets up an important challenge for us: in refusing conventional understandings of photography as a still visual art, how can we use more dispersed accounts of agency and mobility to work through the political paralysis that Sontag identifies?

Original source and licence

M/C Journal, Vol. 12, No. 1 (2009) - 'still', http://journal.media-culture.org.au/index.php/mcjournal/article/viewArticle/125.
Licence: CC-BY NC ND.

References

Adorno, T. (1997) *Prisms*. Cambridge: MIT Press.

Bachner, E. (2004) *At Ease: Navy Men of WWII*. New York: Harry N. Abrams.

Bachner, E. (2007) *Men of WWII: Fighting Men at Ease*. New York: Harry N. Abrams.

Barthes, R. (1980/2000) *Camera Lucida*. London: Vintage.

Benjamin, W. (1999) 'On the Theory of Knowledge, Theory of Progress', in *The Arcardes Project*. Cambridge: Cambridge University Press.

Bogue, R. (2003) *Deleuze on Music, Painting and the Arts*. London: Routledge.

Buck-Morss, S. (1997) *The Dialectics of Seeing: Walter Benjamin and the Arcades Project*. Cambridge: Cambridge University Press.

Butler, J. (2007) 'Torture and the Ethics of Photography', *Environment and Planning D: Society and Space*, (25), 6.

Deleuze, G. (2003) *Francis Bacon: The Logic of Sensation*. London: Continuum.

Deleuze, G. & Guattari, F. (1994) *What is Philosophy?* New York: Columbia University Press.

Lisle, D. (2007) 'Benevolent Patriotism: Art, Dissent and the American Effect', *Security Dialogue*, (38), 2.

Mitchell, W. J. T. (2004) *What Do Pictures Want? The Lives and Loves of Images.* Chicago: University of Chicago Press.

Perez, G. (1983) 'Atget's Stillness', *The Hudson Review,* (36), 2.

Philips, C. (1981) *Steichen at War.* New York: Harry N. Abrams.

Sontag, S. (2004) *Regarding the Pain of Others.* London: Penguin.

Sontag, S. (1971) *On Photography.* London: Penguin.

Steichen, E. (1945) *U.S. Navy War Photographs.* New York: U.S. Camera.

CHAPTER 7

The Cinematograph As an Agent of History

Kamila Kuc

The photographic apparatus as a nonliving agent

For many classic film theorists such as André Bazin, the invention of photography in the 19th century was a response to the human's supposed psychological need for illusion created by 'a mechanical reproduction'. According to Bazin, the arrival of photography was precipitated by a crisis of realism in painting, a crisis that emerged from a certain tension between the 'aesthetic and the psychological' (Bazin, 2005a: 12-13). Bazin believed that photography had 'freed the plastic arts from their obsession with likeness' and, in doing so, addressed a 'psychological' problem: the human need to preserve images for posterity, thus winning the battle against time and 'spiritual death' (Bazin, 2005a: 9). For Bazin photography was characterized by a greater objectivity than painting, as he considered the photographic apparatus a 'nonliving agent': 'for the first time an image of the world is formed automatically, without the creative intervention of a man', he pronounced (Bazin, 2005a: 13). Because of its ability to reproduce movement, cinema took this aspiration to realism a step further as it was capable of capturing, or simply functioning as, 'objectivity in time' (Bazin, 2005a: 14). It was in film that, for the first time in the history of vision, 'the image of things [was] likewise the image of their duration' (Bazin, 2005a: 15).

One could argue that, ever since its emergence, this task of faithfully representing reality has been imposed on cinema because of its ability to capture motion. And it is precisely the notion of movement that brings together – and separates – the complex and interrelated histories of photography and film. Both media have been burdened with claims about their supposed objectivity as something that shapes and defines their ontology. It is also because of its extensive use in science, for example in providing records of surgical operations, that it was traditionally believed, especially in the early days of the medium, that cinema's main destiny was to document reality. Among those who held this view was an internationally renowned Pole, Boleslaw Matuszewski (1856-1944), who was convinced that film's most important role was to capture the world faithfully as it was. Matuszewski was a keen theorist, photographer (he owned two photographic studios: one in Paris, one in Warsaw) and filmmaker. This essay revisits Matuszewski's understanding of the cinematic apparatus as a witness of history in relation to Karen Barad's notion of agential realism. A clear tension between the objective and subjective approach to filmmaking is revealed once we allow the claim that the cinematic apparatus is not just a witness to history but also its active agent. In what follows I will show that, on the one hand, early documentary practices were seen as a rather conventional, straightforward record of reality, as embodied in Matuszewski's *actualities* (aka proto-documentaries) and the principle of 'capturing life unawares'. On the other hand, the 1920s and 1930s avant-garde experiments with documentary allow us to situate this type of filmmaking within the realm of more subjective and, to use Barad's term, more agential storytelling, as seen, for example, in Dziga Vertov's or Walter Ruttmann's city symphonies.

The cinematograph as a creator of history

Matuszewski's seminal article 'The New Source of History: The Creation of a Depository for Historical Cinematography' (1898) is one of the first texts concerning the ontology of the cinematic image.[1] An admirer of both still photography and the cinematograph, Matuszewski believed that the latter was less open to manipulation than photography. For him photographs could be retouched, 'even to the point of transformation. But just try to make identical changes on... microscopic images!' (Matuszewski, 1898a).[2] For Matuszewski the superiority of the cinematograph rested in the fact that, unlike any other medium, it could reliably reproduce movement, and hence life. For him, 'authenticity, exactitude and precision' were intrinsic to 'animated photography' (Matuszewski, 1898b). Matuszewski's belief in the impartiality of the cinematic lens led him to a conviction that film was actually capable of correcting the errors of history. A Polish weekly paper commented on the publication of Matuszewski's 'A New Source of History' as follows:

> As a work of the human mind, every literary or printed source must, from the very nature of things, be more or less reticent. Because of this, historical truth is relative. However, the cinematograph – unmistakably a source of, as they say, mechanical history – is *an absolutely truthful* document: the cinematograph never lies. (Anonymous, 1898).[3]

Matuszewski considered his actuality, *The Visit of President Faure in St Petersburg* (1898), an expression of this view. The film documented the visit of President Faure to St Petersburg. During this visit, Otto von Bismarck accused the French President Félix Faure of breaching a certain diplomatic etiquette by not taking his hat off while reviewing a guard of honour. Matuszewski's footage challenged this claim by showing that Faure did indeed do so, thus preventing a historical error and a possible diplomatic conflict.[4] For Matuszewski this film proved itself a reliable eyewitness, as the cinematograph verified 'verbal testimony' (Matuszewski, 1898a). He believed that 'if human witnesses contradict each other about an event', the cinematograph could 'resolve the disagreement by silencing the one that it belies' (Matuszewski, 1898a).

For this reason, the filmmaker considered a celluloid strip not simply a historical document, but a part of history in its own right. The process of recording reality was thus the very act of creating history for him, which he believed was the filmmaker's greatest responsibility (Matuszewski, 1898a). Such a view conflates different senses of 'history': as a record and document, as well as analysis and discourse. Matuszewski's idea that a celluloid strip constituted a part of history not only granted the cinematograph more seriousness, but it also made a stronger claim for the reliability of the recorded image. This echoes the German historian Leopold von Ranke's concept of writing history. Because of his critical use of documents as the model for historical research and writing in the 19th century, Ranke is often referred to as the 'father of historical science'. Influenced by German Idealist thought and figures such as Johann Gottlieb Fichte and Friedrich Schelling, Ranke's method can be summarised in the idea of holding on 'strictly to the facts of history'.

For Ranke a proper understanding of history required a reconstruction of the past, which stressed the importance of the relevant facts and the use of a strict critical method. This included 'a documentary, penetrating, profound study' as a necessary approach. Ranke considered history an art but, unlike other arts, history required the ability to recreate (Iggers, 2010: xi). The ideal historian, for Ranke, should therefore possess certain qualities, the most important one being his 'pure love of truth' (Ranke, 1830: 12). He believed that 'by recognizing something sublime in the event, the condition, or the person we want to know something about, we acquire a certain esteem for that which has transpired, passed, or appeared' (Ranke, 1830: 12).

However, for Ranke, the factual establishment of events did not yet constitute history and the historian was not a passive observer who merely recorded events: instead, the historian actively recreated a historical subject matter by relying on empirical observation and was 'bound by the reality of his subject matter' (Iggers, 2010: xxvii). The ability to 'portray the forces of history without interjecting one's own set of values is the core of objectivity', thus impartiality was of key importance (Iggers, 2010: 2). For Ranke universal history could never be a mere compilation of national histories, but the history of the nations had to be related to a 'broader course of world history' (Iggers, 2010: 84). He valued an 'honest' historian who could confront the documents and thus attain an objective view of the great facts, 'free from the mutual accusations of the contemporaries and the often restricted view of their posterity' (Iggers, 2010: 84).

According to Ranke, history was given a task of 'judging the past' and 'of instructing the present for the benefit of future ages' (Ranke, 1824: 57). For him a reliable historian should be able to show 'what actually happened' (*'wie es eigentlich gewesen'*) (Ranke, 1824: 57). Similarly, Matuszewski was convinced that the human word failed as the only evidence in the recollection of historical events and that the cinematograph could correct this failure because it offered a reliable and objective view. Like Ranke, Matuszewski thought that history could teach future generations how to avoid political errors: 'Do you believe that some knowledge of past events contains nothing useful which is applicable to the present or future?', asked Ranke (Ranke, 1836: 77). The aim of history was not so much to 'gather facts and to arrange them as to understand them' (Ranke, 1836: 77). Although it is not clear whether Matuszewski had ever read

Ranke, many of Ranke's beliefs, prominent at the time, were reflected in the way Matuszewski perceived the role of film in society.

Matuszewski's appreciation of the cinema's documentary values was echoed in subsequent debates about the processes of recording history. For example, in 1931 the President of the American Historical Association, Carl L. Becker commented on the fact that many historical events are only known 'imperfectly' because we can 'never revive them, never observe or test them directly' (Becker, 1931: 221). Becker continued that once the event had occurred, it had disappeared, 'so that in dealing with it the only objective reality we can observe or test is some material trace which the event had left – usually a written document' (Becker, 1931: 221). As an effect, Becker distinguished two histories: 'the actual series of events that once occurred; and the ideal series that we affirm and hold in memory. The first is absolute and unchanged – it was what it was whatever we do or say about it; the second is relative, always changing in response to the increase or refinement of knowledge' (Becker, 1931: 221).

This complex relationship between the actual and the related events is at the heart of Matuszewski's film, which illustrates the limitation in the process of writing history with words. The numerous imperfections in relating historical events could be successfully avoided in film, as seen in *The Visit of President Felix Faure*. Although Matuszewski claims that the process of recording reality counts as the very act of creating history, often in his discourse the apparatus of cinema, i.e. the actual cinematographic machine, seems to function as an objective and passive agent. Similarly, in his claim about a greater authenticity of photography over painting, Bazin supports himself with an observation that 'the lens' in French is 'the *objectif*, a nuance that seems lost in English (Bazin, 2005a: 13). In the process of revisiting such claims Karen Barad's notion of agential realism, which I will discuss at the end of this essay, will prove instructive.

Actualities and the avant-garde documentary tradition: between objectivity and subjectivity

Matuszewski's own films were of documentary (*Coronation of Tsar Nicolas II*, 1896; *The Jubilee of the Queen of England, Victoria*, 1897 and *The Visit of President Faure in St Petersburg*, 1898), ethnographic (*Travels in Spała and Białowieża*, 1895) and educational character (*Surgical*

Operations in Warsaw, 1895). His practical and theoretical works testify to a certain tension that existed in cinema from its beginning: the one between what filmmakers and critics alike perceived as objective and subjective forms of filmmaking. The key films of the 1920s and 1930s avant-garde were typically seen to be of a documentary nature: for example, Dziga Vertov's *Man with the Movie Camera* (1929, Soviet Union) and Walter Ruttmann's *Berlin: Symphony of a Great City* (1927). These films to a great degree reflected the growing politicization of the avant-gardes, as captured in Hans Richter's 1934 book, *The Struggle for the Film*, in which the filmmaker traced a departure of numerous avant-garde filmmakers from a purist, formalist filmmaking to a politically and socially concerned filmmaking of the late 1920s and 1930s.

By the 1920s the documentary was also one of the most popular film genres in Poland. Productions such as *Praca Polski na morzu* (*Polish Work at the Sea*, produced by Sea and River League, 1928) and Łódź – miasto pracy (Stefan Grodzieński, 1927) (Banaszkiewicz and Witczak, 1989: 245-246) all derived from the early actualities by filmmakers like Matuszewski. Let us first consider the differences between actualities and documentaries, because it is in this distinction that the more creative role of the supposedly realist and representational filmmaking comes to the fore. Tom Gunning understood 'actuality' as 'the practice before World War One', whereas such practices after the Great War are referred to as 'documentary' – the term which has been in use since John Grierson's 1926 review of Robert J. Flaherty's *Moana* (1926) (Gunning, 1997: 23). In Grierson's view Flaherty 'had created a film of documentary value', which nevertheless involved a 'creative treatment of actuality' (Grierson, in Loiperdinger, 1997: 25). The founder of the British Documentary Movement therefore clearly believed that the filming of 'actuality' in itself did not constitute what might be seen as the 'truth'. Actuality footage had to be subjected to a creative process 'to reveal its truth'. He distinguished documentaries from other films made from 'natural material', such as newsreels, scientific and educational films. Film could not just describe and photograph – it needed to analyse and synthesise. Only through this process, Grierson claimed, could creativity emerge, and he believed that his film *The Drifters* (1929) was an expression of such an approach.

This creative approach to the recording of reality discussed by Grierson as a mark of difference between actuality and documentary relies on a particular intervention and embraces the notion of the cut (i.e. edit) in the process of shaping the film's form and content. It is because, as we know well by now, the practice of editing is by no means neutral. Prompted by this realisation, in *Life After New Media: Mediation As a Vital Process* (2012) Sarah Kember and Joanna Zylinska ask: if we must always cut – as writers, photographers and filmmakers, then 'what does it mean to cut well?' (Kember and Zylinska, 2012: 71). One possible answer to this question can be found in Bazin's writings. For the *Cahiers du Cinéma* theorist the decisive cut is not just an aesthetic but also an ethical notion, which is a point that Kember and Zylinska also make. Not one in favour of the fast cutting and montage techniques of Sergei Eisenstein, Bazin preferred the deep focus of Orson Welles and the long takes of the Italian Neorealist directors. He believed that these latter techniques created a greater illusion of reality and thus brought cinema closer to life (Bazin, 2005b). Yet 'reality' remains a highly contested and subjective term, given its reliance on editorial decisions, choices and cuts.

As for the links between documentary and the avant-grade, Bill Nichols argues that what fulfilled Grierson's desire for 'the creative treatment of actuality' most relentlessly was the modernist avant-garde (Nichols, 2001: 592). It can thus be said that the evolution of documentary went hand in had with the development of avant-garde tendencies in film. They both utilised each other's techniques: 'Modernist techniques of fragmentation and juxtaposition lent an artistic aura to documentary that helped to distinguish it from the cruder form of early actualities or newsreels' (Nichols, 2001: 583).

It was the experimental use of film that, according to Nichols, turned an actuality into a documentary. In consequence, 'documentary, like avant-garde film, cast the familiar in a new light...' (Nichols, 2001: 580). Nichols thus considers documentary as a mature version of actuality and an important genre of avant-garde film. For Matuszewski the raw footage of actuality was enough to consider it a faithful representation of reality as the cinema's artistic status rested in its unique qualities as an objective source of historical events. The mission to represent reality faithfully was, he believed, the cinematograph's *raison d'être*. In a similar vein, in his 1935 book *Documentary Film*, Paul Rotha recognised the early actualities' capability of recording 'spontaneity of natural behaviour' as 'a cinematic quality' (Rotha: 1935, 79). Matuszewski's preoccupation with film in the service of the nation and his recognition of film's nation-building qualities resembles not only Polish Romantic beliefs but also an approach employed by such key figures of the international avant-garde film scene as Sergei Eisenstein, Vsevolod Pudovkin and Dziga Vertov.

In his argument for making a connection between documentary and avant-garde films, Nichols points out four elements that contributed to the formation of a documentary film wave. Only one of these elements, Nichols argues, 'had been in place since 1895' (Nichols, 2001: 586). Incidentally, this element is most crucial to my argument as it refers to 'the capacity of cinema to record visible phenomena with great fidelity' (Nichols, 2001: 586). Here Matuszewski's attitude towards shaping historical consciousness through the use of film puts him at the forefront of the debates about the propagandist values of film. His recognition of the propagandist values of cinema corresponds to some degree with that of Sergei Eisenstein's *Battleship Potemkin* (1925) and *October: Ten Days That Shook the World* (1928). Although highly stylized and heavily cut, Eisenstein's films, like Matuszewski's actualities, reflect Nichols's belief in the documentary's power to 'alter our perception of the world' (Nichols, 2001: 596).

Both Matuszewski and Eisenstein shared a certain level of utopian visionary romanticism as far as the role of cinema was concerned. According to Sheila Skaff, Matuszewski's writing was 'informed by the nineteenth century Polish Romantic nationalist literary tradition and its sense for longing identity, which has fallen into a slumber and must be reawakened' (Skaff, 2008: 33). Matuszewski's proposal concerning the importance of preserving aspects of army life is relevant here. He thought that footage of army battles could be shown to the future generations of soldiers and civilians (Matuszewski, 1898a). In this vein, in 1900 Robert W. Paul filmed *The Army Life or How Soldiers Are Made: Mounted Infantry*, a silent propaganda actuality, which featured the King's Own Royal Lancaster Regiment riding over a plain. Both Matuszewski and Paul recognized the nation-building values of the cinematograph and its potential for strengthening patriotic feelings and preserving tradition – a function that, particularly in the occupied Polish territories, was previously performed by literature and painting. In filming soldiers fighting for the freedom of their country, Matuszewski saw the resurrection of national values and the promotion of patriotism, as seen in the art of painting (Mazaraki, 2006: 40). His need to present 'the true' version of history may have been driven by his coming from a country which for many years had been affected by the reversals of history (Mazaraki, 2006: 40). He saw the cinematograph as playing an important part in the process of creating a new national consciousness and cultural identity of the Poles. To this end, Matuszewski considered the role of a filmmaker as that of an orator who offers moral and political guidance to the masses by means of film.

Taking into account Poland's political situation and its geographical positioning in the 19th century, it is no surprise that Matuszewski emphasised the need for objectivity in the process of recording history in an accurate manner. There had been no Polish state since the partition of 1795 (Wandycz, 1996). Divided between the three occupiers: Austria, Prussia and Russia, Poland existed only as an idea. His conviction about the role of the cinematograph as a reliable witness to history is also a reflection of the spirit of nationalism in Europe in the 19th century.

In his ongoing commitment to representing reality faithfully, Matuszewski believed in cinematic truth as the ultimate truth. It was mainly because of the cinematograph's ability to record reality in an accurate manner that he proposed to establish a legitimate film archive, an act which the British film historian Penelope Houston has described as 'one of the most unexpected and remarkable in film history' (Houston, 1994: 10). For Matuszewski, cinematographic documents deserved the same level of authority as any other objects kept in a museum. Matuszewski also wanted to publish a periodical of animated photography with an international editorial board – *Chronotografia i jej zastosowanie* – which was to be used as a platform to discuss film preservation and other issues concerning cinema.

Matuszewski's proposal recalls Robert Paul's 1897 letter to the British Museum, 'Animated Photos of London Life', in which he expressed the need to create an archive devoted to the moving image, for pieces of history to be safely stored (Matuszewski, 1898b). Matuszewski's recognition of the need for a moving image archive brings him close to the preoccupations of the later film avant-gardes, since the question of film archives formed an ongoing debate among numerous avant-garde filmmakers in the late 1920s, particularly since, as Malte Hagener points out, the avant-garde was largely responsible for the naturalization of documentary

(Hagener, 2007: 36). In 1928 Walter Ruttmann highlighted the need for a film archive of sorts. Such an archive, Ruttmann believed, would preserve and make available all those important films 'which failed to be successful' (Ruttmann, in Hagener, 2007: 113). Matuszewski was thus at the forefront of the ideas of archiving and preserving moving image works.

The very process of recording history also makes us reflect on the role of documentary cinema in the avant-garde tradition. As shown here, for theorists such as Nichols the evolution of documentary took place alongside the various developments in avant-garde film, as both genres utilised each other's techniques. This, I suggest, permits us to view Matuszewski's supposedly 'objective' work in the context of more experimental, subjective filmmaking.

In her book *Meeting the Universe Halfway: Quantum Physics and the Entanglement of Matter and Meaning* (2007) Karen Barad proposes to view apparatuses as active agencies and 'boundary-making practices'. For her apparatuses are 'specific material reconfigurings of the world that do not merely emerge in time but interatively reconfigure spacetimematter as part of the ongoing dynamism of becoming' (Barad, 2007: 142). To this end she considers apparatuses as material-discursive practices. They are 'not passively observing instruments' but are capable of producing differences that matter; hence they are boundary-making practices that are 'formative of matter and meaning' (Barad, 2007: 142, 146). The apparatuses can reconfigure the world and here Matuszewski's film proves that the apparatus's record shaped the course of history and helped to avoid a diplomatic disaster. This conclusion corresponds with Barad's agential realism, which proposes that 'phenomena do not merely mark the epistemological inseparability of observer and observed ... rather phenomena are ontological inseparability/entanglement of intra-acting "agencies"' (Barad, 2007: 139). Apparatuses, according to Barad, are themselves phenomena and have no intrinsic boundaries, thus they constitute open-ended practices (Barad, 2027: 142).

Barad's notion of 'intra-actions' suggests that individuals 'do not pre-exist as such but rather materialize in intra-action', which means that they 'only exist within phenomena' (materialized/materializing relations) 'in their ongoing iteratively intra-active reconfiguring' (Barad, in Kleinman, 2012: 77). Most importantly, for Barad, the intra-actions enact 'agential separability' – 'the condition of exteriority within phenomena' (Barad in

Kleinman, 2012: 77). Barad's notion of agential realism does not begin with any predetermined set of fixed differences. Instead, it aims at making inquiries into how differences are made, 'stabilised and destablised' (Barad in Kleinman, 2012: 77). Barad's argument goes beyond the objective/subjective divide: she claims that apparatuses actually shape the history on the material level, beyond the thoughts and passions of their individual human users. Seen in this light, Matuszewski's cinematograph – or, indeed, any other camera – is not a passive witness to history but an active creator and agent of it. The more recent uses of highly portable, digital devices that upload content to various Internet platforms with immediate effect – as seen, for example, in Jehane Noujaim's Oscar-nominated documentary about the Egyptian revolution, *The Square* (2013), in which such small devices played a crucial role – testify to the medium's active (even if not determining) role in all kinds of history-making.

Licence

CC-BY SA

References

Anonymous (1898) 'Z tygodnia na tydzień', *Tygodnik Ilustrowany*, 31.

Banaszkiewicz, W. & Witczak, W. (eds) (1989) *Historia filmu polskiego 1895-1929*, vol.1. Warsaw: Wydawnictwa Artystyczne i Filmowe.

Barad, K. (2007) *Meeting the Universe Halfway*. Durham: Duke University Press.

Bazin, A. (1945/2005a) 'The Ontology of the Photographic Image' in H. Gray (ed.), *What is Cinema?* Vol. 1. Berkeley, Los Angeles, London: University of California Press.

Bazin, A. (1945/2005b) 'The Evolution of the Language of Cinema' in H. Gray (ed.), *What is Cinema?* Vol. 1. Berkeley, Los Angeles, London: University of California Press.

Becker, C. L. (1931) 'Everyman His Own Historian', *American Historical Review* 37 (2).

Gunning, T. (1997) 'Before Documentary: Early Non-fiction Films and the View Aesthetics', in D. Hertogs and N. Klerk (eds), *Uncharted Territory: Essays on Early Nonfiction Film*. Amsterdam: Stichting Nederlands Filmmuseum.

Hagener, M. (2007) *Moving Forward, Looking Back: The European Avant-Garde and the Invention of Film Culture 1919-1939*. Amsterdam: Amsterdam University Press.

Houston, P. (1994) *Keepers of the Frame: The Film*. London: British Film Institute.

Iggers, G. (ed.) (2010) *Leopold von Ranke: The Theory and Practice of History*. London and New York: Routledge.

Kember, S. & Zylinska, J. (2012) *Life After New Media: Mediation As a Vital Process*. Cambridge: MIT Press.

Kleinman, A. (2012) 'Intra-actions: An Interview with Karen Barad', *Mousse*, 34.

Loiperdinger, M. (1997) 'World War I Propaganda Films and the Birth of the Documentary' in D. Hertogs & N. Klerk (eds), *Uncharted Territory. Essays on Early Nonfiction Film*. Amsterdam: Stichting Nederlands Filmmuseum.

Matuszewski, B. (1898a) 'Une nouvelle source de l'histoire (création d'un dépôt de cinématographie historique)', La Trobe University. Translated by Julia Bloch Frey. Accessed on 16 July 2007.

Matuszewski, B. (1898b) 'La photographie animée, ce qu'elle est et ce qu'elle doit être', La Trobe University. Translated by William D. Routt and Danielle Pottier-Lacroix. Accessed on 16 July 2007 [1898]

Mazaraki, M. (ed.) (2006) *Boleslas Matuszewski: Écrits cinématographiques*. Paris: Association française de recherche sur l'histoire du cinéma et Le Cinémathèque Française.

Nichols, B. (2001) 'Documentary Film and the Modernist Avant-Garde', *Critical Inquiry*, 27 (4).

Ranke, L. (1830/2010) 'On the Character of Historical Science', in G. Iggers (ed.), *Leopold von Ranke: The Theory and Practice of History*. London and New York: Routledge.

Ranke, L. (1836/2010) 'On the Relation of and Distinction between History and Politics', in G. Iggers (ed.), *Leopold von Ranke: The Theory and Practice of History*. London and New York: Routledge.

Richter, H. (1934/1986) *The Struggle for the Film*. New York: Scholar Press.

Rotha, P. (1935) *Documentary Film: The Use of Film Medium to Interpret Creatively and in Social Terms the Life of the People as It Exists in Reality*. London: Faber and Faber.

Skaff, S. (2008) *The Law of the Looking Glass: Cinema in Poland, 1896-1939*. Athens: Ohio University Press.

Turvey, M. (2009) 'Epstein, Bergson and Vision' in T. Trifonova (ed.), *European Film Theory*. London and New York: Routledge.

Wandycz, P. S. (1996) *The Lands of Partitioned Poland, 1795-1918*. Seattle and London: University of Washington Press.

Notes

1 Matuszewski's seminal article was written and originally published in French as 'Une nouvelle source de l'histoire (création d'un dépôt de cinématographie historique)'. Here I am using Julia Bloch Frey's translation, with an introduction by William D. Routt at La Trobe University website: no longer available.

2 Matuszewski, 'La photographie animée, ce qu'elle est et ce qu'elle doit être' ('Animated photography. As it is and as it should be') at La Trobe University. Translated by William D. Routt and Danielle Pottier-Lacroix. Accessed on 16 July 2007 [1898].

3 My italics.

4 *Le Figaro* from 12 January 1898 confirmed that Matuszewski's film challenged von Bismarck's claim: 'Or, voici qu'avant-hier le cinématographe reproduisit précisément la scène de l'arrivée de M. Félix Faure a Saint-Pétersbourg. Et chacun put voir le Président s'avancer à pas lents, devant le front, et baisser tout à coup son chapeau, d'un geste large et correct, - ce geste que tous les Parisiens connaissent bien'. *Le Petit Journal* from 15 July 1898 stated that, thanks to documents such as Matuszewski's footage, Bismarck's assertion could have been refuted: 'C'est même grâce à ces documents qu'on a pu réfuter l'assertion de Bismarck, qui prétendait que M. Félix Faure avait omis de se découvrir devant le drapeau russe à son débarquement'.

CHAPTER 8

What is the Value of a Technological History of Cinema?

Lee Grieveson

I was asked some time ago to contribute to a discussion on the function and value of a technological history of cinema.[1] Remarks I made are reproduced here, and I have resisted the temptation to substantially rework them. What is lost from a fully worked out and carefully constructed article is, perhaps, gained in the looser and slightly more polemical framing of this. I am particularly interested here in thinking about how cinema emerged in the context of the broader transformations of the second stage of the Industrial Revolution, itself powered by a particular formation of capitalism, and how in turn this form of media and spectacle helped enable the expansion of that conjuncture across a world system (Grieveson, 2012).

It is a commonplace of industrial history that the last third or so of the nineteenth century saw a second-stage Industrial Revolution driven principally by new discoveries in electricity and chemistry. Around the turn of the century these developments led to the rapid and extensive mechanisation of industrial production that underpinned the diffusion of mass production methods as well as the emergence of new organisational procedures and the formation of new corporate forms (and intra-corporate or monopoly organisation, frequently predicated on the corporate monopolisation of technological intelligence which became essential to profit maximisation: in this way, technological knowledge was increasingly privatised). Industrial capital produced a surplus reinvested as finance capital, motivating globalising practices (either colonialist or, as with the U.S., an economic imperialism increasingly divorced from geographic possession and later supported by ostensibly neutral international institutions like the World Bank). Like it was in the Industrial Revolution, when the steam engine enabled the greater circulation of raw materials and manufactured goods, so it was that the new industrial and economic practices of the echo-boom of the revolution were twinned with developments in transportation and communication technologies – now automobiles, airplanes, telegraphs, telephones – and the construction of large modern technological systems that subtended new economic forms of ever more rapid circulation. All of this was accordingly supported by liberal capitalist states through policies that increased research potential (and here investments in schools and universities were critical); the potential circulation of materials on rails, roads, international canals, airways; and macroeconomic policies that developed safeguards for intellectual property rights, facilitated monopolisation, and weakened worker and subaltern resistance. 'Technology' accordingly became a keyword from the 1930s onwards, recent scholarship suggests, supplanting earlier terms like 'useful arts' that made less and less sense in the face of large-scale technological systems (Schatzberg, 2006). And this shift was facilitated by the close links between universities and business. All to say: it is, then, a truism of modern history that the concurrent emergence or coupling of technology and corporate and increasingly global capitalism, facilitated by liberal states, is one of the most significant developments of the modern world. We live in many ways in the shadow of this.

Likely it is already apparent that the tenor of my answer to the question posed by this discussion – what is the value of a technological history of cinema? – is to push thinking in the direction of addressing cinema's role in a broader technological, and so therefore necessarily economic and political, history. Technology may not be determining, as the Humanities mantra must repeat, but it is increasingly hard to look outside the walls of the cinema and not notice that global economies are quite determining. I personally have next to no interest in a history of cinema technology for its own sake, as a discrete history of a privileged object. Rather, the invitation of this discussion is to pose different questions. What roles, I want to ask, did cinema play in the formation of a corporate liberal political economy? What were the ways that media as a system was integrated with new capitalist practices? What were the logics of capital that made these machines (cameras, kinetoscopes, projectors) or storage substances (celluloid, as a visual and later auditory material and chemical substrate), and what did these machines help make? It is not easy to answer these questions, of course, but let me offer some observations along those lines, some examples drawn from recent scholarship, and some reflections on what this material might do for our understanding of how cinema technology was enmeshed with particular economic and governmental projects.

The connections are, of course, myriad. We might start, for example, with the discovery of photosensitive halogen silver salts, crucial to the establishment of photographic film as an improvement on the technology of glass plates. Eastman Company developed this most thoroughly from the 1870s (from which point, of course, it carved out a system of patents to maximise profits). Eastman's marshalling of chemical knowledge to develop flexible photosensitive film was a critical, formative, technological development for what came to be called cinema. In a 1927 investment report on the moving picture business, the Chicago investment firm of Halsey, Stuart & Co. observed in passing that motion pictures use more silver than the United States mint. What an interesting image. Where did this silver come from? I don't know precisely, but here is what I assume: from silver mines, likely enough those in colonised states, and certainly predicated on exploitative and dangerous labour practices. The film in film technology was always already ensnared in complex histories of extraction and exploitation... Quite some time ago now, at a conference in India, I was told by colleagues there that very few Indian films of the 1940s survive because they were destroyed to release the silver content in them.[2] I suppose this was a wider practice, and that archivists would know a great deal about this, and likely I should have known it myself. In any case, the connections between film, extractive economy, and the conjuncture of 'precious' metals associated with currency, ornamentation, and the chemical basis of photosensitivity is worth remarking upon.

I do know better, because of other people's research, that experiments in serialised photography emerged from, and supported, new conceptions of temporality and the subdivision of time into discrete units – visible in the proliferation of watches from the 1870s – that were fundamentally connected to industrial labour practices. E. P. Thompson's 1966 account of the emergence of time-oriented, as opposed to task-oriented, labour is the classic account of this.[3] It is no coincidence, surely, that Eadweard Muybridge's experiments in serialised photography were sponsored by a railroad magnate and made directly possible by technology borrowed from a telegraph company: driven, we might say, by the twin motors of transportation and communication, and the imperatives of the speeded up circulation of goods and information so central to advanced capitalism. Later experiments by physiologists and industrialists utilised this technology to examine closely the movement of the labouring body, so enabling the extraction of extra surplus value (Braun, 1992; Rabinach, 1992). The fragmentation of flow into discrete and manageable moments was integral to a new rationalised industrial capitalism. Moving pictures facilitated this. Frank Bunker Gilbreth filmed workers completing various tasks – packing and labelling cartons, for example, analysed carefully the film to devise quicker ways of working, and re-filmed the now redesigned task to show clearly the success of his methods.[4]

In my own research on the Ford Motor Company's extensive use of film I discovered some evidence that the Company used film technology as part of its elaboration of the mass assembly line (Grieveson, 2012: 26-7). Time-motion studies at Ford contributed directly to the division of labour into separate and increasingly routinised and mechanised tasks. When combined with the production of machine tools enabling standardisation, this rationalisation process culminated in the momentous establishment in 1913 of the moving assembly line (Hounshell, 1984). It was this innovation that enabled the direct and mechanised control of the movement and pace of workers, dramatically increasing productivity and the extraction of surplus value from labouring bodies (Braverman, 1998: 127-62). Mass assembly and production was fundamental to the establishment of corporate capitalism. And, through the reduction of costs, it underpinned a mass culture of abundance and consumerism that emerged most clearly in the 1920s (Zunz, 1998: 73-92). At Ford, this coercive architecture of production enabled automobiles to be produced, as two contemporary observes noted, 'like the successive negatives on a motion picture film' (Arnold and Faurote, 1915: 360). Another interesting image. We might invert it to say: for a time, the successive frames of motion pictures participated in the process by which the outputs of the labouring body could be maximised to produce quickly the identical Model T's that rolled off the assembly line as perhaps the most emblematic image of the age of mechanical production.

I could likely go on, and remind us all (if it were needed) perhaps that the first significant theorist of the cinema, Hugo Münsterberg, was, in his day job, a scholar of 'attention' and the problem of directing and harnessing workers attention – but let me shift tack, towards a few brief remarks on the state use of cinema technology.[5] It is increasingly clear that many of the technical innovations in the fields of photography and cinema were financed and first tested for warfare and military objectives and thus there was, in the words of Friedrich Kittler, a 'historically perfect collusion of world wars, reconnaissance squadrons, and cinematography' (Münsterberg, 1916: 124). Here we might think specifically about the synergy between the design of automatic weapons and the camera apparatus (Marey's chronophotography derived in part from machine-gun technology); the development of 16mm; portable projection technologies in mobile cinema vans to bring cinema as recreation and propaganda to soldiers and diverse populations; and the broader enmeshing of surveillance and state agendas through visual and sound technologies (General Electric, for example, developed aspects of sound technology under the direction of the U.S. Navy: these connections continue in later media practices, though I would need to be a much, much better historian of the Internet to make the precise connections between military objectives, new media, and surveillance). Virilio reminds us that the nitrocellulose in film stock was used also for explosives; and that searchlight technology filtered back into studio lighting practices (Virilio, 1989: 288).

Liberal and other states used film technology in the state of exception of wartime, certainly, but this practice became regularised, just as – as Giorgio Agamben teaches us – exceptional state practices tend to. In the U.S. the Departments of Agriculture, Interior and Commerce pioneered the production of film beginning in the 1910s and running through the New Deal. Vans carrying films to ever more remote peripheral regions were developed, capable of using electricity generated from their engines to overcome problems of local differences in electricity current to project these films of government practice to isolated rural populations. In the U.K. the Conservative party pioneered this use of mobile cinema vans in the 1920s, carrying the films it financed to working-class populations who had become electorally significant after the Representation of the People's Act in 1918.

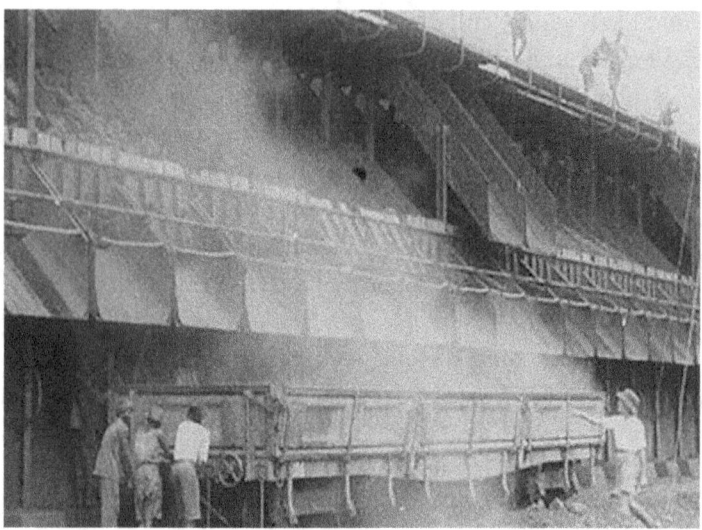

Figure 8.1: Conservative Party's Mobile Cinema Van. Courtesy of the Modern Records Centre at the University of Warwick.

It is relatively well known, I think, the subsequent history of these developments in the formation of the Empire Marketing Board Film Unit in 1927 that pioneered various uses of technology to supplement its attempts to establish a colonial economic bloc: not only mobile cinema vans, but also automatic film projectors placed in train stations in London to advertise imperial produce. This is the direct progenitor of all those screens selling us things that populate public space these days. Media technology operated as part of a wider networked infrastructure working to facilitate and mediate the materials, goods and capital that travelled along the same pathways.

Later, the use of mobile cinemas was imported to the empire, with the intention frequently of using film to 'educate' colonial populations, to create modern colonial subjects, and to bind populations into an imperial collectivity.[6] Exhibition functioned as a performance of modern colonial power, a kind of ritual of state power that started with film itself as the embodiment of the technological modernity that colonial power claimed for itself. Here film technology supplied the 'shock and awe' that facilitated colonial practices. Indeed, EMB and other British colonial films insistently feature technology: a common trope shows raw materials being gathered in the empire, and transported back to the metropole – on the British ships so central to its position of geopolitical and economic primacy in the nineteenth century – where they are fed into great big machines, and turned into the manufactured goods that maintained British economy and the necessary underdevelopment of colonial economies. The fascinated gaze of the camera machine at the various industrial machines that litter the film offers exemplary instances of what Brian Larkin has called 'the colonial sublime', the 'effort to use technology as part of political rule' (Larkin, 2008: 39). The films make a distinction, though, between the way workers interact with machines, for in the sequences in, say, colonial Africa the machines dwarf workers, who are always supervised in their relatively menial work of fetching and carrying by British officials, whereas in the short sequences in British factories the workers are unsupervised and demonstrate a mastery of complex technology.

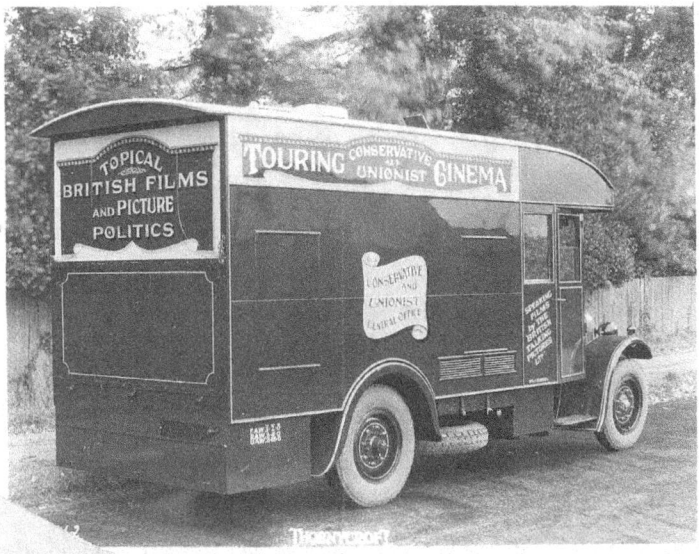

Figure 8.2: *West Africa Calling* (1927). Courtesy of the British Film Institute National Archive.

The gulf of technological superiority legitimises colonial rule. If this representation belies the history of how new technologies of mass production and Fordist work practices deskilled working-class populations, it does so in the goal of a political logic that seeks to cathect the working class to technological modernity and perhaps even more substantively to associate the power of machinery with that of capital and state. The machinery of state powers industrial machinery, witnessed here (and so facilitated) by the actual and figurative machinery of film.

I will end here. I have made no reference to the expansion of commodity capitalism into the sphere of leisure, or to the screen as a technology of display. All the examples I have given have, instead, been from what we might call nontheatrical cinema, or, following Charles Acland and Haidee Wasson, 'useful film': the attempts by various organisations, from states to corporations to educators and reformers, to use film and its related technologies to supplement what I would describe as a corporate liberal political economy. It is in these connections, in the ways cinema gets cathected to – and helps orchestrate – economic and political projects that I see the most value for thinking carefully, again, about cinema and technology.

Original source and licence

Alphaville: Journal of Film and Screen Media (6), Winter 2013. Licence: CC BY NC ND.

References

Acland, C. and Wasson, H. (eds) (2011) *Useful Cinema*. Durham: Duke University Press.

Agamben, G. (2005) *State of Exception*. Chicago: University of Chicago Press.

Arnold, H. L. & Faurote, F. L. (1915) *Ford Methods and Ford Shops*. New York: The Engineering Magazine Company.

Braun, M. (1992) *Picturing Time: The Work of Etienne-Jules Marey (1830–1904)*. Chicago: University of Chicago Press.

Braverman, H. (1998) *Labor and Monopoly Capital: The Degradation of Work in the Twentieth Century*. 1974. New York: Monthly Review Press.

Dagognet, F. (1992) *Etienne-Jules Marey: A Passion for the Trace*. New York: Zone Books.

Grieveson, L. (2011) 'The Cinema and the (Common)Wealth of Nations' in L. Grieveson and C. MacCabe (eds), *Empire and Film*. London: BFI.

Grieveson, L. (2012) 'The Work of Film in the Age of Fordist Mechanization', *Cinema Journal* (51), 3.

Hale, M. Jr. (1980) *Human Science and Social Order: Hugo Münsterberg and the Origins of Applied Psychology*. Philadelphia: Temple University Press.

Halsey, S. (1985) 'The Motion Picture Industry as a Basis for Bond Financing' in T. Balio (ed.), *The American Film Industry*. Madison: University of Wisconsin Press.

Hounshell, D. A. (1894) *From the American System to Mass Production, 1800–1932*. Baltimore: Johns Hopkins University Press.

Kittler, F.A. (1999) *Gramophone, Film, Typewriter*. Stanford: Stanford University Press.

Larkin, B. (2008) *Signal and Noise: Media, Infrastructure, and Urban Culture in Nigeria*. Durham: Duke University Press.

Münsterberg, H. (1916/2002) 'The Photoplay: A Psychological Study in A. Langdale (ed.), *Hugo Münsterberg on Film. The Photoplay: A Psychological Study and Other Writings*. New York: Routledge.

Rabinach, A. (1992) *The Human Motor: Energy, Fatigue, and the Origins of Modernity*. Berkeley: University of California Press.

Schatzberg, E. (2006) 'Technik Comes to America: Changing Meanings of Technology Before 1930', *Technology and Culture*, 47 (3).

Thompson, E.P. (1966) *The Making of the English Working Class*. New York: Vintage.

Virilio, P. (1989) *War and Cinema: The Logistics of Perception*. London: Verso.

Zunz, O. (1998) *Why the American Century?* Chicago: University of Chicago Press.

Notes

1. The 'Impact of Technological Innovations on the Historiography and Theory of Cinema' conference was organised by André Gaudreault and Martin Lefebvre as part of the Permanent Seminar on the History of Film Theories in Montreal in late 2011. My thanks to Martin Lefebvre in particular for the invitation.

2. The conference was held at the English and Foreign Languages University in Hyderabad. My thanks in particular to Madhav Prasad for the invitation.

3. Thompson argued that industrialisation fundamentally changed the understanding of time and of labour practices, shifting production away from workers managing their own schedules in a focus on particular tasks often correlated to seasons or cycles – for example, harvests – to one that subdivided tasks and regularised timings.

4. A compilation of some of these films is available online from Prelinger Archive at http://www.archive.org/details/OriginalFilm.

5. Münsterberg played a significant role in the development of industrial psychology in America and his book *Psychology and Industry Efficiency* (1913) is seen by some as the founding work in the discipline (see Hale, 1980).

6. The history of this process is told on the Colonial Film Website at http://www.colonialfilm.org.uk.

CHAPTER 9

A New/Old Ontology of Film

Rafe McGregor

The purpose of this article is to examine the ontological effects of digital technology, and determine whether digital films, traditional films, and pre-traditional motion pictures belong to the same category. I begin by defining the parameters of my inquiry, and then consider the two most significant consequences of the new technology. §2 proposes a decisive refutation of the causal relationship between reality and photography. §3 identifies an end to the dominance of photorealistic film over animation, and argues for an inversion of that relationship, whereby animation is paramount. Finally, I consider the implications of these consequences for film ontology, compare theories, and conclude in favour of Berys Gaut, for whom digital film is the latest incarnation of a history of moving pictures that stretches back for centuries.

Defining the question: terminology and technology

The fundamental problem with the question 'what is film?' is that it presupposes a certain kind of answer. In fact, the words 'film', 'motion picture', and 'movie' all make the question redundant. The term 'film' is derived from film stock, the photosensitive chemical material used to record rebounding light. The conversion of light into film produces a negative, which is then photographed itself to produce an original print. The photochemical process has been labelled 'traditional', and produces both still photographs and the sequences of still images called 'films'. So it seems that asking what film is limits the answer to the projection of photographic images onto screens, exhibited through the medium of cinema from 1895. Although photographic film is still used, the success of George Lucas's Star Wars: Episode II – Attack of the Clones in 2002 heralded the entry of digital cinema to the mainstream market. James Cameron's Avatar (2009), a three-dimensional (3D) digital production, is the most commercially successful film to date at the time of writing, and a return to photographic film in the future appears highly unlikely.

The use of 'motion picture' and 'movie' is no less prescriptive. The etymology of 'movie' is uncertain, but is probably an abbreviation for 'moving image' or 'moving pictures'. I shall regard 'moving image', 'moving pictures', and 'motion picture' as synonymous for my purposes. If the inquiry concerns moving pictures rather than film, then it extends back well beyond 1895. Berys Gaut identifies three different categories of motion picture: object-generated, handmade, and mechanically-generated (2010: 6-10). Object-generated motion pictures have existed since at least the tenth century CE, in the form of Indonesian and Chinese shadow puppet plays. Handmade motion pictures include simple flipbooks, magic lanterns, the thaumatrope, the phenatakistocope (1832), the zoetrope (1833), the choreutoscope (1866), and the praxinoscope (1877). Mechanically generated motion pictures began with Edison's kinetoscope and the Lumière *cinématographe* – both of which used film stock – and the category includes subsequent electronic and digital developments.

While Gaut maintains that all three types of moving image share a common ontology, Noël Carroll restricts motion pictures to the mechanically-generated (Gaut, 1996: 127-130). I wish to avoid asking a redundant question and limiting the scope of film or motion pictures without justification. I shall therefore use 'film' and 'motion picture' interchangeably, with both referring to the exhibition of moving images in the broadest possible sense, i.e. not restricted to either photochemical stock or photorealistic pictures. I include animated features in the category of traditional film due to the fact that until *Toy Story* (John Lasseter, 1995) animated films consisted of photographs of either illustrations or objects (for stop motion animation, e.g. *Wallace and Gromit* [Nick Park and Nick Rushton, 1989-2010]).

Carroll distinguishes film from similar art forms like theatre and puppet shows by stipulating the moving image as two-dimensional (2D) (Carroll, 1996: 130). With the post-*Avatar* revival of 3D film, this distinction might seem outdated, but 3D cinema has existed since the screening of *The Power of Love* in 1922, so the issue is neither new nor linked to digital cinema (Zone, 2007: 1-2). I endorse Carroll's distinction, specifying that motion pictures *are* 2D even though they may *appear* 3D. The images are generated on a two-dimensional surface; they may be drawn on this surface directly, in the case of a flip-book or a zoetrope, or projected onto a flat screen, in the case of a shadow play or traditional film. I can now identify the question, which is 'what is film?' where 'film' is the art form involving the exhibition of 2D moving pictures, and 'a film' or 'motion picture' is a specific instance of this category. I have noted the possible beginnings of the art as shadow plays, mentioned the more recent precursors to traditional film, and given a very brief description of the photochemical process. A summary of the digital revolution in film follows.

In contrast with the photographic process, where light is converted to film, digital image recording converts light into streams of binary numbers. Digital recording employs a charge-coupled device (CCD) to first convert light levels to voltages and then convert them to the number streams, which are stored in bitmaps, i.e. grids of pixels.[1] The bitmap is a mathematical representation and thus has no physical relation to the image, which is manufactured by the interpretation of numbers. The images can be recorded either on digital tape or as digital files. Aside from the use of a CCD, there are two other methods of producing digital images: by hand with a software tool, and computer synthesis. The former creates images by digital painting; the latter involves the construction of a vector graphic or 3D model to generate bitmaps. All three methods of manufacture can be combined seamlessly. The digital image does not suffer degradation when it is replicated, and duplication produces a clone rather than a copy (Gaut, 2010: 12-16).

'Computer-generated imagery' (CGI) describes the application of pre- and post-production digital painting and computer synthesis to film, and is fundamentally 'a form of computer animation' (Cook, 2004: 882). Steven Spielberg's *Jurassic Park* (1993) was the first extensive use of CGI in a photorealistic film, and met with unprecedented commercial success (Cook, 2004: 890-891). Two years later *Toy Story* became the first digital feature film, i.e. the first film created entirely with CGI. *Star Wars: Episode I – The Phantom Menace* (George Lucas, 1999) made even more use of CGI than *Jurassic Park*, and was exhibited in digital screenings in addition to its traditional cinema release (Gaut, 2010: 10-11). The success of the sequel in 2002 ushered in a new era of motion pictures. The philosophical implications of digital cinema are both far-reaching and complex, but I believe it has finally quashed the various positions that reject photography as a representational art.

Another long goodbye: photography as presentation

Gregory Currie bade a conclusive farewell to the persistent – but insubstantial – hypothesis that the ontology of film was that it constituted a particular kind of language. The argument he calls the 'presentation thesis' has been just as persistent, with as little substance (Currie, 1995: 48). Currie describes the presentation thesis as the claim that photography presents rather than represents the world, and focuses on Kendall Walton's transparency argument. Gaut maintains that there are two distinct objections to photography as art within transparency – causal and reproductive – and although I disagree, I shall mention all four of the arguments opposing representation in photography (Gaut, 2010: 21-22).

André Bazin held that photography was essentially objective, by which he meant that the photographic image was (the same as) the thing itself: 'Photography enjoys a certain advantage in view of this transference of reality from the thing to its reproduction' (Bazin, 1960: 8). For Bazin, to look at an old family photograph was to see the deceased relatives themselves, rather than to see a representation thereof. Rudolf Arnheim interpreted Charles Baudelaire's comments on photography imitating reality as the idea that photography 'was nothing but a mechanical copy of nature' (1974: 155). If this is indeed the case, then photography has no capacity to express artistic intention. Roger Scruton contrasted photography with painting: where the latter stood in an intentional relation to its subject (due to the representational act), the former stood in a causal relation, and could not be considered a representational art (Scruton, 1981: 578-598). Looking at an object through a camera lens (or at the resultant photograph) was thus the same as looking at a mirror or looking through a telescope; it merely presented the reality. Finally, Kendall Walton argued that to see a photograph of X was to see X, while to see a painting of X was not: 'Photographs are *transparent*. We see *through* them' (Walton, 1984: 251). This transparency causes photographs to put one in perceptual contact with the object photographed.

I believe these four theses – objectivity, reproduction, causal relativity, and transparency – all present a single challenge to photography as representational art, and I use 'presentation thesis' to describe this challenge. I shall first show why the presentation thesis does not hold – even for traditional photography – and then show the effect of digital photography on the debate before considering the implications for film. It is worth noting an observation by Currie at the outset: most advocates of the presentation thesis have limited their claims to photographic images that have not been significantly altered subsequent to exposure (Currie, 1995: 48). So the presentation thesis is subject to a qualification, and even its proponents do not accept that seeing (a photograph) is always believing (the reality). Scruton is even more restrictive, limiting his observations to a 'logical ideal' (Scruton, 1981: 578). One could argue that if photographs are not *always* objective, reproductions, causally related, or transparent, then there *is* a capacity (of some sort) for representation inherent in the medium, but the move is not necessary.

Gaut provides a conclusive and entertaining refutation of the presentation thesis, using the example of Jean Auguste Dominique Ingres's painting, *Madame Moitessier* (1856) (Gaut, 2010: 30-31). He identifies a number of ideas expressed by Ingres in the work, and then imagines that the woman depicted had been painted by Oscar Kokoshka and Lucian Freud. Gaut notes the differences in intention and appearance likely to have resulted, e.g., from skin as pure as marble (Ingres) to skin that looks like raw meat (Freud). He then extends the thought experiment to photography, suggesting that parallel differences in appearance would result if the subject was photographed by Sir Cecil Beaton, Julia Margaret Cameron, and Diane Arbus. The photograph perceived by the viewer would differ significantly in all three cases – just as the painting by each artist would differ. These differences are caused by the intentions of the photographers and the capacity of photography to express these intentions indicates that it is a representational medium. I believe Gaut's thought experiment is sufficient to turn the tables on the presentation thesis. There is no justification for regarding all unaltered photographs as presentations of reality; many photographs are representations, so the presentation thesis should be confined to those depictions where the intention of the photographer is to present (rather than represent) an object. One might acknowledge that, e.g., photojournalists and crime scene photographers typically present reality, but even this claim is debatable.

The appearance of Kevin Carter's Pulitzer Prize-winning *Starving Child in the Sudan* in the *New York Times* in March 1993 resulted in public concern for the infant portrayed (Keller, 1994). When readers saw the photograph they believed that there was a real starving girl, and that the event captured in the image – a vulture awaiting her demise – really happened at a certain time and place. The assumption was correct, and would not have been made if the picture printed in the newspaper had been an illustration, no matter how life-like. When one sees a photograph in a context like a newspaper one tends to think of it as presenting reality. There seem to be degrees of realism: from actual perception, to looking at a photograph, to looking at a painting. Thus looking at Carter's photograph is not as horrific as actually being in the Sudan with the child and the vulture, but is more horrific than seeing a sketch of her. Walton makes this point by contrasting the immediacy of Francisco Goya's 'Even Worse' (1810), part of *The Disasters of War*, with Timothy H. O'Sullivan's photograph, *Death on a Misty Morning* (1883) (Walton, 1984: 247-248).

Walton has selected a particularly visceral portrayal of the aftermath of a battle, but his choice is unfortunate for his argument: O'Sullivan was believed to have moved the bodies of the corpses he photographed in order to create a more dramatic effect, i.e. to express his intentions in his representations of dead soldiers.[2] While (most) photographs undoubtedly appear more real than (most) other pictures, even photojournalistic images do not necessarily present reality. Two of the most famous photographic images ever taken serve as examples. There is an ongoing debate about Robert Capa's *Falling Soldier* (1936). The question is not only whether the image was posed, as I have suggested in Walton's example, but where it was actually taken: on the battlefield as claimed, or at a safer position behind the front lines (Mitchell, 1992: 40-43). When Dorothea Lange took the photograph *Migrant Mother* (1936) she failed to notice that her subject had grasped a tent pole in order to steady her sleeping child. The thumb and finger that appeared in the foreground of the image were subsequently edited out (Curtis, 1986: 17-20).

My point is that in two paradigmatic cases of photojournalism there is room for doubt as to the reality, and room for expression on the part of the photographer. William J. Mitchell mentions the response to an international incident between the United States and Libya in January 1989 as an exemplary instance of photographic evidence being contested

– contested on the very basis that it does not present reality (Mitchell, 1992: 22-24). Hoaxes like the Cottingley Fairies (1917) and the surgeon's photograph of the Loch Ness Monster (1934) reveal that the capacity for deception afforded by photographic evidence is not a recent development. I offer these examples as a supplement to Gaut's argument, to show that there is always – and has always been – a possibility for representation in photography, even when it appears at its most transparent.[3] If this is true of traditional photographs, then the opportunity for representation in digital photographs is even greater, due to the increased possibilities in editing.

Gaut maintains that the digital image is correctly identified as: 'a mélange (or blended) image – that is, it can be produced by any of three distinct techniques and each technique may vary in the proportion it has in the making of a particular image' (Gaut, 2010: 45). He claims that even if one restricts one's inquiry to the digital *photograph*, the software packages accompanying digital cameras allow photographers of all proficiencies a wide range of editing options. Mitchell believes that digital images should never be called photographs, even if created with a digital camera, as they differ as much from a traditional photograph as a photograph from a painting (Mitchell, 1992: 3). Gaut rejects this radical distinction on the basis of the similar generative methods employed in traditional and digital photography (Gaut, 2010: 49). I agree with his assessment, though I shall show that he underestimates the impact of his own falsification of the presentation thesis.

I have considered the presentation thesis in some detail due its implications for the ontology of film. If photography could only present rather than represent reality, then photorealistic film would be similarly limited as an art form. Scruton is convinced that a film presents a drama, and that while drama is a representative art, the filming or photographing thereof is not (Scruton, 1981: 598-603). He holds that photography hinders rather than assists dramatic representation, because of the limits it places on interpretation and its link to fantasy rather than the imagination. For Scruton, therefore, the ontology of film is that it is no more than photographed drama. Arnheim contemplated the consequences of the thesis for contrasting reasons, and was concerned about the inevitable and undesirable conclusion that there could be no artistic expression in film (Arnheim, 1974: 155). With the presentation thesis refuted, however, film can take its rightful place as an art form.[4] The digital revolution has not only strengthened the argument for film as art, but also – I shall argue – indicated the category of art to which digital and traditional film belong.

The digital film: photorealistic animation

Gaut defines digital cinema as 'the medium of moving images generated by bitmaps' (Gaut, 2010: 14), and Lev Manovich identifies it as 'a particular case of animation which uses live action footage as one of its many elements' (Manovich, 1995). They both note a number of essential differences between digital and traditional film (Manovich, 1995; Gaut, 2010: 17-18). All three types of digital image are subject to direct manipulation, with the result that the visual realism of photography has a plasticity that was formerly confined to animated film. In digital cinema, the traditional distinction between the ease of editing (a sequence) and the difficulty of image manipulation (special effects) has been eroded, and the spatial and temporal qualities of images can now be rearranged with equal ease. As there are no longer any aesthetic features linking film to film stock, digital cinema also has a purity from its physical origin. Once live action material is digitised, the existing relation to reality is lost as the digital images become raw material (grids of pixels) for manipulation. Digital technology has eroded the distinctions between creation and modification, production and postproduction, as every image – whatever its source – is processed through various computer programs before the final cut. Lastly, the speed of computer processing has opened up new possibilities for interactivity in digital cinema.

Even the most cursory examination of the philosophy, theory, and criticism of film reveals an overwhelming bias in favour of photorealistic – as opposed to animated – films. Gaut states that the 'philosophy of film has concentrated almost exclusively on traditional photographic images' (Gaut, 2010: 19). Manovich takes an even stronger line, describing the marginalisation as resulting in animation being 'cinema's bastard relative, its supplement, its shadow' (Manovich, 1995). Works of reference on film frequently pay scant attention to animated features, and many philosophers exclude them from their definitions and ontologies of film. When the American Film Institute published a list of the hundred best American motion pictures made from 1898 to 1998, it included only two animated films: *Snow White and the Seven Dwarves* (David Hand et al., 1937), forty-ninth, and *Fantasia* (James Algar et al., 1940), fifty-eighth. When the list was revised in 2007, it included *Toy Story* at a rather disappointing – given its significance in the history of film – ninety-ninth place, and at the expense of *Fantasia* (which was dropped) (American Film Institute). Animated films have nonetheless played a significant role in the film industry, from the commercial success of *Snow White and the Seven Dwarves* to the artistry of *Beauty and the Beast* (Gary Trousdale and Kirk Wise, 1991), and the groundbreaking technological advances of *Toy Story* and *The Polar Express* (Robert Zemeckis, 2004).

Gaut believes that digital technology has undermined the dominance of the photograph in film (Gaut, 2010: 17). The (literal) photographic essence of traditional film, the link between film and film stock, has been severed. Live action photography is now merely one of several methods – methods which are themselves frequently combined – of producing the moving pictures that comprise a particular film. Manovich notes that digital technology has introduced the possibility of a feature film of one hundred and twenty-nine thousand, six hundred frames that is both indistinguishable from a photorealistic film, and created entirely by digital painting (Manovich, 1995). He maintains that the combination of live action material, painting, image processing, compositing, 2D and 3D animation that constitutes digital film has returned the moving image to its roots, which lie in the animation used in devices such as magic lanterns, zoetropes, and praxinoscopes. For Manovich, therefore, digital film has reversed the traditional relationship between photography and animation, with the latter now dominating.

Perhaps digital film is best described by Gaut, as a mélange. Certainly my first thoughts on seeing a trailer for *Avatar* were, 'what is it, a film or a cartoon?'[5] There seem to be two equally valid answers: 'both', in that it was created with live actors (using motion capture) and digital painting; and 'neither', because it doesn't fit into either traditional category. David A. Cook presents an interesting study by comparing the representation of the Japanese attack on Pearl Harbour in *From Here to Eternity* (Fred Zinnemann, 1953) and *Pearl Harbor* (Michael Bay, 2001) (Cook, 2004: 921-926). The former relied heavily on the use of actual documentary footage from 1941, but appeared much less realistic than the latter, which involved extensive use of CGI. Simulated reality, created by the combination of digital photography, digital painting, and computer synthesis, is thus more 'real' than the photo-chemically-recorded reality. Cook believes that the two films cannot be compared by the same standards, and agrees with Manovich that the digital revolution has created a new aesthetic where film has become a type of animation, and where production is the first stage of postproduction (Cook, 2004: 925-926).

Cook uses 'photorealistic animation' to refer to animation that resembles photography in its attention to detail, but I believe the term appropriates the sense in which animation can replicate reality more successfully than photography (Cook, 2004: 883). Film can no longer be differentiated from animation because the development of digital cinema has completely blurred the distinction. Peter Jackson deliberately used CGI techniques with a strong photographic basis for *The Lord of the Rings* trilogy (2001-2003). He successfully created an appearance of reality, yet one of the main characters – Gollum – is entirely computer-generated. Robert Zemeckis's *The Polar Express* is an apparently clear case of an animated film, yet his paradigmatic use of motion capture brings an almost disturbing element of realism to the characters. Films like *Avatar* and *Alice in Wonderland* (Tim Burton, 2010) – their 3D aside – fall somewhere in between, and these examples of the cross-pollination of photography and painting show that the line between photorealism and animation is not only unclear, but irrelevant. The distinction may continue to be made for marketing purposes, but the two types of film have converged in a single category, digital film. Photorealism *and* animation have been replaced by *photorealistic animation*.

Whether one regards the digital film as animated (Manovich) or mélange (Gaut), the photograph is obviously no longer as significant to the phenomenon as it once was. I believe that film has been freed from the restrictions imposed by photography, with the result that the scope for representation has increased exponentially. Drawing on Walton's work (1970: 143-145), Gaut (2010: 37-38) elucidates the link between artistic expression and the perception of film and reality. Perceiving a film and perceiving reality diverge in a number of ways. Where the divergence is fixed, e.g. the lighting in the theatre and the 2D structure of the screen, one cannot regard it as communicating any artistic intention. Where divergence is variable, e.g. the shape of the image on the screen and the movement of the camera, one can attribute intention and expression. The point can be generalised to all art: when there is choice, there is a potential for the expression of meaning; and the greater the capacity for choice, the greater the capacity for expression.

I have mentioned the increase in choice in the change from traditional to digital photography, and the case is even more extreme for the moving image. The bewildering number of options available to contemporary film directors means that they have increased opportunities for expressing their intentions, and it is this intentional relation to the subject that makes film a representational art. Gaut holds that the digital revolution has resulted in a more compelling argument for film as art; indeed, Scruton's claim that film is merely a recording of representative drama is simply implausible for the digital variety (Gaut, 2010: 49). Gaut also notes the intentionality of digital film in that it 'possesses the possibility, in its non-photographic modes, of creating expressive content that does not require the recording of any reality at all' (Gaut, 2010: 50). I believe, however, that he understates the importance of digital developments.

Although photographs continue to be used in film, they have become one of several kinds of mathematical representations that constitute the raw material from which the finished product is created. The photographic element of film is no longer any more significant than, e.g., computer synthesis, and Manovich has noted that even photorealism need not involve any photography. The fact that digital film does not require the recording of reality not only means that the art form has the potential to stand in a purely intentional relation to its subject, but that it actually does so. The reason can be found in Walton's standard and variable properties, alluded to by Gaut. In photorealistic traditional film the use of photography was a standard (fixed) property, like the 2D screen, i.e. there was no other option available. In photorealistic digital film, the use of photographs has become a variable property. Live footage has become one of several options for the director, and the decision to use it has thus become an expression of intention. Digital film, like painting, is always intentional. A contemporary director who used only photographs (of either type) in a feature film would be exercising a meaningful choice, and that choice would convey his intention. The consequence of this intentionality is that digital film is indisputably a representational art.

What is film in the 21st century?

I began by defining the scope of my inquiry as the art form of moving pictures, where the movement may be actual or apparent, and where the picture – despite appearances – is understood in the ordinary sense of being presented on a flat surface.[6] I have established that all four categories of traditional and digital photography and film offer possibilities for representation, and noted that the digital film is a development of traditional film characterised by what I have called 'photorealistic animation'. I shall now answer the question 'what is film?', taking into account both traditional and digital varieties, and consider the restrictions an ontology of film should impose in order to make an enlightening classification of the art form.

Currie produced the first comprehensive philosophy of film in the analytic tradition with *Image and Mind* in 1995. Although the ontology of film he proposed has much to recommend it, Currie's position on non-photographic film is opaque. He cites animation as an example that 'more distant causes' of the cinematic experience need not be photographic, but subsequently excludes all reference to animated film (Currie, 1995: 4). It seems that he is either concerned purely with photorealistic film or – at most – film produced with film stock. By linking film to photography, Currie is committed to the view that *Toy Story* – produced with CGI – is not a film, and that *Toy Story* and *Snow White* are therefore different phenomena. The position is clearly erroneous.

Digital technology – in the form of CGI – has been applied to photochemical film over a period of at least forty years, with notable early examples like *2001: A Space Odyssey* (Stanley Kubrick, 1968) and *Westworld* (Michael Crichton, 1973). CGI has been used incrementally, as technology developed, and even *Toy Story* was recorded onto celluloid for screening, and thus used photochemical material. There is some dispute over the first film produced and released without employing any photochemical process, but the success of *Star Wars: Episode II – Attack of the Clones* in 2002 popularised the fully-digital film (Gaut, 2010: 11-12). It would be unfair to attribute the view that digital films are not films to Currie, and I think it much more likely that he simply failed to foresee the consequences of the digital revolution.[7]

Carroll was quicker to realise the implications of the new technology: in 1996, he noted the advances made in electronic cinema and predicted the possibility of films being produced on CD-ROMs (Carroll, 1996: 115), and the future film as 'digitally synthesized images' (Carroll, 1996: 122). He believes that the domain of film is moving images, which seems a promising start in the light of subsequent developments. He stipulates 'moving images' as opposed to 'moving pictures' in order to include abstract, nonrepresentational, and non-objective film (Carroll, 1996: 126). Carroll's ontology of moving images identifies five necessary (but not jointly sufficient) conditions: they must have the potential to appear to move, be a detached display, be 2D, and be generated by a template that is a token such that performance tokens are not works of art (Carroll, 1996: 130). That an image must have the potential to appear to move seems obvious. By 'detached display' Carroll means that the images must not contain egocentric information, i.e. tell the viewer where he is in relation to the space depicted.[8] Thus watching *Jurassic Park* does not tell me how to find the park in question, nor identify my position in relation to the dinosaurs roaming on screen. I have already accepted the 2D requirement, which is implied in 'picture' (although not in 'image'). So far, therefore, Carroll's ontology is applicable to digital and traditional film, and the range of motion pictures that preceded traditional film.

Carroll uses the type-token distinction to contrast film with theatre (Carroll, 1996: 127-129). The play *Richard III* is a type, and its performance is generated by an interpretation. I may, e.g., have the option of seeing two *Richard III*s, one at the university and one at a theatre in town. The interpretation of Shakespeare's text will differ according to the tastes and skills of the different directors and actors involved. These interpretations are themselves types, and they generate the token performances, e.g. a week of six shows from Monday to Saturday at the university. These tokens will ideally be identical, but the two interpretations may differ substantially. In a play the text, the interpretation, and the performance are all subject to artistic evaluation. Richard Loncraine's 1995 film *Richard III* differs entirely, however. I could have seen exactly the same performance no matter what film theatre I went to because the token – the particular screening I did in fact see – was generated by a template, which would have been a film print in 1995, and could be a film print or a digital file fifteen years later. The template is itself a token of the type, with the result that the performance I see is a token generated by another token. Neither the template nor the performance are subject to artistic evaluation, only the type, Loncraine's *Richard III*. The interpretation, acting, cinematography, and other aesthetic elements of the film are all contained in the type. The template and the screening may be faulty, but such problems are technical rather than artistic.

It should be evident that Carroll's use of type and token differentiates plays and, e.g., puppet shows, from traditional and digital film, and is thus satisfactory in dealing with bitmap-generated motion pictures. Strangely, Carroll describes his ontology as 'overly inclusive' for 'what we typically call motion pictures' (Carroll, 1996: 131). He specifically excludes mass produced flip books and the zoetrope from the art form he is attempting to identify because they 'do not seem to be the kind of phenomena that one has in mind when speaking of moving pictures in ordinary language' (Carroll, 1996: 131). I believe Carroll is in error here, for if he is attempting to establish an ontology of photographic film, then there should have been some reference to photography or film stock in his criteria. If he is seeking a broader ontology of moving images, however, then the ordinary usage of 'motion picture' for 'traditional film' is of little relevance. There is an inconsistency in investigating the moving image and restricting the results to its current popular incarnation.

Inconsistency notwithstanding, there is a further problem with Carroll's ontology in that it excludes both hand-crafted flip books (as he admits) and any moving picture presentation where the performance is an art. With regard to the latter, I have mentioned that the requirement that the moving image be generated by a template is an implicit link to Gaut's mechanically-generated category. While the template might apply to mass-produced thaumatropes and zoetropes – and perhaps even certain magic lantern shows – it would definitely exclude the shadow puppet plays, where the performance is not produced by a template and is itself a source of artistry. Perhaps this is not a fault in Carroll. If one considers watching *Avatar* in 3D and watching a shadow play, one might well conclude that they are not the same kind of thing. Yet Carroll's ontology includes the flip book and the zoetrope, which seem much closer to the shadow play than the digital film in category. Why can a zoetrope be a moving image, but not a shadow play; and why can a mass-produced flip book be a moving image, but not a handmade one? Though Carroll's ontology is remarkable in anticipating and including digital cinema, I believe it ultimately fails by excluding object-generated and handmade moving pictures without sufficient justification.

Manovich's characterisation of film as a particular type of animation may serve better, for animation seems to be – literally – the art of moving pictures. Manovich's ontology of film is in fact more radical than this. He maintains that the return to handmade motion pictures epitomized in digital manipulation is not merely a return to animated moving pictures, but 'a particular branch of painting – painting in time' (1995). His answer to the ontological question is thus that a film is a series of paintings. The proposal is intriguing, but while there are aspects of digital cinema that are indeed a return to handmade motion pictures, the particular synthesis between human artistry and mechanical computer production in digital images appears to be a new development rather than a return to painting. One might, e.g., possibly conceive of *Avatar* as a series of paintings, but I'm not convinced that describing Rob Marshall's *Nine* (2009) as series of paintings would be in any way enlightening. Although Guy Ritchie achieved the photorealism in *Sherlock Holmes* (2009) by animation, Manovich's answer to the question 'what is it?' still seems confusing. Even if one agrees with Manovich entirely, however, his ontology excludes traditional film, and the many similarities between digital and traditional film indicate that the former is a development of the latter rather than a new art form (in the same way that digital photography is a development of traditional photography).

I believe that digital film is the same kind of 'thing' as traditional film and its predecessors, and that choreutoscopes and phenatakistocopes are similarly related to their own predecessors, magic lanterns and shadow puppet plays. They are all displays of *motion pictures* – or moving images – and while any two examples of the category may appear quite different, there is evidence of a linear development through history, particularly from the beginning of the nineteenth century. I agree with Manovich that the latest technology has asserted the dominance of animation over film, and reversed the relationship that persisted through the twentieth century. For all my criticism of Carroll, he had a seer's vision in stating, '[t]he epoch of photographic film... may represent nothing but a brief interlude in the artform' (Carroll, 1996: 122). Ultimately, however, Gaut's description of the many kinds of cinema is the most convincing. Cinema, and moving pictures, have existed for centuries, and the current sovereignty of animation in digital imaging serves as a reminder that the moving picture pre-dated photography. What is a film? A series of pictures in motion. What is a digital film? The latest incarnation of the motion picture. Motion pictures can, as Gaut claims, be produced by objects, hand, or machine, but nonetheless belong to the same ontological category.

The concept of film is currently in crisis, as it was eighty-odd years ago when the 'talkie' replaced the silent film. The talkie was seen by many as a threat, or a different kind of art form, but increased the opportunities for expression in the established art of film. The digital revolution has enriched the art form no less – perhaps even more so – returning the motion picture to its roots in animation, and creating new horizons for expression. Digital technology has created new possibilities for interactivity and mass-produced virtual reality. The consequences of virtual reality 'total cinema' and the threat of interactivity to the traditional unity of the art work are beyond the scope of my inquiry, and may produce questions to which a contemporary answer would be premature. At this point in the second decade of the twenty-first century, however, digital film remains – like traditional film and its predecessors – the art of moving pictures.[9]

Original source and licence

Film-Philosophy (17), 1, 2013. Licence: CC-BY.

References

Anonymous (n.d.) 'AFI's 100 Years...100 Movies', American Film Institute, at: http://www.afi.com/tvevents/100years/movies.aspx. Accessed on 12 May 2010.

Arnheim, R. (1974) 'On the Nature of Photography', *Critical Inquiry*, 1 (1).

Bazin, A. (1945/1960) 'The Ontology of the Photographic Image', *Film Quarterly*, 13 (4).

Buser, T. (2006) *Experiencing Art Around Us*. Belmont, CA: Thomson Wadsworth.

Carroll, N. (1996/2006) *Defining the Moving Image* in N. Carroll & J. Choi (eds), *Philosophy of Film and Motion Pictures*. Oxford: Blackwell.

Cook, D. A. (2004) *A History of Narrative Film*. New York: W.W. Norton.

Currie, G. (1993/2006) *The Long Goodbye: The Imaginary Language of Film* in N. Carroll & J. Choi (eds), *Philosophy of Film and Motion Pictures*. Oxford: Blackwell.

Currie, G. (1995/2008) *Image and Mind: Film, Philosophy, and Cognitive Science*. Cambridge: Cambridge University Press.

Currie, G. (1997) 'The Film Theory that Never Was: A Nervous Manifesto' in R. Allen & M. Smith (eds), *Film Theory and Philosophy*. Oxford: Oxford University Press.

Curtis, J.C. (1986) 'Dorothea Lange, Migrant Mother, and the Culture of the Great Depression', *Winterthur Portfolio*, 21 (1).

Gaut, B. (2010) *A Philosophy of Cinematic Art*. Cambridge: Cambridge University Press.

Kania, A. (2002) 'The Illusion of Realism in Film', *British Journal of Aesthetics*, 42 (3).

Keller, B. (1994) 'Kevin Carter, a Pulitzer Winner For Sudan Photo, Is Dead at 33' *New York Times*, 10 August, at: http://www.nytimes.com/1994/07/29/world/kevin-carter-a-pulitzerwinner- for-sudan-photo-is-dead-at-33.html. Accessed on 11 May 2010.

Manovich, Lev (1995) 'What is Digital Cinema?', Lev Manovich Online at: http://www.manovich.net/TEXT/digitalcinema. Accessed on 7 May 2010.

Mitchell, W. J. (1992) *The Reconfigured Eye: Visual Truth in the Post-Photographic Era*. Cambridge, MA: MIT Press.

Rohter, L. (2009) 'New Doubts Raised Over Famous War Photo', *New York Times*, 17 August, at http://www.nytimes.com/2009/08/18/arts/design/18capa.html?_r=1. Accessed on 11 May 2010.

Scruton, R. (1981) 'Photography and Representation', *Critical Inquiry*, 7 (3).

Seels, J. (1997) 'The Eye of History: 1860-65', *Journal of Visual Literacy*, 17 (1).

Walton, K. L. (1970/2008) 'Categories of Art' in P. Lamarque & S. Olsen (eds), *Aesthetics and the Philosophy of Art*. Oxford: Blackwell.

Walton, K. L. (1984) 'Transparent Pictures: On the Nature of Photographic Realism', *Critical Inquiry*, 11 (2).

Zone, R. (2007), *Stereoscopic Cinema & the Origins of 3-D Film, 1838- 1952*. Lexington: University Press of Kentucky.

Notes

1. Electronic recording also uses a CCD, converting light to an electric pulse, and has been primarily employed in television and video (Gaut, 2010: 9-10). I do not discuss electronic cinema as its innovations have been overshadowed by digital technology.

2. I am not aware of conclusive evidence that O'Sullivan engaged in the practice, but several American Civil War photographers did, including his colleague Alexander Gardner. See Buser (2006: 214); Mitchell (1992: 43-45); Seels (1997: 48-51).

3. Photographs created with instant cameras, the production of which was dominated by the Polaroid Corporation from 1948-2008, are a possible exception.

4. Interestingly, Polavision – the Polaroid Corporation's instant movie camera – was a commercial failure, being discontinued two years after its launch in 1977.

5. The word 'cartoon', with its juvenile, trivial connotations, is a product of the peripheral status of animation in the twentieth century.

6. The question of whether the images projected by a film actually move or only appear to move is much debated. See Currie (1995: 28-47) and Kania (2002) for contrasting views.

7. Significantly, Currie subsequently changed his conception of 'film' to anything that displayed moving images (1997: 47).

8. This has also been disputed, however. See Currie (1995: 22-27).

9. I am indebted to Maarten Steenhagen and David Tallerman for their assistance with this paper.

II Hybrid Photomediations

CHAPTER 10

Notes on a Painting of a Painted Photograph

Ajay Sinha

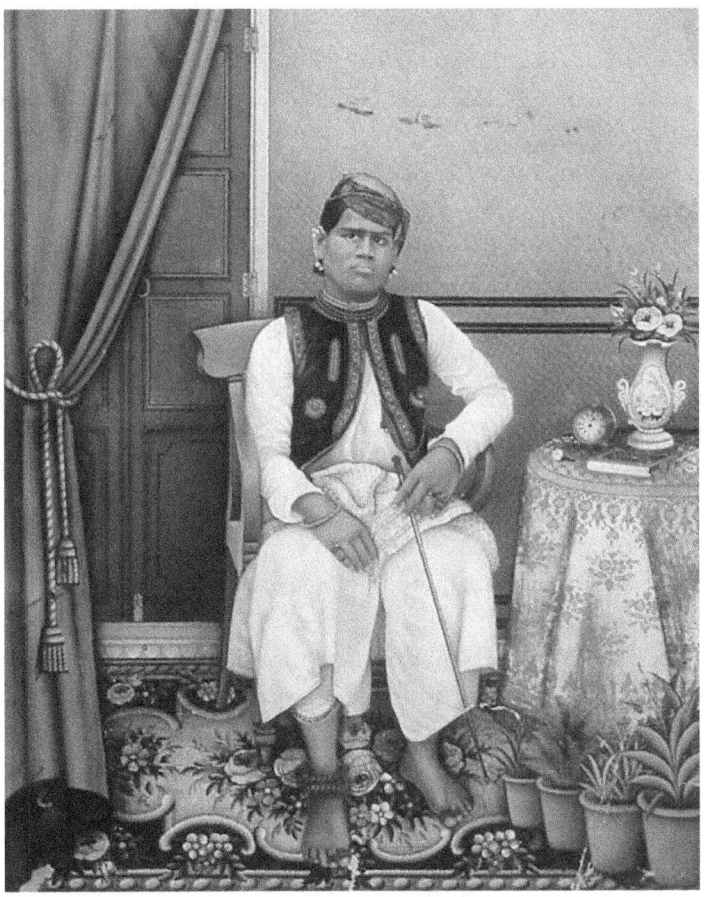

Figure 10.1: Unknown artist, *Portrait of a Young Prince*, 19th century, watercolor on paper, National Gallery of Modern Art, New Delhi, India, Acc. No. 14759, Courtesy National Gallery of Modern Art, New Delhi.

This is not a painted photograph. It is an opaque watercolor painting on paper that resembles a painted photograph. Conventions of a painted photograph are closely followed. A heavy green curtain on the left introduces us to the seated figure next to a table, as in a studio photograph. The painter also embellishes this basic setup. On the table, the blue chinoiserie vase painted like wallpaper, the sacred book with metal clasps, and the clock are picked out and made legible against the bright pink Victorian table cover. The chair, sculpted in sharp chiaroscuro, flares out unusually to accommodate the sitter's outstretched left elbow. The spotted scarf on the sitter's lap looks creaturely. On the floor, the carpet pops out at us in bold relief, flattening the pictorial space, while more than necessary potted plants, graded from bright to dull green, dramatize perspective and depth.

Unusual among these standard features of a painted photograph, however, is the background. It is neither a backdrop of fantastic locales rendered in atmospheric perspective nor a glowing, opaque ground against which figures magically levitate (Pinney, 2003: 202). A closed wooden door set on a marble threshold returns us instead to the banal setting of the original black-and-white photograph, which may have been taken not in a studio but rather in a room belonging, presumably, to the royal sitter's mansion. Oddest is the sitter's defiant look away from the camera, this in spite of the chance artists usually take for adjusting it toward a frontal gaze, as is conventional in painted photographs.[1] The look is an anomaly. It recalls not the painted photograph of which this is a copy, but instead the very first, unpainted photograph from which this painting is twice removed.

In the history of world photography, the interaction of photography and opaque paint is unique to India and quite unlike tinting the surface of the photographic emulsion found generally in the 19th and 20th centuries (Gutman, 1982: 103-32).[2] For scholars of Indian photography, opaque paint covering the grey photographic emulsion using techniques of Indian miniature painting marks the local ways of socializing the modern technology. In such a hybrid image, clashing interests in flat, bright colors as well as exaggerated depth and perspective also indicate a painterly resistance to the scopic regimes of British colonial photography in India. In this image, however, paint is used not only to reproduce bright colors but also to paint in the surface greyness and indexical details that might have been left untouched in the original painted photograph, thus reversing the inquiry. Instead of asking about painterly inventiveness operating on photography, the question to be posed, somewhat counterintuitively, is: What motivates a painter to use his miniature painting style to underscore, not obscure, the shady presence of the photographic emulsion?

This essay offers five loosely connected thoughts regarding possible motivations for this choice as a way of suggesting the web of visual and cultural relations in which this image was involved.

1. It is possible that the image is simply a copy of a pre-existing photograph of a deceased ancestor. The painting is in the Jaya Appasamy collection at the National Gallery of Modern Art, New Delhi, where the sitter is identified as an unknown, late-19th-century tribal prince from central India. The figure and his Victorian setting certainly capture the 19th-century conventions of painted photography, but the copy could also belong to the early 20th century, when an old, fading image required renewal.[3] The NGMA has no documentation of the provenance of the image, and the artist is unknown. Unmistakable, nevertheless, is the impulse to imitate, not embellish, the original photograph. The painter maintains its appearance exactly, without alteration. A conspicuous indicator of this choice is the sitter's skin, in which shades of grey are visible through the brownish tint, pointing to the natural chemical layer of a photographic image. Whereas artists usually try to tint and inflect the deathly grey of the photographic image or cover it with opaque paint, here the painter mixes chalk white and soot black to match the combination of grey and brown of the sitter's skin in the photograph. The observation leads me to suggest that the intention here is simply to preserve in an exact pictorial form a photographic image that is possibly beyond repair. At the same time, it leads me also to ask why the artist, or the patron, subjected the revered ancestor to such a museological impulse and not a painterly one that could have transformed the fraying photograph into a living presence, as is common in pictorial practices.

2. It is possible that the patron prefers a painting even while desiring photographic effects in the image. Exploring mechanically reproducing images of Indian gods and other social individuals, Christopher Pinney makes an argument for a preference for chromolithography over

photography on the grounds that Indian consumers of images usually looked beyond mere appearance for signs of 'extra-mundane' qualities of the subject, for which 'photography was deemed a phenomenological failure' (Pinney, 2009: 79).[4] I suggest that the NGMA image is reaching for the 'extra-mundane' qualities of the sitter by converting the photograph into a painted copy. Miniature paintings have performed the function of bestowing power and status to royal patrons within India's courtly culture since the 16th century.[5] Painters invented elaborate iconographic frames for their sitters, giving them sacred attributes and exquisite halos, and located them in settings designed to convey their importance in a hierarchy of power relations (Aitken, 2010: 111-53). It is this traditional role and value of painting that extends to the NGMA image.

One could even propose that the NGMA image returns the painted photograph to the cultural valence of painting. When court painters picked up photography, in the mid-19th century, photography certainly took over some of the concerns of traditional painting.[6] The genre of painted photograph is one result, but painted photographs were also used for making other kinds of images instead of being an end in themselves, as is usually assumed.[7] Tryna Lyons documents a large mural portrait of the Maharaja Rana Zalim Singh II of Jhalawar, dated to about 1918–1920, in Garh-Mahal in Jhalawar, Rajasthan, and calls it the 'photo studio' type because it resembles a painted photograph except for its large scale (Lyons, 2004: 170). The young Maharaja sits on a chair in three-quarter view, resting his right elbow against the marble-top table, while details of the carpet and the fine muslin tunic, as well as the blurred, romanticized backdrop with a classical column, are painted to closely imitate a painted photograph. The difference between the mural and the NGMA painting is the latter's small size – made to be framed, displayed, and handled exactly like a photograph, not stretched on a wall from floor to ceiling.

3. The NGMA image differs from the Jhalawar mural discussed above in one more significant way. The mural filters out the chemical greyness of the painted photograph and retains, in fresco secco, only the warm orange and brown tints of the sitter's skin. By contrast, the NGMA image reproduces both the grey photographic emulsion and the brown tint the original painter might have introduced in the painted photograph. Thus, the use of a photograph as a model, to be reworked into an adequate image

of the sanguine sitter, is understandable in the mural but not in the miniature painting. Surely the painter of miniatures demonstrates his ability to observe and emulate, but he applies that ability to reproduce the original model exactly, not to transform it according to the sitter's sense of himself. In other words, this is a case not of realism but of photorealism, the almost mechanical reproduction of a photographic image. The painting accurately documents what is being encountered in the original painted photograph, including a somewhat irregular mixture of both depth and flatness and photogenic facts such as residual indexical details and chemical greyness. To put it another way, the copy merely declares the painted photograph as a material object in itself.

4. Like gold, or lapis lazuli in an earlier era of miniature painting, the grey chemical underlayer of the photographic emulsion in this copy now gains a material presence. It is neither to be removed, as in the mural, nor inflected or covered up, as in a painted photograph, nor overlooked in order to get to the 'real' photographic referent, as in black-and-white photography. Instead, grey becomes one among several layers of paint to be burnished, reworked, and brought to a shiny finish as in the tradition of miniature painting. Furthermore, the greyness of the image is highlighted when seen against the pink table, the colorful vase, and the gold embroidery on the sitter's black jacket. One could argue from this treatment that brightly painted details were considered standard, conventional features of a painted photograph by the early 20th century, but what is added in this image is a sensuous response to the photographic emulsion. Our awareness of greyness is heightened when we realize that we are looking at a painting, not a photograph, in which greyness is unavoidable and normalized. The material presence of greyness is especially worked out in the back wall, which was probably left unpainted in the original image. In the copy, crosshatching and lightly variegated white spots give the wall a 'physical substantiality' employing techniques previously used to depict fleshy, erotic figures by early-19th-century Rajasthani artists such as Chokha (Beach et al., 2005: 81).

5. How should we approach and evaluate the 'substantiality' of photogenic greyness in the NGMA image? One could suggest at least two possibilities: First, in bringing attention to the greyness of the image, the

painter could be looking at photography with the same fascination late-18th- and early-19th-century Rajasthani artists, Chokha among them, showed toward other modern visual effects, such as linear perspective, light and shade, and panoramic view, disregarding scholarly arguments on the subject of Indian painting's, and by extension Indian photography's, preoccupation with a flat pictorial surface.[8] In other words, the photogenic greyness of the NGMA image relates better to the broader historical context of visual exchanges in early-modern India. In addition, although the Indian viewers may have preferred brightly colored chromolithographs against the 'phenomenological failure' of three-dimensional space and chemical greyness of colonial photography, as Pinney suggests, the NGMA image may be elevating the grey surface of the photographic emulsion itself to an 'extra-mundane' level.

Second, the photogenic qualities of the image could have seemed to the painter to be an integral part of the sitter's appearance, even perhaps his 'extra-mundane' personality. This strange fact can be explained by what could be called the linguistic or iconographic approach in Indian miniature painting. Artists of the traditions of courtly miniature painting rendered painted portraits from models preserved in sketchbooks, not directly from real life. Thus, painting became a matter of giving a visual syntax to dispersed visual elements and attributes taken from those sketchbooks.[9] The practice also means that the likeness of a sitter was a renewal, or reornamentation, of an earlier model. That a portrait was a collection of well-practiced iconographic motifs is especially true for venerable figures, whose 'extra-mundane' qualities the finished design was meant to incorporate.[10] Within this traditional framework, to which the NGMA image belongs, the original painted photograph could have appeared as a visual model for describing the venerable attributes of the sitter. In this view, the photogenic greyness of the image could have appeared as one more attribute, the newest one, to be included in the finished portrait along with the sitter's pose in the chair, the curtain, and the table containing a vase, a clock, a writing quill, and a sacred book.

What kind of 'attribute' is this photogenic greyness? I suggest it marks the individual in the image with an immanent sense of 'nowness', a connotation relating to the modern technology of photography itself. This greyness is a product of alchemy – a combination of sunlight, the not readily available silver nitrate, camera lens, and darkroom – as well as investment of clients in the power of this alchemy to absorb the world. The alchemy is what attracts clients to the camera and to photo studios, and holds their enchanted presence in an image, throughout the global history of photography. Greyness, with a hint of silver underlying the shiny surface of the chemical image, is also what relates photography to the moving image in the early 20th century. If photography lends an aura to an individual sitter's social presence, the moving image, tinted or not, makes palpable to viewers myths, dreams, and spectacles of faraway worlds. It is this greyness of the technological image that is incorporated in this painting.

Coda

The photogenic greyness of the NGMA image goes unnoticed in the current discussion of Indian painted photographs, in which it is connected only with the colonial technology to be resisted through opaque paint. Grey, however, spreads across image practices in early-20th-century India, and is seen in secular as well as religious images. Tryna Lyons reproduces a remarkable image of the Hindu god Krishna, datable to 1900-1910, painted by Ghasiram, a well-known artist and photographer practicing in the religious town of Nathadwara, in Rajasthan. In that image, Krishna's body is painted blue, as is usual, except for his face. Krishna's face is treated with the grey tonal shades of a black-and-white photograph, made vivid also by surrounding details, such as his yellow turban, gold ornaments, a peacock feather, and the pink lotus blossoms he holds.[11] The Nathadwara image documents the disappearance of photography into the sacred shimmer of a god, and it is this shimmer that is rekindled within the secular portraiture in the NGMA image.

Original source and licence

Local Culture/Global Photography special issue. *Trans-Asia Photography Review*, Volume 3, Issue 2, Spring 2013. http://hdl.handle.net/2027/spo.7977573.0003.205. © Ajay Sinha. Permission to republish granted.

References

Alkazi, E., Allana, R. & Kumar, P. (eds) (2008) *Painted Photographs: Coloured Portraiture in India*. Ahmedabad: Mapin Publishing, in association with the Alkazi Collection of Photography.

Aitken, M. E. (2010) *The Intelligence of Tradition in Rajput Court Painting*. New Haven and London: Yale University Press.

Beach, M. et al. (2005) 'Master Artists at Devgarh' in *Artibus Asiae Supplement* 46. Zurich: Museum Rietburg.

Davis, S. (2008) *The Bikaner School: Usta Artisans and Their Heritage*. Jodhpur: RMG Exports.

Dewan, D. (2012) *Embellished Reality: Indian Painted Photographs: Towards a Transcultural History of Photography*. Toronto: Royal Ontario Museum Press.

Goswamy, B. N. & Dallapiccola, A. L. (1983) *A Place Apart: Painting in Kutch, 1720–1820*. Bombay and New York: Oxford University Press.

Gutman, J. M. (1982) *Through Indian Eyes*. New York: Oxford University Press / International Center of Photography.

Koch, E. (1997) 'The Hierarchical Principles of Shah-Jahani Painting' in *King of the World: The Padshahnama*. London: Azimuth Editions.

Lyons, T. (2004) *The Artists of Nathadwara: The Practice of Painting in Rajasthan*. Bloomington: Indiana University Press.

Pinney, C. (1997) *Camera Indica: The Social Life of Indian Photographs*. Chicago: University of Chicago Press.

Pinney, C. (2003) 'Notes from the Surface of the Image: Photography, Postcolonialism, and Vernacular Modernism' in C. Pinney and N. Peterson (eds), *Photography's Other Histories*. Durham and London: Duke University Press.

Pinney, C. (2009) 'Mechanical Reproduction in India' in G. Sinha (ed.), *Art and Visual Culture in India*. Mumbai: Marg Publications.

Notes

1. Even in memorial portraits made from a photograph taken of a person after death, the artist paints in bright, open eyes looking straight at the viewer. (Pinney, 1997: 139-140 and fig. 122)

2. See also Alkazi, Allana, and Kumar (2008) and Dewan (2012).

3. Assigning a date to the moment of painting as opposed to the moment when the photograph was taken can be tricky. See Allana (2008) for the artist Pannalal Gaur (c. 1880–1950), whose earliest-known work is on a photograph of the Maharana Swarup Singh of Udaipur by an unknown photographer, datable to c. 1861, when the Maharaja presumably died (fig. 7). Based on the artist's own dates, Allana concludes that the painting could have been done years only after the photograph was taken. From Gaur's very long career, the last work reproduced in the catalogue, a portrait of the Maharaja Kumar Bhagwat Singh of Udaipur, dates from c. 1940.

4. The phrase suggests a certain quality that exceeds, but is also indicated in, the visual image and the network of exchanges in which it participates.

5. For the 'conflation of Krishna with Rajasthan's rulers' as a 'common trope' in Rajasthani paintings, see Aitken (2010: 49).

6. For photographer-painters in the Mewar court of Rajasthan, in western India, see Lyons (2004: 170).

7. For a detailed discussion and typology of various painting techniques by which photographs were finished, see Dewan (2012).

8. For flatness in photography, see Gutman (1982: 81); Goswamy and Dallapiccola (1983); Lyons (2004); Aitken (2010).

9. See Davis (2008); Lyons (2004) and Aitken (2010) for detailed documentation of sketchbooks and their usage in Rajasthani painting.

10. On the iconography of one such feature, the profile, in imperial Mughal portraiture, see Koch (1997: 130-43). On 'eye as an iconographic form' in Rajasthani portraits, see Aitken (2010: 260-65).

11. See Lyons (2004: 151). In this image, Ghasiram might be exploring possibilities for visualizing Krishna's body as shyama (darkness), which is neither blue nor black.

CHAPTER 11

Boredom and Baroque Space

David Bate

André Bazin argues in 'The Ontology of the Photographic Image' that 'In achieving the aims of baroque art, photography has freed the plastic arts from their obsession with likeness' (Bazin, 1980: 240). Photography and the cinema, he says, have satisfied our 'appetite for illusion'. The invention of myriad computer imagery shows this to be otherwise. The appetite for illusion shows no bounds, just as the psychoanalytic proposition of Jacques Lacan regarding the 'metonymy of desire' reminds us that desire itself is an endless process. In this context, new computer-based practices of representation are, without knowing it, precipitating a mutation in representational space. There is an uncanny 'return of the repressed' which moves us out of twentieth-century photographic realism. It is a Baroque trend of spatial illusions, theatrical imagination and intense feelings, where an image is a representation of the thing it represents through a relation of meaning, a kind of 'psychological realism', rather than through a mere mimetic likeness or literal resemblance.

The attitude of Baroque art, according to Erwin Panofsky, can be defined as 'based on an objective conflict between antagonistic forces, which, however, merge into a subjective feeling of freedom and even pleasure...' (Panofsky, 1997: 38). The paradigmatic example of this for Panofsky is a sculpture, the *Ecstasy of St. Theresa* (1644–47) by Bernini. This famous altar piece in Rome dedicated to Saint Theresa depicts the moment in her story when an angel of the Lord has pierced her heart with a golden flaming arrow. She is shown swooning, filled with pain *and* erotic ecstasy. Her facial expression is intended to express this emotional intensity, while streams of light in the form of golden rays suggest the movement of her rising to heaven. The drapes around her body also suggest movement with their crisp dishevelled and whirling forms. Intended to be seen from a single point of view, as in the modern photographic image, the three-dimensional statue combines picture, relief and plastic grouping. Thus, for Panofsky, 'Baroque art came to abolish the borderline between the "three arts", and even art and nature, and also brought forth the modern landscape in the full sense of the word, meaning a visualization of unlimited space captured in, and represented by, a section of it, so that human figures became debased to a mere "staffage" and finally could be dispensed with altogether' (Panofsky, 1997: 45, 51).

For Michel Foucault 'the Baroque' period is 'the privileged age of *trompe-l'oeil* painting, of the cosmic illusion, of the play that duplicates itself by representing another play, of the *quid pro quo*, of dreams and visions; it is the age of the deceiving senses' (Foucault, 1985: 51). Celestial frescos, anamorphic distortions, the illusion of doors, windows and other images where they do not exist, all move the spatial representation of the world away from one of resemblance. For Foucault, this is the 'essential rupture of knowledge in the Western world, what has become important is no longer resemblances but identities and differences'. If somewhere like Versailles is 'baroque', it is its grand plan, its 'grotesque', 'excessive ornamentation', the 'decorative' components that spiral off into an infinity of minute differences. The vases in the garden: each one the same identity (as vase) yet different in decoration. Decoration is not extra or unnecessary in the baroque, but constitutive of differing identities, of an infinite difference. Where representation had been based in resemblance and similitude in the sixteenth century, the seventeenth century world was represented in signs without guaranteed meaning. While comparison and similitude had revealed the ordering of the world, baroque rhetoric made representation (of the world) a question of analysis. The logic of likeness, resemblance, the 'chimera of similitude', was represented as such. It is no coincidence that the Baroque was also the age of allegory where a sign is always already a collection of other signs. Laid bare, the illusion of space where there is none (i.e. the *trompe-l'oeil*), may be read allegorically as a critique of the structure of social space and social relations within them. Whether viewed as ugly or beautiful, the common sense of baroque as 'excessive decoration', of an exaggerated, unnecessary artfulness, only shows our distance from an understanding of the Baroque rhetoric of visual splendour. Pleasure is the measure of intelligence and boredom is the signified of a lack of eloquence. A common-sense view of baroque is associated with decadence and a grotesque, as things that grew out of an 'ennui', the result of a boredom with the existing spatial and representational conventions. In courtly life of the period where speech was the equivalent of thinking, a bored response signified a refusal or rejection of the speaker's thought. A boring speech was one composed of boring thoughts, or rather, for the listener, no libidinal investment or stimulus in the speaker's words. Therefore, 'Plato is boring because he is not eloquent' (Lichtenstein, 1993: 29).

The term Baroque initially begins as an insult, a term of abuse and derision to describe – or criticise – the bold, 'over-ornate' style. The use of the word boredom similarly describes a negative state of being bored by something. But boredom is a question of what one does with space. 'Nothing to do' or 'nothing to see' does not mean that there is literally not anything to see, but rather that the subject cannot see it. Vision is colonized, inhibited, by boredom. The bored person is the one for whom seeing is blasé, the sense of sight, supposedly, as it is commonly said, is 'dulled through over-stimulation' (Fenichel, 1954: 302). As Otto Fenichel argues, what such situations really describe is the damming up of a libido. Repressed, the libidinal energy turns around on the subject and disperses through it as a kind of paralysis of any aim (or rather, boredom is now the manifestation of that aim). This boredom is like anxiety, it similarly petrifies the subject into non-action. Boredom and anxiety are defences against libidinal excitement. This can be seen as the 'passive' type of boredom. The 'active' type of boredom, in turn, is exemplified in the idea of the 'Sunday neurotic': the person who cannot abide the idea of vacation, they are bored by it. When there is no duty to fulfil, the libidinal energy comes rushing out, only to be inhibited and dammed up as 'I'm bored'. At work such a person strives to disperse their desire for intense excitement in the demands of work duties. Once these duties are removed, the anxiety of how to disperse the libidinal energy emerges again in boredom. The activity of work thus offers an escape from the pain of boredom.

The sort of 'clutter' associated with Baroque architecture, sculpture, painting and rhetoric is not merely ornamental, but a constitutive component of the style. If this style is 'irritating' to someone, it is because it invokes anxiety and boredom. There is too much 'emotion' in it, too many signifying components, it is 'over-stated'. Baroque work itself seems to characterize the active aim of boredom. The 'eclectic' sticking together of 'disconnected styles', the ceilings filled with an imaginary space, the portraits that are crowded allegorical personifications, everything is doubly filled with meanings and details. It is as though the whole age of Baroque recognised the illusion of the Renaissance representational space. Perspective, where a horizon is the vanishing-point of the lines that meet in the infinite distance, hides the anxiety that there is nothing beyond the perspectival horizon. The anxiety of cosmic space is 'filled in' in Renaissance representation by the horizons of Quattrocento perspective. Revealed in the Baroque as a chimera, this perspectival logic is obsessively covered over and simultaneously revealed. The anxiety of there being nothing beyond is actually represented and embodied in the signifying forms of the Baroque. This is the symptom of the Baroque age.

The painting by Velasquez of the maids of honour called *Las Meninas* (1656) holds for Michel Foucault the representation 'of Classical representation, and the definition of the space it opens up to us' (Foucault, 1985: 16). Much earlier Hans Holbein's *The Ambassadors* (1533) had combined two points of view, literally 'perspectives' (one anamorphic), into the same picture plane, simultaneously revealing the supplement of mercantile capitalism and the accumulation of worldly goods: death. The spatial 'distortion' of the anamorphic skull or flying pancake (I am reminded, distractedly, of Lacan's 'hommlette' joke) as it appears from the 'normal' point of view interferes with, and cuts across, the normal perspectival logic of the picture. It is such 'distortions' that the computer enables to be produced fairly simply, such that these images become absorbed into the dominant signifying practices of our visual culture as 'normal'. We are again in a period of chimerical representation, of eclectic styles, an obsessive covering over of the holes in existence, which both reveals them and denies them. As Baroque art 'upped the stakes' in the demand for the ever new with a spiral of invention – new combinations of contradictions – so its use of the devices and ornaments inevitably multiplied. On the one hand, Baroque invention appears as a kind of 'Sunday neurosis', the crowding of signifiers, a constant work of signification, to avoid the anxiety and boredom of 'nothing to see'. On the other hand, these eclectic signifiers fill a space, which offers no comfort for the subject of a passive boredom. A bored subject is one who craves stimulation. But boredom is not a property of the object, it is a problem of the subject. Thus, whatever the signifier, the signified is always 'boring'. Stimulation is repressed, such that it manifests as a bored response, a constant deferral of dealing with the passing of time. With the *speed* of new technologies, the distance between things is collapsed, simultaneously different spaces are collapsed into the same time.

Today's culture of the 'visual', based in a logic of the photographic image, is potentially thrown into a baroque 'deception' when the indexical-iconic field of resemblance is constantly disturbed by the new capacities for illusion. If the computer is giving a twist to the uncertainty of the historical kaleidoscope of representation, we may find ourselves in the space of a baroque dream.

Licence

© David Bate.

References

Bazin, A. (1980/1945) 'The Ontology of the Photographic Image', in A. Trachtenberg (ed.), *Classic Essays on Photography*. New Haven: Leete's Island.

Fenichel, O. & Rapaport, D. (eds) (1954) *The Collected Papers of Otto Fenichel*, Vol.1. London: Routledge and Kegan Paul.

Foucault, M. (1985) *The Order of Things*. London: Tavistock.

Lichtenstein, J. (1993) *The Eloquence of Color*. Berkeley: University of California Press.

Panofsky, E. (1997) 'What is Baroque?', in *Three Essays on Style*. Cambridge, MA: MIT Press.

CHAPTER 12

Differential Interventions: Images as Operative Tools

AUD SISSEL HOEL AND FRANK LINDSETH

Advanced imaging technologies are currently transforming operating theaters into sophisticated augmented reality studios. State-of-the-art operating rooms are run like modern media laboratories exploring recent developments in communication technology, including computer visualizations, positioning and navigation applications, and the expansion of network systems. Surgeons interact with various displays permitting indirect observation of the surgical field through high definition videoscopes (microscopes, endoscopes), supplemented with scans obtained before the operation in combination with image and tracking data acquired during the procedure. Surgical imaging and navigation challenge established frameworks for understanding images, just as much as they belie the idea, widespread in early-stage theories of digital images, of digitization corrupting the detecting capacity of images. While being highly interventional and artificial, and sometimes entirely computer-generated and synthetic, medical images and visualizations undoubtedly reveal pertinent aspects of reality. How are we to make sense of them?

Images used for guidance during surgical procedures exemplify a category of images that in recent literature has been characterized as 'operative' (Farocki, 2004; Kogge, 2004; Krämer, 2009). Operative images are images that, in the words of Harun Farocki, 'do not represent an object, but rather are part of an operation' (Farocki, 2004: 17). The images in question typically serve practical purposes tied to specialized tasks, such as, in the case of navigated brain tumor surgery, to localize a tumor and control the removal of pathological tissue. The active and performative work of digital images is also emphasized by new media scholars investigating digital image applications such as Photosynth, Augmented Reality, and Google Street View (Uricchio, 2011; Verhoeff, 2012; Hoelzl and Marie, forthcoming). As pointed out by William Uricchio, algorithmic intermediation reconfigures the relation between the viewing subject and the object viewed in a way that 'ultimately determines *what* we see, and even *how* we see it' (Uricchio, 2011: 33). Algorithmically enabled image applications do not simply reproduce pre-given realities but exercise transformative powers on both ends of the subject-object relationship (Carusi, 2012). This is why established representational approaches fall short of accounting for the active roles of digital image applications, and this is why new theorizations of images are needed.

Operational approaches provide promising possibilities for rethinking images for at least three reasons: first, they offer dynamic approaches that analyze phenomena into doings and happenings rather than into things and static entities; second, they offer relational approaches that conceive identity in terms of open-ended processes of becoming; and third, by so doing, they allow us to ascribe agency to images, and crucially, to conceive agency as distributed across interconnected assemblages of people, practices, and mediating artifacts. In the following, we contribute to the ongoing efforts to rethink images in dynamic terms by probing more closely into neurosurgical imaging and navigation practices where images are literally used as operative tools. By zooming in on critical moments of the image-guided neurosurgical process, we draw out key features of an operational understanding of images, with the aim of developing it further as a 'differential' theory of images (Hoel, 2011a and 2011b).

Contemporary neurosurgery relies heavily on computer-assisted navigation technologies. Neuronavigation, which is a further development of stereotactic surgery (Enchev, 2009), is a set of methods that makes use of three-dimensional coordinate systems for frameless guidance, orientation, and localization of structures during brain surgery. Neuronavigation systems transfer multimodal image data into the surgical field, track surgical tools, and overlay the position of important instruments on medical image maps of the patient. A major challenge for neuronavigation is the shift in position of the brain anatomy as the operation progresses, commonly referred to as 'brain shift'. To compensate for this shift, updated maps are acquired during the operation on the surgeon's request (Lindseth et al., 2013).

Differential Interventions: Images as Operative Tools   179

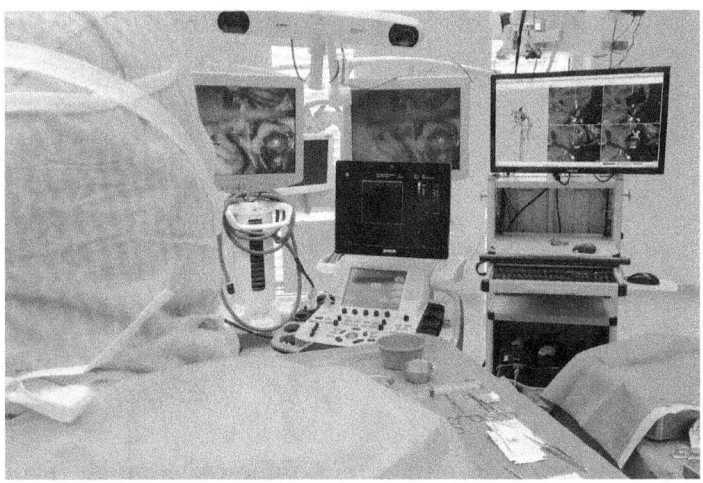

Figure 12.1. The surgeon's view in the operating room.

In a tumor removal procedure that we observed, the navigation system included preoperative magnetic resonance images, live video images from a surgical microscope, intraoperative ultrasound images, and optical tracking of surgical instruments. The image and tracking information was shown on a multimodal display unit facing the surgeon (figure 12.1), either as corresponding views in separate display windows, or as integrated navigation scenes mixing features from different imaging modalities (figure 12.2). In addition to this, the surgeon could change the magnification levels of the images and flip between different modes within each imaging modality.[1] Apart from that, the operating room was populated with additional screens displaying the microscope images as well as the patient's vital signs during anesthesia. At critical points in the operation (before, during, and after the removal of tumor tissue), ultrasound volumes were obtained to show the extent of brain shift. Far from being passive reflections of pre-given realities, medical images rely on active interventions. Magnetic resonance imaging produces images using the magnetic properties of hydrogen atoms, which abound in the human body, especially in tissues such as fat and water. When the patient is placed in an MRI scanner, the system generates images by producing a strong uniform magnetic field that aligns the axes of the protons parallel or antiparallel to the field, emitting a radiofrequency pulse at the right frequency and duration, and altering the magnetic field on a local level using gradient magnets to determine the location of the image 'slices'.

When the radio-wave transmitter is turned off, the protons start to 'relax', producing radio wave signals as they release their energy and return to their equilibrium state. The signals are picked up by the system's receiver coils and transformed into gray level intensities for each pixel in a cross-sectional image. Since protons in different tissues have different relaxation times, various scanning sequences can be used to distinguish between different types of tissue, say, fat and water, or pathological tissue and normal tissue. Conventional 2D ultrasound also builds cross-sectional grayscale images of the anatomy at hand, this time by a transducer probe emitting a high frequency sound pulse into the patient. As the sound waves travel into the body, they hit boundaries and interfaces between various tissue types and some of the sound waves are reflected back to the probe. In ultrasonic imaging, each sound pulse is followed by 'listening' for these sound echoes. By measuring the time taken for echoes to return, the system calculates the distance to anatomical structures and displays the strength of the echoes as a grayscale image.

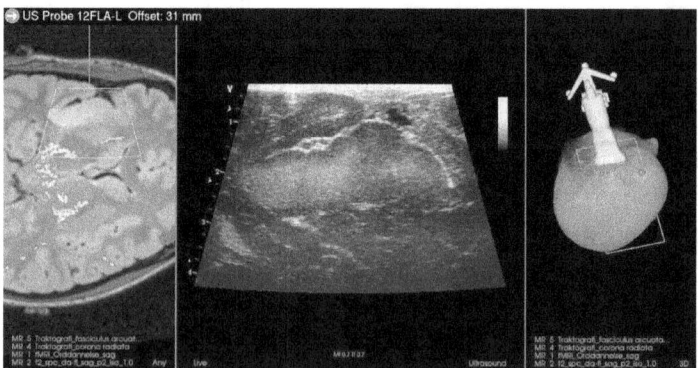

Figure 12.2. Navigation display. Corresponding MR (left) and ultrasound (middle) slices, as well as an overview showing the position of the ultrasound probe relative to the head.

We have zeroed in on technical details of medical image generation in order to show that MR and ultrasound imaging are based on *contrasts*. The patterns shown are not simply *found*; they stand out only to the extent that the areas of interest are subjected to targeted excitations, tissues and organs being provoked to answer back along the lines specified by the parametric setup. Each imaging method has a highly selective range, disregarding anatomical or functional features that fall outside its scope. The point we want to make, however, goes beyond the familiar one concerning the selective nature of imaging methods. Rather, the point is that these methods stand in a *generative* relation to the imaged features: each imaging method *differentially intervenes* into the phenomena under examination, delineating and sustaining a characteristic pattern or structure not detectable in the same way by other methods.

In order for images to support navigation, the image data have to be registered to the patient coordinate system. The registration process makes the coordinates of anatomical features in physical space and the various image spaces coincide. During surgery, 3D ultrasound can also be used to update the preoperative image maps, shifting the positions of imaged features by means of advanced algorithms (Lindseth et al., 2013). In the observed operation, fiducial markers were placed on the patient's skull before entering the MRI scanner. When the patient was immobilized on the operating table, the markers, visible in the MR images, were used by the surgeon to identify the corresponding points on the patient's head by means of a tracked pointer. As the procedure progressed, ultrasound was used for direct guidance (figure 12.3).

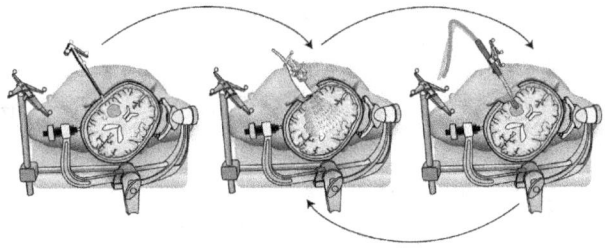

Figure 12.3. Ultrasound-guided surgery. Preoperative planning using a tracked pointer (left), acquisition of a new ultrasound volume using a tracked ultrasound probe (middle), and removal of tumor tissue using a tracked resection instrument guided by updated ultrasound images.

Images used for neuronavigation are clearly 'part of an operation'; they are active, transformative, and most definitely reconfigure the subject-object relationship. For all that, even if they are considered here as 'agents', they are not understood to operate on their own. Further, even if they are made to be processed by computers, the images are ultimately aimed at human eyes. First, when it comes to objects, it is important to note that the imaged features are *relational* and *dynamic* entities. The objects revealed by one method are not strictly speaking the same as the objects revealed by another method. Each method establishes, so to speak, a 'working object' (Daston and Galison, 2007), natural objects being too plentiful and unrefined to usefully cooperate in systematic comparisons. Second, when it comes to subjects, imaging methods enact a *productive displacement of the human sensorium*, bringing information that is naturally beyond us into the purview of the human senses. By enhancing human sensitivity, they expand the human action range. In neuronavigation, agency is *distributed* as humans, apparatuses, and tissues form an integrated system.

Thus, if we replace the framework of representation with a dynamic and relational framework, the 'operational' understanding of images can be further specified as 'differential': images serve to discern differences; differential intervention is their mode of operation. However, if we truly endorse a dynamic and relational framework, we soon come to realize that in fact *all* images, even the pre-digital ones, are operative and differential tools.

Original source and licence

The New Everyday: A MediaCommons Project, 'The Operative Image' cluster curated by Ingrid Hoelzl, http://mediacommons.futureofthebook.org/tne/cluster/operative-image January 24, 2014. Licence: CC-BY ND SA.

References

Carusi, A. (2012) 'Making the Visual Visible in the Philosophy of Science,' *Spontaneous Generations*, 6/1: 106-114, DOI 10.4245/sponge.v6i1.16141.

Daston, L. & Galison, P. (2007) *Objectivity*. New York: Zone Books.

Enchev, Y. (2009) 'Neuronavigation: Geneology, Reality, and Prospects', *Neurosurgical Focus* 27/3: 1-18.

Farocki, H. (2004) 'Phantom Images', *Public*, 29 (2004): 12-24.

Hoel, A. S. (2011a) 'Differential Images', in J. Elkins & M. Naef (eds), *What Is an Image?* University Park: Penn State University Press, 152-4.

Hoel, A. S. (2011b) 'Thinking "Difference" Differently: Cassirer versus Derrida on Symbolic Mediation', *Synthese*, 179/1: 75-91.

Hoelzl, I. & Marie, R. (forthcoming), 'Google Street View: Navigating the Operative Image,' *Visual Studies*.

Kogge, W. (2004) 'Lev Manovich: Society of the Screen', in D. Lauer & A. Lagaay (eds), *Medientheorien: Eine philosophische Einführung*. Frankfurt: Campus Verlag, 297-315.

Krämer, S. (2009) 'Operative Bildlichkeit: Von der "Grammatologie" zu einer "Diagrammatologie"? Reflexionen über erkennendes "Sehen"', in M. Hessler & D. Mersch (eds), *Logik des Bildlichen: Zur Kritik der ikonischen Vernunft*. Bielefeld: Transcript, 94-123.

Lindseth, F. et al. (2013) 'Ultrasound-Based Guidance and Therapy', in Gunti Gunarathne (ed.), *Advancements and Breakthroughs in Ultrasound Imaging* (InTech), DOI: 10.5772/55884.

Uricchio, W. (2011) 'The Algorithmic Turn: Photosynth, Augmented Reality and the Changing Implications of the Image', *Visual Studies*, 26/1: 25-34.

Verhoeff, N. (2012) *Mobile Screens: The Visual Regime of Navigation*. Amsterdam: Amsterdam University Press.

Notes

1   T1, T2, FLAIR, MR angiography, fMRI, and DTI tracts for the magnetic resonance images, and B-mode and Doppler for the ultrasound images.

CHAPTER 13

Glitch Studies Manifesto

Rosa Menkman

1. The dominant, continuing search for a noiseless channel has been – and will always be – no more than a regrettable, ill-fated dogma.

Acknowledge that although the constant search for complete transparency brings newer, 'better' media, every one of these improved techniques will always possess their own inherent fingerprints of imperfection.

2. Dispute the operating templates of creative practice. Fight genres, interfaces and expectations!

Refuse to stay locked into one medium or between contradictions like real vs. virtual, obsolete vs. up-to-date, open vs. proprietary or digital vs. analog. Surf the vortex of technology, the in-between, the art of artifacts!

3. Get away from the established action scripts and join the avant-garde of the unknown. Become a nomad of noise artifacts!

The static, linear notion of information-transmission can be interrupted on three occasions: during encoding-decoding (compression), feedback or when a glitch (an unexpected break within the flow of technology) occurs. Noise artists must exploit these noise artifacts and explore the new opportunities they provide.

4. Employ bends and breaks as metaphors for différance. Use the glitch as an exoskeleton for progress.

Find catharsis in disintegration, ruptures and cracks; manipulate, bend and break any medium towards the point where it becomes something new; create *glitch art*.

5. *Realize that the gospel of glitch art also tells about new standards implemented by corruption.*

Not all glitch art is progressive or *something new*. The popularization and cultivation of the avant-garde of mishaps has become predestined and unavoidable. Be aware of easily reproducible *glitch effects* automated by software and plug-ins. What is now a glitch will become a fashion.

6. *Force the audience to voyage through the acousmatic videoscape.*

Create conceptually synaesthetic artworks that exploit both visual and aural glitch (or other noise) artifacts at the same time. Employ these noise artifacts as a nebula to shroud the technology and its inner workings and to compel an audience to listen and watch more exhaustively.

7. *Rejoice in the critical trans-media aesthetics of glitch artifacts.*

Utilize glitches to bring any medium into a critical state of hypertrophy, to (subsequently) criticize its inherent politics.

8. *Employ Glitchspeak (as opposed to Newspeak) and study what is outside of knowledge. Glitch theory is what you can just get away with!*

Flow cannot be understood without interruption, nor function without glitching. This is why glitch studies is necessary.

Original source and licence

Rosa Menkman (2011) *The Glitch Moment(um)*. Network Notebooks 04. Amsterdam: Institute of Network Cultures. http://networkcultures.org/blog/publication/no-04-the-glitch-momentum-rosa-menkman/. Licence: CC-BY NC ND 3.0.

CHAPTER 14

NewFotoScapes:
An Interview with Charlotte Cotton

JONATHAN SHAW

A creative life

NewFotoScapes (Jonathan Shaw as NFS): We are here in the offices of Michael Mack in the heart of London talking to Charlotte Cotton. Welcome and many thanks for agreeing to take part in the conversation for *NewFotoScapes*. I think it would be fair to say that you describe yourself as a writer, curator and sometimes educator of photography?

Charlotte Cotton (CC): Yes

NFS: I was fascinated to hear earlier this year, at the Association of Photography in Higher Education conference in Wales, how photography became your destiny and I wondered if you could share this with our community here?

CC: I was talking about the fact that at the moment I'm thinking a lot about an earlier point in my own life when I was seventeen or eighteen years of age, and what I remember needing to reinforce my aspirations to have a creative adult life. It didn't really take much contact with cultural spaces for me to feel as if it would be possible to have a creative adult life. I was 17 and studying for my A-levels when I came up to London and went to the V&A and the Boilerhouse, which was hosting a programme of exhibitions, including photographers such as Irving Penn, that felt sophisticated and relevant and exactly what I would want to look at. I think I then ended up at The Photographers' Gallery off Leicester Square. I really wanted to see what I should wear, how I should interact and exchange and converse if I was going to have an adult creative life. And I am not even really that sure how I knew those two places existed, pre-internet age. But I did, and I think that antenna that you have when you are young is one of the most remarkable things! I really am concerned about what it would mean, what tangible evidence and support I would find if I was trying to navigate an entry into creative life if I was going through it in this era.

Conservatism and creativity

NFS: Why is that?

CC: For a number of reasons. One of them is, we are in a situation that is equally economically challenging for young creative people as the late 1980s. One thing that has happened within the creative industries in the twenty-first century has been an ageing of creative industries and their workforces. For example, if you think about fashion photography, through the post-war period it was an area where somebody who was young, whether it was a photographer, a fashion editor, a designer, a model, could innovate, could inject real life and the currency of 'the new' into image-making culture.

That dynamic took place in Britain through the post-war period, including when I was young in the late 1980s early 1990s, with what got labelled 'grunge' photography and photographers such as Corrine Day, Juergen Teller, Nigel Shafrab and David Sims, and stylists including Melanie Ward, Venetia Scott, Edward Enninful, and i-D magazine and The Face. It is within our active memory that there has been a period when it was possible for a group of very young creative people to literally visualise what was going on within culture. Fashion photography post-9/11 became deeply conservative. We saw this impact across the commercial world: it was the time to get rid of the creatively opinionated, to say all bets are off, things are going to work in a different way, where creative vision was far from sacred and the risks in bringing in new and audacious talent would be made only sparingly.

NFS: And you saw the photographers' day rates tumble…

CC: Right, you saw the mere handful of fashion photographers who represent the pinnacle that many aspire to taking cuts in their day rate, taking jobs they would have discounted five years before. And what got broken was that quid pro quo of commercial image-making, namely that as a young person wanting to begin a career in fashion photography, you work like hell, you subsidise the costs of your first editorial shoots, you practically subsidise the editorial pages of youth magazines.

NFS: Yes, because it was about the portfolio of photographs.

CC: You build a portfolio and you reach a point where somebody picks you out of obscurity, and you are in line for a lucrative advertising campaign, which brings in enough money for you to go off and do your own photography and also make a name for yourself as a new talent. That system was severely damaged in the commercial fragility of the US (the commercial home of fashion image-making) in the aftermath of 9/11. And even today, over a decade later, you pretty much see the same list of top fashion photographers as in 2000.

Revolutions and radical change

NFS: So broadening that out and thinking of the breadth of routes that the new landscape of photography offers, do you feel that it is still governed by the economics associated with photography then, in terms of the type of image-making that is produced or the type of work that is getting seen? Is it now more about free labour as opposed to really trying to push and enhance ideas?

CC: Well, those two things are not mutually exclusive, but I think when there is a client involved in the production of photography, you are visually problem solving for someone else. If you are ambitious and audacious and are given the space, you might also produce something which is the visualisation of a moment in time, and all of this is magical and worth chasing after. I think this dynamic does move to other areas of photographic practice. You could say that there is a parallel or even a precedent with editorial photography and the economy of documentary photography. The idea of defining your practice as an editorial documentary photographer or photojournalist has been under debate for a number of decades now. What we saw in the 1990s and early 2000s was the movement of some documentary photography into the new axis points for the cultural appraisal of photography in the book form and into exhibitions for non-profit spaces, museums and art galleries. However, it is a misunderstanding to suggest that that has been a secure and vital place for documentary photography, or that there is full career as a documentarian who produces books and exhibitions.

NFS: That sense of change and of considering the photographic object reminds me a little of your conversation with Aaron Schumann for FOAM's project, 'What's next?'. A particular quote that stood out for me was where you said you 'do fetishize revolutions and moments of radical change, that you really enjoy them and that you are enjoying this moment'.

CC: Yes.

NFS: That seems to suggest something very upbeat, because there could be a debate in terms of how we have approached our conversation up to now, the finances go down, and the demand is going down, a deep conservatism. But that quote very much suggest something different, a different way of looking at this kind of change?

CC: They are actually connected and I think the first stage of emancipation is to abandon hope that the situation is any less challenging or in need of radical change than it really is. Across the world, creative people in the fields of photography, curation, activism, writing, filmmaking, know that the money is spent. That is the first step, to know that there isn't a reassuring paternalistic structure that you can literally buy your way into. It doesn't exist, and if anyone promises you that they are lying to you. They might be lying to themselves as well. They might have too much of a vested interest in keeping that idea of pedagogy and creative industry alive to admit the possibility of any other reality.

But it is over, and owning that is the first step, and I don't see that as a negative. I actually think that's a really positive thing in life to know where you are because this is the key to all things – to your mental health, to the sustainability of your creativity: you can only start from where you are, not from where you hope or wish to. You can only start where you are. I think that's what the quote from the conversation with Aaron was really about.

NFS: What's really interesting there is that often, and especially around academia, we talk about authority and institutions, and the canons of photography being the authorities, and I think there's something quite powerful about freeing ourselves from that paternalistic notion, the idea of trying to please somebody. Maybe we should think about that time when we are young and creativity is the tool that we have to express ourselves – that actually maybe this is the space photography and broader creative fields can explore now and open up some really interesting possibilities?

Questioning authority and expertise

CC: Yeah, absolutely. I think the other thing to be said here is that authority and expertise are notions that are definitely under question with the dismantling of cultural structures that privilege such terms. Obviously, I am not thrilled at the idea that expertise is something that has become optional to the development of culture, but the reality is that no one is an expert on the future, especially in a time of change.

NFS: That's true... But is there something in particular that you feel or believe has been a defining factor and that has seen such a shift in the landscape of the lens, a particular moment or any other elements that have shifted things? We've talked about finance, for example?

CC: I think the shape of commercial image making post-9/11, and also the decline of printed news media, are two of the biggest militating forces for the shape of what it means to be a photographer in the professional sense right now. But we should look at the other two important areas in relation to photography: what happened to independent artistic photography and also the idea of the amateur or citizen photographer. Both of these facets have seeded profound shifts in the character of photography, even if they are not entirely evident to us yet in the behaviour of institutions. Shall I talk about those two things?

NFS: Yes, what would be interesting to hear is how that really is informing and changing your interpretation of your response to this field of practice.

CC: Contemporary art photography has become much more specialised and rarefied. In the early 2000s, we had a strong market for photographs that were printed large and laminated behind Plexiglas; it felt like a bubble market for photography. We're at a period now where I think we are in a really good place, much leaner and more precise. Making photographic prints or using photographic language within artistic practice is something few people decide to do. At its best, it's not a lifestyle choice and it's not a career. It's actually a very old school idea of the artisan, somebody who crafts and renders something. Personally, I work more with artists who don't necessarily come from a photographic training now, because the point we have reached within contemporary art is one where photography is a set of materials rather than a separate discipline. As you know from my writing I think one of the big things that we are grappling with is whether the structures to legitimise photography as an independent art form that began in the 1970s are going to work so well for what happens next in the story of photography. Those historic structures often relied on monographic narratives and separatist ideas of photography and its history, as devices to align photography with more established independent artistic disciplines. And all of those things actually are not very useful for interpreting contemporary photographic culture.

To think about photography at large at this terrifically exciting moment is where the innovative potential for cultural institutions lies. If you spend a lot of time with contemporary art, as I do, visiting exhibitions and making studio visits, I'd guess that as much as half of what is under artistic discussion uses the materials of photography and video. And very, very little of this critical mass would fit within the tail end of a separatist history of photography as proclaimed by most photography institutions and museum departments. I really want cultural institutions to offer points of view on the real practices of photography and to support emergent talents to know that photography is one tool amongst many that you can use to express yourself. The artists who I think will define this moment, who do define this moment for other artists, are actually invisible to most cultural institutions.

NFS: This quest for more from our cultural institutions seems to push the ideas you were writing about in *The Photograph as Contemporary Art* back in 2004. Interestingly, in preparation for our meeting today, I came across an article where you were saying that, even at the time of writing the book, you were bored of that debate and really you felt it was kind of over before you put it out there.

CC: The title wasn't my choice, I thought it could just be 'Contemporary Art Photography' because I really felt that was a statement of fact by 2004. But I am actually really glad that the commissioning editor, Andrew Brown, persisted with the title, because it suggests an active election of photography as art, as opposed to all of the other facets of the medium's character. And of course what happened afterwards was the central idea of photography moving to the vital arena of amateur and citizen practices, and Andrew was right to give the book an equivocal title.

NFS: What becomes a testament to that is the fact that the projects you have been part of, and the ideas you are exploring, have consistently put you at the forefront of thinking around what photography is or where photography is going. As that example illustrates, that was the point where your book became a key title on a university reading list that students read, and are still reading, and one they continually refer back to. Is there an inherent danger that through the form and function of a printed book over time you lose the currency of its content? As such learners both inside and outside of the education system perhaps still focus on that debate. So really the question is what do you see as the key debates now? What would you hope that learners today would be looking at now? And how would you like them to read your writings from eight to nine years ago? Photography in that time has become a very different beast, so what do you see those key debates as being?

Communities and conversations

CC: You're right; photography *has* changed during that time, but the book was still the best way for me to represent that moment, in as much as it was quite a definitive moment, and that's what books do – they are definitive rather than iterative. But in my own practices I have also been interested in creating structures for iterative processes, because we are at a time that is not definitive in a conventional sense – it is in flux. I started thinking seriously about how you might develop ideas within a self-elected community in 2006 when I was living in New York, and I wasn't working for a museum, so it was the first time in a long while that conversation didn't just come to me in my place of work.

NFS: You mean you had to seek it out?

CC: I think it was a more normal experience of how ideas and opinions develop. Working as a curator in a national museum is a very specific thing – it's a vocation that I really believe in. For me it was the best way in which to engage with photography, within an environment where the stakes are very, very high. However, the reality of the way we discover and change our mind about culture, and especially in the 2000s when I think many of us were changing our minds about lots of things, well, I didn't feel that those definitive processes of printed books and institutional exhibitions at best reflected what was actually happening in terms of ideas around photography. The jury was (and maybe still is) out about who is going to make visual culture, how the creative industries will reform, what we will consider to be the pivotal issues for visual practice. Where does the energy of photography at large move at a time like this? I mean, we are all to a certain degree blinded by the empirical mass of citizen and orphan photography, and only to a certain degree have we began to analyse that. 'Words without Pictures' was the first iterative discussion project that I staged, and it was borne out of the fact that some of the most meaningful conversations I was having around photography were outside institutional frameworks. These were important conversations for me because of the quality of opinions and an openness, a discursiveness, that was just in the air, in the absence of anyone or any institution having the answer.

NFS: Very much so, and this is totally at the heart of the NewFotoScapes project. A time to stop worrying that the landscapes are not formed. To stop trying to work out what is true, what is fact, what is finished, what is complete, and perhaps think more about how can we develop and evolve the tools. So, if we adopt the analogy of using a map and a compass, our focus is perhaps more on the decisions and the paths that we navigate ourselves around. It would be true to say that our senses become heightened and we are far more aware when we travel somewhere alien, somewhere unknown. I think and wonder what might happen if we consider ourselves at this point of the journey to discovery? And this seems to really chime with your earlier description of being young, and reminds me of one of your recent interviews, where you referred to the practitioners or processes or thinkers that you seek out to act as your antennae. Who are they and why have you chosen those people?

CC: I think you are referring to my introduction to the spring 2013 Aperture Photo Book Review, which I guest edited. The well of the publication is a series of conversations I asked people that I talk to about photography and creative culture to 'perform' for the publication. I had an email this morning from someone I met very briefly a couple of years ago, and they had been reading the review and they told me why they liked it. They said it was because I really had asked my friends to talk as they would talk to me. They appreciated that I hadn't edited it in such a way that looked down on an audience, and I had just assumed that everyone is conversing in the same way. Actually I think it's human nature to have people whose opinions you seek out and to make the time to meet up and really talk it through. I think it's a more useful way to form an understanding of this creative moment.

NFS: What is really important and ultimately compelling about this approach and way of working is that honesty and desire to offer clarity to an audience. It starts with that openness and transparency, rather than the hierarchy and 'by invitation only' philosophy. It acknowledges the strength of a community and then seeks to build engagement and invite a wider audience to participate. We will talk a little bit more about 'Words Without Pictures' shortly, but that would be a perfect example of how you consider the audience: not in a way to look down on them, as you say, but to seek to either engage them or look at methods of building networks or communities. And I think what is great is that you also speak about the importance for photographers to look at building their own networks.

CC: Yes, definitely.

NFS: Which makes for really exciting times for photographers today, and moves us further away from seeking approval from the institution or the gatekeeper. This could equally be quite challenging. Is it possible to just open up a little bit more about how you consider the process of engagement?

CC: I have been a curator for coming up to twenty years. I feel very happy with the role of curator, as somebody who does creative things for other people – there is always an audience with curating. I'm not an artist. Although I'm a very self-aware person, I'm not directly exploring the internal questions that I have for myself as an artist does. I don't think a photographer needs to be a curator at heart, but I think a photographer does need to understand the curatorial mode of their practice for sure.

NFS: You have talked about this idea that you are mostly curating experiences, whether it's digital, whether it's online, or whether it's a physical live event, which I think is a really important way to consider our roles as the field progresses.

It is a good reminder that we need to consider our purpose, not the apparatus. But we could perhaps suggest there have been experiential precedents. The camera obscura and the cinema: an immersive experience within a darkened environment, illuminated by a single project revealing and interpreting an 'outside or alternative' world. I also enjoy the similarities between today's digital tablet and the early drawings of a painter's canvas using a camera obscura. Similarly, we seem to have forgotten that the book is a piece of technology, so it really just reinforces the message that technology has and will always continually evolve and change. I think, interestingly, your approach seems to seek to maximise the experience of a particular platform or mechanism, and in that way truly consider engagement and participation with an audience. Would you say that is true?

CC: There is a multitude of modes to most creative people's practices. The way that #phonar is structured consciously seems to address that, given the emphasis placed on not only the 'photographer-as-artisan' training, but also, importantly, the 'photographer-as-editor' and 'photographer-as-curator', 'photographer-as-researcher'. That's the wonder of now – suddenly the true plurality of photographic practice isn't something that you are supposed to keep hidden.

NFS: During the San Francisco Museum of Modern Art 'Is Photography Over?' debate that you were part of, there is one particular thing George Baker, who I think you have worked with before, said that I thought was great, where he talks about the forgotten potentials of the medium. It seems that photography has almost become dominated by particular forms, by particular methods of commissioning, etc. And that actually it was all there in the beginning, and that maybe we simply need to go back to remembering or look at those potentials and begin to re-explore them.

CC: Geoffrey Batchen's writing about the earliest era of photography has been really instrumental in us thinking of photography as not an invention but a conception; suggesting that there was something in the cultural psyche that meant that photography happened when it did, and it was not just reliant on technological innovation. I think that the academic field of comparative media studies is an amazingly well developed area that is usefully applied to thinking about contemporary photography. I was speaking at a conference recently and really enjoyed the thoughts of art historian David Joselit, who talked about photography as 'the many' and related our contemporary sense of 'image overload' to the early 20th century, and the wholesale adoption of photomechanical reproduction methods. He talked very convincingly about how avant-garde and contemporary artists are negotiating parallel issues of what it means to create singular, artistic images in eras when photography embodies 'the many'.

Genuinely open

NFS: Absolutely. This would seem to be a good time to talk about a couple of your recent projects, 'Words Without Pictures' and 'eitherand'. You've mentioned 'Words Without Pictures' earlier; I wondered if you might summarise how and why that project came about. You have previously mentioned a sense of frustration?

CC: I think my sense of frustration is very quickly followed by, 'You might as well do it yourself – what's the worst thing that could happen?'. The worst thing that can happen is that somebody else does it and not as well as you could if you'd put your mind to it! 'Words Without Pictures' was essentially driven by both my conversations with people I met in New York, as I mentioned earlier, and then finding the right context to develop the idea. I had just started as curator at Los Angeles County Museum of Art and I needed to rebuild a community around the photography department. I didn't want to build a community based on explorations of the collection, which might have been the obvious place for a photography department in a museum! But I wanted to make an invitation to photographic practitioners living in Los Angeles to think of LACMA as a place where the crucial conversations about photography could happen. One of the areas I still feel very strongly that museums need to provide for, is those years after college when you want to know where you can go for a really serious debate about the creative sphere you are passionate about.

NFS: It's about that sense of the institution being regarded as safe and trusted, so you know the information you are going to receive has been filtered through your peers, which I think is vital.

CC: Yes, just think how radically we have shifted our view about peer-reviewing and editing of photography. Even five years ago it was still something that institutions were very suspicious of endorsing. 'Words Without Pictures' was one of a small number of projects that arts institutions initiated, which were genuinely open and which released editorial control. The smart institutions really did that. They saw that there was nothing advantageous in censoring or institutionalising the language of this particular moment and, instead, that we just needed to be generous hosts to the thoughtfulness of creative people thinking aloud and together. [...]

NFS: I am intrigued by how you planned and mapped out the legacy of 'Words Without Pictures' in the context of the web as an open and free domain. You knew you wanted to have clear parameters for its timeframe: so that project had twelve months, with new stimuli on a monthly basis, mixed with live events, and then as the culminating physical resource. The book went from being print-on-demand, to its new association with Aperture, and in fact to being published by Aperture. Why isn't it online anymore? Why take it away, close the door down in that sense?

CC: Obviously I'm not working at LACMA anymore so I am not in control of the evolution of the project. I decided from the outset that the website would only exist for a year, as I felt a year was the maximum amount of time before the behaviour of the site would become institutionalised. The next phase of the life of the project happened in other places, offline, mainly in classrooms where the essays began to be used as prompts to live discussions. The pdf versions of the essays rippled out in the world and appear on curriculum reading lists. We didn't work with a sort of modernist idea of the original 'Words Without Pictures', so all of these permutations, all of these iterations of the project, are part of it. Our success criteria for the project was that we wanted to create a framework for a discussion to be had, and I was happy that we only had 300 readers a day and a new response to the monthly essay came in very slowly, because we found the quality of the engagement was astounding.

NFS: I think that's an interesting point, though, only 300 readers a day. If we equate that to a physical lecture theatre in the largest universities, that is often the size of one room. So the scale you cite, I think still makes a serious impact. But almost more importantly it demonstrates an active engagement with the subject that you wouldn't be guaranteed in that same lecture theatre. Having a desire for the project to achieve more, do you think that framework was enabled through technology? Was it able to become more viral or more permeable?

CC: It was beautifully planned and beautifully designed; it was very true all the way through. There was real thoughtfulness within the concept and throughout the design. David Reinfurt is an incredible designer. The amazing Alex Klein, who is an artist and a curator, was the editor overseeing all aspects, every day. The most important thing is to use these platforms in a way, which is really true to what it is you want to do, and all we wanted to do was to create a framework for the discussion to happen.

Mixed economies

NFS: I'd like to end with two questions. We have talked about the obstacles and challenges facing photography, and how perhaps these have at times shaped your future. What is your next project that begins to address or look at those and question them?

CC: I think I am going to continue to live in a mixed economy which sees me sometimes as the author with researched and definitive opinions, as a participant in things that I think are really interesting but I am not an expert in, and as a collaborator developing ideas with creative people who come from other areas of expertise. My next text book is under development. It's going to take me a while but the title is 'Photographic'. Contemporary photography is beautifully faceted – photography remains a prompt for social change. It is a vital vehicle for ideas. It is an astounding empirical mass. Photographic technology is an author of the ways we perceive the world. And photographic industries are challenged but reforming, and photography is of course a material form. I want to offer useful reading to people embarking on their creative, photographic lives that really embodies the current debates.

NFS: That sounds fantastic. My other question was really going to be about what would potential projects for you, thinking in five years' time, look like, in light of this change and these exciting yet challenging developments? And I think what you are suggesting is that they would have multiple elements, but importantly that they should be a prompt for something more, something different. That's maybe the space we are entering into, where being able to be fluid and responsive is going to be key.

CC: Yes, but within that, is having your own internal critical framework for what it is you do. [...]

Antennae

As a way of extending the initial conversation Charlotte Cotton has offered the following list of writers whose ideas are inspiring her in the continuation of her practice:

Fred Ritchin, Professor of Photography and Imaging at New York University's Tisch School of the Arts. He has written three critically acclaimed books on photography, In Our Own Image; After Photography and, most recently, Bending the Frame.

Katherine Hayles, Professor of Literature at Duke University. Her recent book How We Think seeks to embrace the idea that we think through, with, and alongside media.

Julian Stallabrass is a writer, curator and photographer. He is Professor in Art History at the Courtauld Institute of Art, London. He is noted for his controversial views on the art world and for his observations on the major transformations and opportunities afforded to artists by technological developments in production and distribution.

Grant Kester is Professor of Art History in the Visual Arts department at the University of California. Kester's 2011 book The One and the Many provides an overview of the broader continuum of collaborative art practices.

David Joselit is the Carnegie Professor of Art History at Yale University. His latest book After Art defines a shift in the status of art under the dual pressures of digital technology.

Original source and licence

Shaw, J. (ed.) (2014) *NewFotoScapes*. Birmingham: The Library of Birmingham: 69-88. Also available online at http://newfotoscapes.org/. Licence: CC BY NC-SA 4.0. This version has been slightly edited from the original.

CHAPTER 15

The Creative Power of Nonhuman Photography

JOANNA ZYLINSKA

Photography as philosophy

This article offers a philosophical exposition of the concept of 'nonhuman photography'. What is meant by nonhuman photography here is not just photos taken by agents that are not human, such as CCTV cameras, body scanners, space satellites or Google Street View, although some of these examples will be referenced throughout the piece. Yet the principal aim of this article is to suggest that there is more to photography than meets the (human) eye and that all photography is to some extent nonhuman. With this, no doubt still somewhat cryptic, proposition in mind, let us take a small detour from philosophising to look at a photographic project which introduces the key ideas behind this article.

Called *Topia daedala* (figures 15.1-15.4), this series of twelve black and white photographs[1] arises out of an ongoing exploration on my part of various forms of manufactured landscape. Taken from two vantage points on both sides of a window, the composite images that make up the series interweave human and nonhuman creativity by overlaying the outer world of cloud formation with the inner space of sculptural arrangement. Remediating the tradition of the sublime as embraced by J.M.W. Turner's landscape paintings and Ansel Adams' national park photographs, the series foregrounds the inherent manufacturedness of what counts as 'landscape' and of the conventions of its visual representation. Through this, *Topia daedala* performs a micro-sublime for the Anthropocene era, a period in which the human has become identified as a geological agent whose impact on the geo- and biosphere has been irreversible. It also raises questions for the role of plastic – as both construction material and debris – in the age of petrochemical urgency.

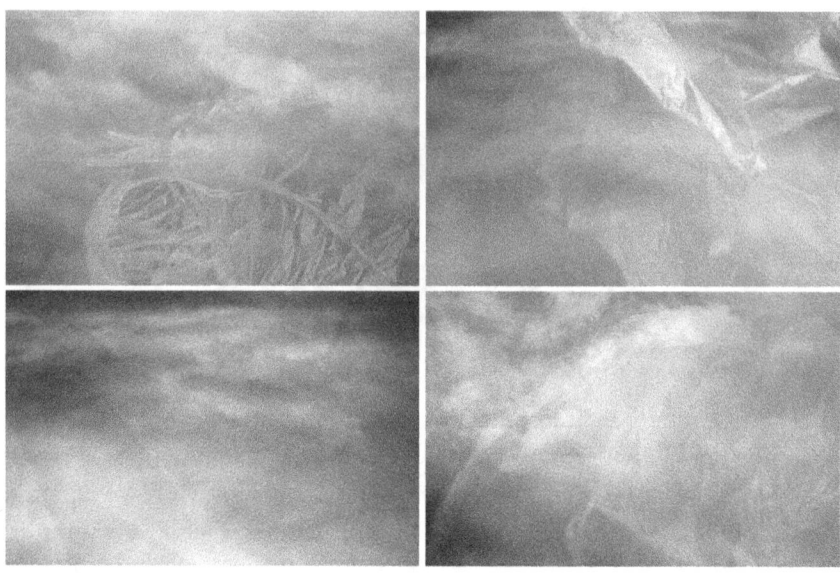

Figures 15.1-15.4. Joanna Zylinska, from *Topia daedala*, 2014.

Topia daedala is not meant to serve as a direct illustration of the concept of nonhuman photography this article engages with. However, it does introduce us to a wider problematic of human-nonhuman relations, raising at the same time the politico-ethical question about our human responsibility in the world in which the agency of the majority of actants – such as wind, rain or earthquake – goes beyond that of human decision or will, even if it may be influenced by human action. The question of human responsibility in the universe which is quintessentially entangled, on both a cellular and cosmic level (with us all being 'made of starstuff'),[2] is an important one. Even if we cannot be entirely sure what this fragile human 'we' actually stands for, the responsibility to face, and give an account of, the unfoldings of this world – which is made up of human and nonhuman entities and relations – *belongs to us humans in a singular way*. Philosophy, in particular ethics, has typically been a way of addressing the problem of responsibility.[3] But written linear argument is only one mode of enquiry through which this problem can be approached. Alongside philosophical writing, over the recent years I have been attempting to experiment with other, less verbal, modes of addressing ethical and political issues: those enabled by art, and, more specifically, photography. These experiments have been driven by one overarching question: is it possible to *practice philosophy as a form of art*, while also *engaging in art-making and photography as ways of philosophising*? The reason photography may lend itself to this kind of cross-modal experimentation is because of its ontological, or world-making (rather than *just* representational), capabilities. We can turn here for support to literary critic Walter Benn Michaels, who, while upholding 'the impossibility (and the undesirability) of simply denying the indexicality of the photograph' (Michaels, 2007: 447), also argues that 'It is precisely because there are ways in which photographs *are not* just representations that photography and the theory of photography have been so important' (445). My proposition about photography's ontological capabilities entails a stronger claim than the one made by Michael Fried in the Conclusion to his book, *Why Photography Matters as Art as Never Before*, in which photography as practiced by representatives of what Fried calls 'the anti-theatrical tradition' such as Jeff Wall, Thomas Struth or Berndt and Hilda Becher is positioned as 'an ontological medium', because it 'makes a positive contribution' to ontological thought via its engagement with issues such as absorption and worldhood (Fried, 2008: 347). While for Fried photography just *makes philosophy better*, my claim in this article is that *photography makes philosophy*, full stop – and also, more importantly, that *photography makes worldhood*, rather than just commenting on it.

It may seem at this point that what was meant to be an account of nonhuman photography is revealing itself to be quite strongly attached to the concept of the human – as philosopher, photographer or art critic. This is true, because there is nothing more humanist than any unexamined singular gesture of trying to 'move beyond the human'. My ambition here, as in my other work, is therefore to explore the possibility of continuing to work with the concept of the human *in the light of the posthumanist critique*,[4] taking the latter seriously as both an injunction and a set of possibilities. The reasons for this proposed retention of the human have nothing to do with any kind of residual humanism or species nostalgia. Instead, they spring from the recognition of a *strategic* role of the concept of the human in any kind of artistic, creative, political or ethical project worth its salt, while also remaining aware of the fact that in many works of recent posthumanist theory the human has been successfully exposed as nothing more than a fantasy of unity and selfhood. This fantasy has been premised on the exclusion of the human's dependency, both material and conceptual, on other beings and non-living entities. Seen as too Eurocentric and masculinist by postcolonial and feminist theory, the human has also been revealed by various sciences to be just an arbitrary cut off point in the line of species continuity on the basis of characteristics shared across the species barrier: communication, emotions or tool use. This (non- or posthumanist) human this article retains as the anchor point of its enquiry is thus premised on the realisation that we are in (philosophical) trouble as soon as we start speaking about the human, but it also shows a certain intransigence that makes (some of) us hang on to the vestiges of the concept that has structured our thinking, philosophy and art for many centuries. So, onto a posthumanist theory of nonhuman photography, as articulated by a human, all too human, philosopher-photographer...

Towards nonhuman photography (and all the way back)

By way of contextualising our discussion of nonhuman photography, I want to look at two important texts in photography theory in which the relationship between human and nonhuman agents, technologies and practices has been addressed explicitly: a 2008 essay by John Tagg called 'Mindless Photography' and a 2009 book by Fred Ritchin titled *After Photography*. Tagg's essay is a commentary on the supposed withering of the critical paradigm in both photographic practice and its interpretation, a paradigm articulated by Victor Burgin in his 1984 seminal text *Thinking Photography* and subsequently adopted by many scholars and students of photography. In his article Tagg references two then recent phenomena which, in his view, had radically altered the relationship between photography and the human: the CCTV system introduced in 2003 to monitor the implementation of congestion charge in central London and the visual rendering of data captured by a radio telescope, in June 2005, of solar dust cloud radiation in the Taurus Molecular Cloud, with the data representing an event that 'took place in 1585, or thereabouts' (Tagg, 2008: 21). While in the 1970s and early 1980s 'photography was framed as a site of human meanings that called the human into place', the more recent developments cited by Tagg are said to have undermined 'this confident assumption' (24). Tagg seems disturbed by the fact that, in the London traffic surveillance system, the relationship between the embodied human subject and the technical apparatus has been irrevocably broken, with the technological circuit which consists of 'cameras, records, files and computers' (19) doing away with visual presentation, 'communication, psychic investment, a subject, or even a bodily organ' (21) – until the visual data concerning the car with a given number plate that has missed the congestion charge payment reaches the court. Tagg is similarly troubled by the severance of the relationship between photography and human sensation, between stimulus and response, in space photography. He goes so far as to suggest that in those new technological developments

> photography loses its function as a representation of the ego and the eye and even as a pleasure machine built to excite the body. In place of those figures, photography is encountered as an utterly dead thing; mindless in a much blunter sense than imagined [by Burgin] twenty-five years ago... [It is] driving towards a systemic disembodiment that, accelerating in the technologies of cybernetics and informatics, has sought to prepare what has been hailed as the 'postbiological' or 'posthuman' body for its insertions into a new machinic enslavement. (25)

Photography which is unable to provide stimulation and pleasure for the human is then immediately linked by Tagg with mindlessness, emptiness and, ultimately, death. It may seem that, with this articulation, Tagg is engaging in a belated attempt to rescue photography from its longstanding association with mortality established by canonical texts such as Roland Barthes' *Camera Lucida*, and to retrospectively postulate *the possibility of photography acting as a life-giving force*. However, this no doubt radical possibility, briefly hinted at in the above cited passage, is immediately withdrawn. Photography does not deliver life to the human any more and, for Tagg, it is only the human that can be both life's subject and its arbiter. This is of course a familiar philosophical gesture, first enacted by Aristotle, whereby technology is reduced to a mere tool for human existence, survival or improvement and is then assessed on the basis of how well it performs this function (rather than being understood as a dynamic network of forces the way Michel Foucault and Bernard Stiegler respectively suggest, or as an 'intrinsic correlation of functions'[5] between the human and the apparatus the way Vilém Flusser apprehends it). Conceived in these instrumental terms, as the human's opponent and enemy – and not part of the originary techno-logic that brings forth the human in the world, and the world itself as a space occupied by human and nonhuman entities – photography must inevitably fail.

It would be unfair not to mention the political motivation that underpins Tagg's argument. His concern with 'machinic enslavement' is driven by what he sees as the deprivation of the human subject of both corporeal integrity and political subjectivity as a result of the encroachment of those new photoimaging technologies, in which 'there is nothing to be seen', on our lives (Tagg, 2008: 24). This concern no doubt becomes even more pressing in the era of global networked surveillance enacted by the likes of the NSA, GCHQ, Facebook and Google. Yet to blame photography for the immoral and inhumane actions of its users is to misidentify the enemy, while also weakening the power of a political critique developed in its ambit. In his essay Tagg takes some significant steps towards analysing the changes occurring to photographic practice at the beginning of the twenty-first century but then recoils in horror from the brink of his own analysis. What could have served as a stepping stone towards developing both a radical posthumanist photography theory *and* a radical posthumanist political analysis ends up retreating into a place of melancholia for the human of yesteryear, one who was supposedly in control of both his personal body and the body politic but who can now only tilt at windmills – which are turning into drones in front of his very eyes.

If only Tagg had allowed himself to hear the exhortation from another photography theory radical, Fred Ritchin! Admittedly, Ritchin's work is not free from a sense of melancholia espoused by Tagg: in *After Photography* Ritchin clearly reveals how he misses the time when people believed in images and when images could be used to solve conflict and serve justice. Yet, even though his book opens up with a rather dispiriting account of the changes occurring to the photographic medium and its representationalist ambitions, it ends with an affirmation of *life in photography*. Dazzled by the horizon of scale opened by telescopy and physics in a similar way Tagg was, Ritchin nevertheless admits that 'in the digital-quantum world, it might be just possible ... to use an emerging post-photography to delineate, document, and explore the posthuman. To dance with ambiguity. To introduce humility to the observer, as well as a sense of belonging. To say yes, and simultaneously, no' (2009: 183).

(*Always*) *nonhuman photography*

It is precisely in this critical-philosophical spirit, of saying yes and, simultaneously, no, that my opening proposition that *all photography is to some extent nonhuman* should be read. While I am aware of, and concerned with, ways in which the nonhuman aspect of photography can produce inhumane practices, I also want to suggest that it is precisely in its nonhuman aspect that photography's creative, or world-making, side can be identified. Therefore, rather than contribute to recent jeremiads about photography, what with it being seen as supposedly dying in the digital era because it is no longer authentic or material enough, or imploding due to its excessiveness and banality as evidenced on Instagram and in the much maligned selfie phenomenon, I want to argue in what follows that it is precisely through focusing on its nonhuman aspect that we can find life in photography. This line of argument is partly indebted to the work of Flusser, who, in *Towards a Philosophy of Photography*, writes: 'The photographic apparatus lies in wait for photography; it sharpens its teeth in readiness. This readiness to spring into action on the part of apparatuses, their similarity to wild animals, is something to grasp hold of in the attempt to define the term etymologically' (2000: 21-22). Flusser builds here on the Latin origins of the term 'apparatus', which derives from *apparare*, 'make ready for' (as a combination of the prefix *ad-*, 'toward', and *parare*, 'make ready'). This leads him to read photography as facilitated by, or even proto-inscribed in, the nexus of image-capture devices, various chemical and electronic components and processes, as well as sight- and technology-equipped humans.

Flusser's proposition challenges the humanist narrative of invention as an outcome of singular human genius: it recognises the significance of the technological set-up in the emergence of various human practices. This is not to say that these practices function *outside* the human but rather that the concepts of self-contained human intentionality and sovereign human agency may be too limited to describe the emergence of specific technological processes at a particular moment in time. Flusser's idea seems to be (unwittingly) reflected in Geoffrey Batchen's proposition outlined in *Burning with Desire* that photography was invented – seemingly repeatedly, by Nicéphore Niépce, Louis Daguerre, Hyppolyte Bayard and William Fox Talbot, among others – due to the fact that in the early nineteenth century there already existed a desire for it. This desire manifested itself in the proliferation of the discourses and ideas about the possibility of capturing images and fixing them, and of the technologies – 'the camera obscura and the chemistry necessary to reproduce' (Batchen, 1999: 25) the images taken with it – that would facilitate such a development. We could therefore perhaps go so far as to say that the photographic apparatus, which for Batchen contains but also exceeds a discrete human component, was awaiting the very invention of photography.

The above discussed ideas on the photographic apparatus will eventually point me not just towards rethinking the photographic medium but also towards a possibility (one that has been withheld by Tagg) of a posthumanist political analysis. For now, taking inspiration from Flusser, I want to suggest that human-driven photography – where an act of conscious looking through a viewfinder or, more frequently nowadays, at an LCD screen held at arm's level – is only one small part of what goes on in the field of photography, even though it is often made to stand in for photography *as such*. The execution of human agency in photographic practice, be it professional or amateur, ostensibly manifests itself in decisions about the subject matter (the 'what') and about ways of capturing this subject matter with a digital or analogue apparatus (the 'how'). Yet in amateur, snapshot-type photography these supposed human-centric decisions are often affective reactions to events quickly unfolding in front of the photographer's eyes. Such reactions happen too quickly, or we could even say *automatically*, for any conscious processes of decision-making to be involved – bar that original decision to actually have, bring and use a camera, rather than not. This automatism in photography also manifests itself in the fact that these kinds of 'snap' reactions are usually rechanneled through a whole database of standardised, pre-programmed, pre-existing image-frames, whose significance we are already familiar with and which we are trying to recreate in a unique way, under the umbrella of so-called individual experience: 'toddler running towards mother'; 'girl blowing a candle on a birthday cake'; 'couple posing in front of the Taj Mahal'. It is in this sense that, as Flusser has it, 'weddings conform to a photographic program' (Flusser, 2001: 56).

Similar representationalist ambitions accompany many professional photographic activities, including those undertaken by photojournalists who aim to show us, objectively and without judging, what war, poverty and 'the pain of others', to borrow Susan Sontag's phrase (2003), are 'really' like, or those performed by photographic artists. Even prior to any moment of making a picture actually occur, fine art photographers tend to remain invested in the modernist idea of an artist as a human agent with a particular vocation, one whose aesthetic and conceptual gestures are aimed at capturing something unique, or at least capturing it uniquely, with an image-making device. And thus we get works of formal portraiture; images of different types of vegetation or geological formations that are made to constitute 'landscapes'; still-life projects of aestheticised domesticity, including close-ups of kitchen utensils, fraying carpets or light traces on a wall; and, last but not least, all those works that can be gathered into that rag-bag called 'conceptual photography'.[6] In this way, images inscribe themselves in a cybernetic loop of familiarity, with minor variations to style, colour and the (re)presented object made to stand for creativity, originality or even 'genius'.

The automated image

Through the decisions of artists and amateurs about their practice, photography becomes an act of *making something significant*, even if not necessarily *making it signify something* in any straightforward way. It is a practice of focusing on what is in its very nature multifocal, of literally casting light on what would have otherwise remained obscure, of carving a fragment from the flow of life and turning it into a splinter of what, post-factum, becomes known as 'reality'. Traditionally, this moment of selection – referred to as 'decisive' by followers of the documentary tradition in photography – was associated with the pressing of the button to open the camera's shutter. However, with the introduction of the Lytro camera on to the market in 2012, the temporality of this seemingly unique and transient photographic moment has been stretched into both the past and the future. Lytro captures the entire light field rather than a single plane of light, thus allowing the photographer to change and readjust the focus on a computer in postproduction. Interestingly, Lytro is advertised as 'The only camera that captures life in living pictures' – a poetic formulation which is underpinned by the ongoing industry claim to 'absolute novelty', but which merely exacerbates and visualises the inherent instability of *all* photographic practice and *all* photographic objects. Lytro is thus just one more element in the long-term humanist narrative about 'man's dominion over the earth', a narrative that drives the progressive automatisation of many of our everyday devices, including cameras, cars and refrigerators. Giving us an illusion of control over technology by making cameras smaller and domestic equipment more user-friendly, the technoscientific industry actually exacerbates the gap between technology and the human by relieving us from the responsibility of getting to know and engage with the increasingly software-driven 'black boxes'.

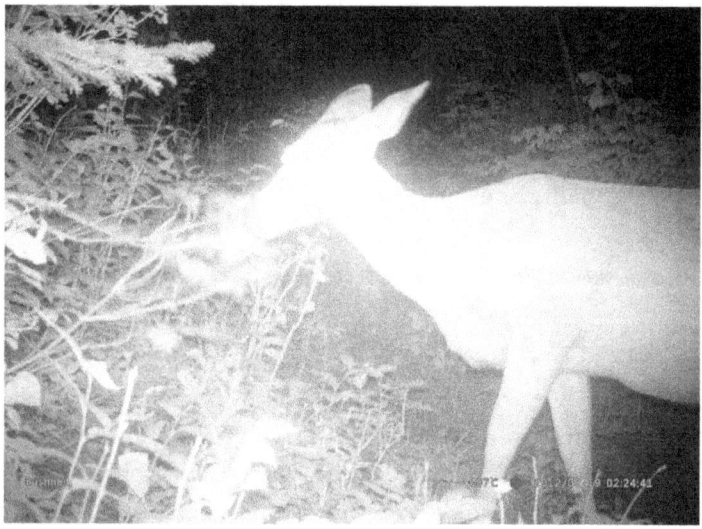

Figure 15.5. Véronique Ducharme, *Encounters*, 2012-2013.

In the light of the dominance of the humanist paradigm in photography, a paradigm that is premised on the supposed human control of both the practice of image-making and the equipment, it is important to ask what gets elided in such conceptualisations. Of course, I am not the only one who is asking this question: the problem of nonhuman agency in photography has been explored by other theorists, artists and curators. One recent photography event that brought many of these ideas to the fore was *Drone: The Automated Image*, a series of shows taking place under the umbrella of the photography biennale Le Mois de la Photo in Montreal, curated by Paul Wombell, in 2013.[7] The uniqueness of this 13th edition of the Montreal biennale lay not so much in highlighting the machinic aspect of photographic and video practice, as this aspect had already been mobilised in the early days of photography – for example, in the works of Alexander Rodchenko or László Moholy-Nagy. *Drone: The Automated Image* (which was concerned with much more than just drones) took one step further on this road towards not just nonhuman but also posthumanist photography by actually departing from the human-centric visualisation process. In many of the works shown, the very act and process of capture were relegated to a computer, a camera mounted atop a moving vehicle, a robot or a dog. To mention just one example, Canadian artist Véronique Ducharme presented a photography-based installation called *Encounters*, consisting of images taken by automatic hunting cameras (figure 15.5). As the artist herself explains:

> Over the course of one year, automatic cameras, installed in various parts of the Quebec landscape, recorded images from the forest. The images included animals, sunrise, wind and other actants susceptible of triggering the shutter of the cameras. These digital images, including the 'mistakes' of the cameras (i.e., blacked-out or overexposed images) were then transferred onto slide film in order to be projected in the gallery space using slide projectors. Accompanied by its rhythmic mechanical click, each machine has been programmed to sporadically and unpredictably project the images around the space, leaving the viewer entangled within the dialogue created by the machines and the images. (2014: non-pag.)

Ducharme's project offers a thought-provoking intervention into the debate about (human) intentionality in photography theory, whereby the former is seen as a condition and a guarantee of the medium being considered a form of art.[8] Photographic agency is distributed here amongst a network of participants, which includes not just nonhuman but also inanimate actors – even if 'the beholder' of the installation is still envisaged to be a human gallery-goer.

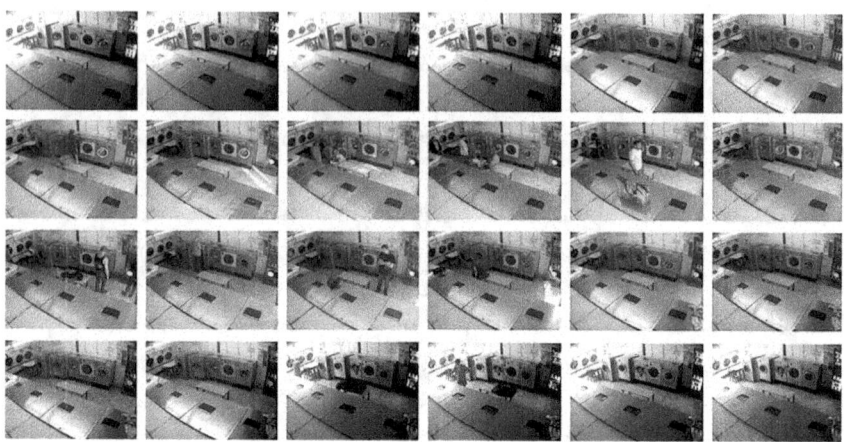

Figure 15.6. Juliet Ferguson, *Stolen Images*, 2011.

Ducharme's work has similarities with another project which foregrounds and remediates nonhuman photographic agency without reneging on its human dimension: *Stolen Images* by British photographer Juliet Ferguson (figure 15.6), published in the London independent photography magazine *Flip* in 2012 and online in *Photomediations Machine* in 2013. Accessing CCTV cameras using appropriate search terms via Google as part of her journalism job, Ferguson was able 'to see through the all-seeing eyes of the CCTV camera places' (Ferguson, 2013: non-pag.) what she would not have access to in the real world – without leaving her sofa. The process led her to reflect 'on what it means to take a photograph' and to pose the following questions: 'The majority of the cameras I used I could pan, zoom and focus. Is this any less photography than someone using a fully automatic camera and taking a picture from a designated panorama point at a beauty spot? Does photography demand a presence or are photographs taken using appropriated cameras controlled from another country in another time zone just as valid as "created" images?' (Ferguson, 2013: non-pag.). Ferguson has revealed that, in the process, she began 'to see a certain beauty in the images as they became removed from their original intention of surveillance. Instead, they offered a unique perspective on the ebb and flow of a day, from a vantage point and rigidity that ordinary photography doesn't offer' (non-pag.).

The photographic condition

These two projects discussed above demonstrate that art practice is merely part of a wider *photographic condition*, with things photographing themselves, without always being brought back to the human spectrum of vision as the ultimate channel of perception and of things perceived. Naturally, humans form part of this photographic continuum – as artists, photojournalists, festival organisers, computer programmers, engineers, printers, Instagram users, and, last but not least, spectators. However, what the examples just presented make explicit is that we are all part of that photographic flow of things being incessantly photographed, and of trying to make interventions from within the midst of it. In this way, Ducharme's and Ferguson's projects fall into a category that we might term 'insignificant photography' – not in the sense that they are mindless (as Tagg would perhaps have it), irrelevant and of no consequence, but rather in the sense of allowing us to see things that have been captured almost incidentally and in passing, with the thematic 'what' not being the key impulse behind the execution of the images. It is worth emphasising that this idea of insignificant photography has not just come to the fore with the development of networked digital technologies but was actually present in the early discourse of photography, even if the latter tended to confine photography's nonhuman aspect to the fairly conservative idea of 'objective observation'. Steve Edwards explains that

> Throughout its history, the camera has repeatedly been seen as an objective machine that captures information without any interference from the artist. ... in the early years of photography this was an often repeated theme: it was assumed that the sun made the picture, or the camera did, or even that the object in question depicted itself (Talbot spoke of his country pile, Lacock Abbey, as the first building 'that was ever yet known to have drawn its own picture'). (Edwards, 2006: 19)

The separation between the mechanism of photography as 'objective observation' and the human-centric notion of the 'intentionality' of the photographer has been used as a disciplinary device in art history: as signalled before, the elevation of photography to the status of art has been premised upon it.[9] It is this separation that the work of many contemporary photographers such as Ducharme and Ferguson troubles to a significant extent.

So what is meant by this notion of *photographic condition*, and does the postulation of its existence stand up to philosophical and experiential scrutiny? To explore these questions, let us start from a very simple proposition: *there is life in photography*. If living in the so-called media age has become tantamount to being photographed on a permanent basis, with our identity constituted and verified by the ongoing development of our photo galleries and photo streams on mobile phones, tablets and social media platforms such as Facebook, Tumblr and Pinterest, not to mention the thousands of security cameras quietly and often invisibly registering our image when we pass through city centres, shopping malls and airports, then, contrary to its more typical Barthesian association with the passage of time and death, photography can be understood more productively as a life-making process. As Sarah Kember and I argue in *Life after New Media*, it is 'precisely in its efforts to arrest duration, to capture or still the flow of life – beyond singular photographs' success or failure at representing *this* or *that* referent – that photography's vital forces are activated' (Kember & Zylinska, 2012: 72). Photography lends itself to being understood in a critical vitalist framework due to its positioning in a network of dynamic relations between present and past, movement and stasis, flow and cut. In making cuts into duration, in stabilising the temporal flow into entities, photography is inherently involved with time. Significantly, for vitalist philosophers such as Henri Bergson and Gilles Deleuze, time, duration and movement stand precisely for life itself. As Bergson provocatively asks, 'But is it not obvious that the photograph, if photograph there be, is already taken, already developed in the very heart of things and at all the points of space?' (1911: 31). Photography's proximity to life is therefore revealed in its temporal aspect, which is enacted in photography's dual ontology, whereby it can be seen as both object and practice, as both snapshot and all the other virtual snapshots that could have potentially been there, and, last but not least, as both being something here and now and as something always unfolding into something else. It is also in this dual ontology that the nonhuman side of photography comes to the fore, enacted as it is through agents as diverse as CCTV, aerial camera systems, satellites, endoscopy equipment and webcams as well as camera- and mobile-phone-sporting humans. It is perhaps worth making a quick reservation here that, to acknowledge the life-making aspect of photography is not necessarily to condone the politically suspicious yet increasingly widespread technologies of ubiquitous surveillance, control and loss of privacy enabled by various kinds of cameras. However, much has already been written about the latter, with little acknowledgement so far of the vital potentiality of photography – which, in an ontological sense, *does not have to* be an agent of control, even if it often is. There is therefore a danger of moralising photography in academic and public discourses before its potential has been truly explored. The foregrounding of the inherently creative power of photography as a practice is part of the philosophical argument of this article, although issues of politics never disappear from its agenda.

Photography and life

The on-off activity of the photographic process, which carves life into fragments while simultaneously reconnecting them to the imagistic flow, may allow us to conclude not only that *there is life in photography*, but also that *life itself is photographic*. Interestingly, Claire Colebrook explains this process of creative becoming in and of life by drawing on the very concept of image production, or 'imaging'. She writes: 'All life, according to Bergson and to Deleuze after him, can be considered as a form of perception or "imaging" where there is not one being that apprehends or represents another being, but two vectors of creativity where one potential for differentiation encounters another and from that potential forms a relatively stable tendency or manner' (2010: 11). This idea has its root in Bergson's *Matter and Memory*, where our experience of the world, which is always a way of sensing the world, comes in the form of images. We should mention here that, on the whole, Bergson is somewhat hesitant about the role played by images in cognition: in *Creative Evolution* he dismisses them as mere 'snapshots' of perception, post-factum reductions of duration and time to a sequence of the latter's frozen slices.[10] It may therefore seem strange to be revisiting the work of a philosopher who only used the concept of photography negatively, to outline a 'better', i.e. more intuitive and more fluid, mode of perception and cognition, in an attempt to say something new about photography. However, my argument here, as in my previous work,[11] is that Bergson's error is first and foremost media-specific and not philosophical *per se*: namely, he misunderstands photography's inherently creative and dynamic power by reducing it to a sequence of already fossilised artefacts, with the mind fragmenting the world into a sequence of 'snapshots'. This is why I want to suggest that, its mystical underpinnings aside, we can mobilise Bergson's *philosophical* writings on duration understood as a manifestation of élan vital to rethink photography as a quintessential practice of life. Indeed, photography is one possible (and historically specific) enactment of the creative practice of imaging, with the cuts into duration it makes always remaining connected to the flow of time. If we accept the fact that cutting – be it with our visual or conceptual apparatus – is inevitable to the processes of making sense of the world, then we can see any outcomes of the photographic cut, i.e. photographs and other products of the image-making process, as temporary stabilisations of the flow of duration that still bear a trace of life – rather than as frozen and ultimately deadly mementoes of the past. It is important to point out that, in order to recognise any kind of process *as a process*, we need to see it against the concept of a temporary stabilisation, interruption or cut into this process. A photograph is one possible form such stabilisations take, and a rather ubiquitous one at that. It is precisely because of its ubiquity and its increasingly intuitive technological apparatus that it serves as a perfect illustration of Bergson's ideas – or rather, of my own 'differentiated reading' of Bergson. Bergson himself foregrounds this mutually constitutive relationship between process and stoppage when he says that 'Things are constituted by the instantaneous cut which the understanding practices, at a given moment, on a flux of this kind, and what is mysterious when we compare the cuts together becomes clear when we relate them to the flux' (1944: 272). This supposition allows us to posit photography as an ultimately salutary and creative force in managing the duration of the world by the human as a species with limited cognitive and sensory capacity.

The notion of the creative role of the imaging process in life has also recently made its manifestation in the work of radical biologists, such as

Lynn Margulis. As she puts it in a book co-authored with her son Dorian Sagan, 'All living beings, not just animals, but plants and microorganisms, perceive. To survive, an organic being must perceive – it must seek, or at least recognize, food and avoid environmental danger' (Margulis & Sagan, 2000: 27). This act of perception, which involves the seeking out and recognition of something else, involves the making of an image of that something else (food, predator, sexual partner), one that needs to be at least temporarily fixed in order for the required proximity – for consumption or sex – to be accomplished. We could perhaps therefore suggest that imaging is a form of proto-photography, planting the seed of the combined human-machinic 'desire' explored by Batchen that came to its own in the early nineteenth century. After Bergson, images (which are not yet photographs) stand for 'a certain existence which is more than that which the idealist calls a representation, but less than that which the realist calls a thing – an existence placed half-way between the "thing" and the "representation"' (Bergson, 1911: vii). It is precisely through images that novelty comes into the world, which is why images should not be reduced to mere representations but should rather be understood as creations, 'some of which are philosophical, some artistic, some scientific' (Colebrook, 2010: 23). To put this another way, the creative impulse of life takes it beyond representation as a form of picturing what already exists: instead, life is a creation of images in the most radical sense, a way of temporarily stabilising matter into forms. Photographic practice as we conventionally know it, with all the automatism it entails, is just one instantiation of this creative process of life.

If all life is indeed photographic, the notion of the photographic apparatus that embraces yet also goes beyond the human becomes fundamental to our understanding of what we have called the *photographic condition*. To speak of the photographic apparatus is of course not just to argue for a straightforward replacement of the human vision with a machinic one, but rather to recognise the mutual intertwining and co-constitution of the organic and the machinic, the technical and the discursive, in the production of vision, and hence of the world. In her work on the use of apparatuses in physics experiments, the philosopher and quantum physicist Karen Barad argues that such devices are not just 'passive observing instruments; on the contrary, they are productive of (and part of) phenomena' (2007: 142). We could easily apply this argument to photography, where the camera as a viewing device, the photographic frame both in the viewfinder and as the circumference of a photographic print, the enlarger, the computer, the printer, the photographer (who, in many instances, such as surveillance or speed cameras, is replaced by the camera-eye), and, last but not least, the discourses about photography and vision *that produce them as objects for us humans* are all active agents in the constitution of a photograph. In other words, they are all part of what we understand by photography.

Becoming a camera

As signalled earlier, it is not just philosophy that helps us envisage this nonhuman, machinic dimension of photography: photographic, and, more broadly, artistic practice is even better predisposed to enact it (rather than just provide an argument *about* it). A series of works by British artist Lindsay Seers is a case in point. Exhibited, among other places, at Matt's Gallery in London as *It Has To Be This Way* in 2009, and accompanied by an aptly titled book, *Human Camera*, Seers' ongoing project consists of a number of seemingly autobiographic films. These are full of bizarre yet just-about-believable adventures occurring to their heroine, all verified by a body of 'experts' – from doctors and critics through to family members – that appear in the films but also leave behind 'evidence' in the form of numerous written accounts, photographs and documentary records. In one of the films, a young girl, positioned as 'Lindsay Seers', is living her life unable to make a distinction between herself and the world, or between the world and its representations. The girl is gifted with exceptional memory so, like a camera that is permanently switched on, she records and remembers practically everything. 'It is as if I was in a kaleidoscope, a bead in the mesmerising and constantly shifting pattern. Everything was in flux, every single moment and every single object rewritten at every turn', as 'Lindsay Seers' recalls in a short piece called 'Becoming Something' included in *Human Camera* (Seers, 2007: 36). This terrifyingly magnificent gift is lost once the girl sees a photograph of herself. She then spends her adult life clothed in a black sack, photographing things obsessively. In this way, she is literally trying to 'become a camera' by making photographs on light-sensitive paper inserted into her mouth, with the images produced 'bathed in the red light' of her body (figure 15.7). This ambition is later replaced by an attempt to 'become a projector' by creating things ex nihilo through the emanation of light. Some of Seers' films presented in the show are screened in a black hut modelled on Thomas Edison's *Black Maria*, his New Jersey film studio that was used for projection as well as photography. With this, Seers invites us not just to witness her process of becoming a camera but also to enter a giant camera ourselves, to literally step into the world of imaging, to re-connect us to the technicity of our own being.

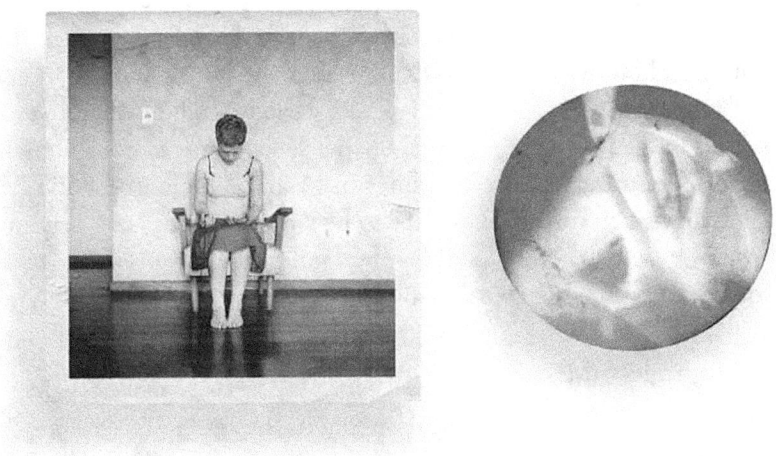

Figure 15.7. Lindsay Seers, *Optogram (mouth camera)*, 2010.

Although Bergson's argument about life as a form of imaging is posited as transhistorical, we can add a unique inflection to it by returning to Flusser, and, in particular, his study of the relation between the human and the technical apparatus. For Flusser, that relation changed significantly after the Industrial Revolution, a state of events in which 'photographers are inside their apparatus and bound up with it... It is a new kind of function in which human beings and apparatus merge into a unity' (2000: 27). Consequently, human beings now 'function as a function of apparatuses' (26), limited as they are to the execution of the camera's programme from the range of seemingly infinite possibilities which are nevertheless determined by the machine's algorithm. Arguably, humans themselves are enactors of such a programme, a sequence of possibilities enabled by various couplings of adenine, cytosine, guanine and thymine, arranged into a double helix of life. To state this is not to postulate some kind of uncritical technological or biological determinism that would remove from 'us' any possibility of action – as artists, photographers, critics, or spectators – and any responsibility for the actions we are to take. It is merely to acknowledge our kinship with other living beings across the evolutionary spectrum, with our lives remaining subject to biochemical reactions that we cannot always understand, control or overcome (from blushing through to ageing and dying). Just as 'the imagination of the camera is greater than that of every single photographer and that of all photographers put together' (Flusser, 2000: 30), the imagination of 'the programme called life' in which we all participate (and which is an outcome of multiple processes running across various scale of the universe) far exceeds our human imagination. Such a recognition of our entanglement as sentient and discursive beings in complex biological and technical networks is necessary if we are to become involved, seriously and responsibly, in any kind of photography, philosophy or other critical or everyday activity in which we aim to exercise 'free will'.

Re-forming the world

By reconnecting us to the technical apparatus, by letting us explore our machinic kinship, artists such as the appropriately named Seers and the other image-makers discussed in this article are all engaged (even if they are not always up-front about it or perhaps even entirely aware of it) in exploring the fundamental problem that many philosophers of technology who take science seriously have been grappling with: given that 'there is no place for human freedom within the area of automated, programmed and programming apparatuses', how can we 'show a way in which it is nevertheless possible to open up a space for freedom'? (Flusser, 2000: 81-82). Such an undertaking is very much needed, according to Flusser, 'because it is the only form of revolution open to us' (82). Flusser points to 'envisioners', that is 'people who try to turn an automatic apparatus against its own condition of being automatic' (Flusser, 2001: 19), as those who will be able to undertake the task of standing 'against the world', by pointing 'at it with their fingertips to inform it'. In this perspective, codification and visualisation are seen as radical interventions into the world, and ways of re-*forming* it, rather than as ways of dehumanising it the way Tagg seemed to suggest.

Any prudent and effective way of envisaging and picturing a transformation of our relation to the universe must thus be conducted not in terms of a human struggle against the machine but rather in terms of our mutual co-constitution, as a recognition of our shared kinship. This recognition of the photographic condition that encompasses yet goes beyond the human, and of the photographic apparatus that extends well beyond our eyes and beyond the devices supposedly under our control, should prompt us human philosophers, photographers and spectators to mobilise the ongoing creative impulse of life, where the whole world is a camera, and put it to creative rather than conservative uses. The conceptual expansion of processes of image-making beyond the human can also allow us to work towards escaping what Colebrook calls the 'privatization of the eye in late capitalism' (2010: 17), where what starts out as a defence of our right to look often ends up as a defence of our right to look at the small screen. In challenging the self-possessive individualism of the human eye, photography that seriously and consciously engages with its own expansive ontological condition and its nonhuman genealogy may therefore be seen as a truly revolutionary practice. Indeed, the concept and practice of nonhuman photography reconnects us to other beings and processes across the universe: including those of the Taurus Molecular Cloud. It serves as a reminder that the short moment in natural history when the human species has folded 'the world around its own, increasingly myopic, point of view' (Colebrook, 2014: 22), and that has allowed it to become 'seduced, spellbound, distracted and captivated by inanity' (15), should not obscure the wider horizon of our openness to the world, our relationality with it through originary perception. Nonhuman photography can therefore serve as both a response to 'man's tendency to reify himself' (Colebrook, 2014: 15) and an opening towards a radical posthumanist political analysis. It can do this by highlighting that there is more than just one point of view and that, by tearing the eye from the body and embracing the distributed machinic vision, it may be possible to see the drone as a more than just a killing machine – although of course there are no guarantees.[12]

Original source and licence

Mika Elo and Marko Karo, with Marc Goodwin (eds) (2015) *Photographic Powers*. Helsinki: Aalto ARTS. Licence: CC BY 4.0.

References

Barad, K. (2007) *Meeting the Universe Halfway: Quantum Physics and the Entanglement of Matter and Meaning*. Durham: Duke University Press.

Batchen, G. (1999) *Burning with Desire: The Conception of Photography*. Cambridge, MA: MIT Press.

Bergson, H. (1944) *Creative Evolution*. New York: Random House, The Modern Library (first published in 1911).

Bergson, H. (1911) *Matter and Memory*. London: George Allen & Unwinn Ltd.

Colebrook, C. (2010) *Deleuze and the Meaning of Life*. London and New York: Continuum, 2010.

Colebrook, C. (2014) *Death of the PostHuman: Essays on Extinction, Vol. 1*. Ann Arbor: Open Humanities Press.

Ducharme V. (2014) *Encounters*, 15.02, *Photomediations Machine*, http://photomediationsmachine.net/2014/02/15/encounters/

Edwards, S. (2006) *Photography: A Very Short Introduction*. Oxford: Oxford University Press.

Ferguson, J. (2013) *Stolen Images*, 29.04, *Photomediations Machine*, http://photomediationsmachine.net/2013/04/29/stolen-images

Flusser, V. (2000) *Towards a Philosophy of Photography*. London: Reaktion Books.

Flusser, V. (2011) *Into the Universe of Technical Images*. Minneapolis: University of Minnesota Press.

Fried, M. (2008) *Why Photography Matters as Art as Never Before*. New Haven: Yale University Press.

Kember, S. & Zylinska, J. (2012) *Life After New Media: Mediation as a Vital Process*. Cambridge, MA: MIT Press.

Margulis, L. & Sagan, D. (2000) *What Is Life?* Berkeley and Los Angeles: University of California.

Michaels, W. B. (2007) 'Photographs and Fossils', in J. Elkin (ed.), *Photography Theory*. New York and London: Routledge, 431-50.

Ritchin, F. (2009) *After Photography*. New York: W. W. Norton & Company.

Seers, L. (2007) *Human Camera*. Birmingham: Article Press.

Sontag, S. (2003) *Regarding the Pain of Others*. New York: Picador.

Tagg, J. (2008) 'Mindless Photography', in J. J. Long, A. Noble & E. Welch (eds), *Photography: Theoretical Snapshots*. London and New York: Routledge, 16-30.

Zielinski, S. (2013) [... *After the Media*]. Minneapolis: Univocal.

Notes

1. This series was developed as a visual track for my book, *Minimal Ethics for the Anthropocene* (Ann Arbor: Open Humanities Press, 2014).

2. This is a famous line by physicist Carl Sagan from his documentary TV series, *Cosmos*.

3. In my books *Minimal Ethics for the Anthropocene* (Ann Arbor: Open Humanities Press, 2014), *Bioethics in the Age of New Media* (Cambridge, MA: MIT Press, 2009) and *The Ethics of Cultural Studies* (London and New York: Continuum, 2005) I explored this question of responsibility by taking some steps towards outlining a non-prescriptive, non-moralistic, content-free ethics.

4. Although the tradition of posthumanist critique in the humanities extends as far back as at least the work of Charles Darwin and Sigmund Freud, and includes writings by authors such as Michel Foucault, Jacques Derrida and Donna Haraway, some of the recent key texts that critically expound the concept of posthumanism include: N. Katherine Hayles (1999) *How We Became Posthuman: Virtual Bodies in Cybernetics, Literature, and Informatics*. Chicago: University of Chicago Press; Cary Wolfe (2009) *What Is Posthumanism?*. Minneapolis: University of Minnesota Press; Rosi Braidotti (2013) *The Posthuman*. Cambridge: Polity; and Stefan Herbrechter (2013) *Posthumanism: A Critical Analysis*. London: Bloomsbury.

5. Cited from a letter written by Flusser in Zielinski (2013: 114). Zielinski explains that, for Flusser, 'the apparatus does what the human wants it to do, and the human can only want what the apparatus is able to do' (114).

6   There are of course many ways of systematising art photography, with additional categories and subcategories – such as 'abstraction', 'architecture' or 'nude' – being frequently listed. The quick typology proposed here does not aim to be comprehensive or scholarly: rather, my aim is to highlight the traditional categories frequently used by professional fine art photography exhibition and competitions, as well as amateur artist photo hosting sites. The last category, 'conceptual photography', is perhaps the most open and the most contentious. I am using the term here in the expanded sense it has gained on many art photography websites. To cite from one of them, Fotoblur (www.fotoblur.com), conceptual photography is a 'genre of photography in which the artist makes a photograph of a concept or idea'.

7   This article arises out of a catalogue essay I wrote for this exhibition: J. Zylinska (2013) 'All the World's a Camera: Notes on Nonhuman Photography', in Paul Wombell (ed.), *Drone: The Automated Image*. Bielefeld: Kerber.

8   For the exposition of this argument, developed in response to the writings of Michael Fried on the work of Thomas Demand, see Michaels (2007: 443-44).

9   Fried's *Why Photography Matters as Art as Never Before* espouses this point of view.

10 Bemoaning our suppression of intuition – which can offer us a more accurate and less fragmented picture of the world – Bergson highlights our overreliance on the intellect in the cognitive process:

> Instead of attaching ourselves to the inner becoming of things, we place ourselves outside them in order to recompose their becoming artificially. We take snapshots, as it were, of the passing reality, and, as these are characteristic of the reality, we have only to string them on a becoming, abstract, uniform and invisible, situated at the back of the apparatus of knowledge, in order to imitate what there is that is characteristic in this becoming itself. Perception, intellection, language so proceed in general. Whether we would think becoming, or express it, or even perceive it, we hardly do anything else than set going a kind of cinematograph inside us. (1944: 362)

11 This section develops some of the ideas discussed in chapter 3 of Kember and Zylinska, *Life After New Media*.

12 For a playful, tactical media-style exploration of what a drone would do in times of peace see IOCOSE's project, *Drone Selfies*, 2014, http://photomediationsmachine.net/2014/08/06/drone-selfies/.

IV The Networked Image

CHAPTER 16

Benjamin, BitTorrent, Bootlegs: Auratic Piracy Cultures?

Raúl Rodríguez-Ferrándiz

Seventy-five years ago, Walter Benjamin showed us that the line between 'production' and 'reproduction' had begun to blur. Reproduction was no longer optional, consequential, and degrading (the shredding of the original's aura), but was instead being transformed into a principle of production itself: something was produced bearing in mind how it was to be reproduced. No longer did the original exist (in photography, film, music recordings), but instead, there was diffusion, exhibition. The work existed precisely at the time and place of its enjoyment. Today, the cultural pirates of the new digital era take this principle to the extreme, with a certain characteristic also foreseen by Benjamin: a yearning to participate, to post-produce something captured in order to later return it to the Internet, modified in some way and made available to others. This postproduction is what is now often mixed up with reception, just as production and reproduction were in Benjamin's day. Postproduction on the receiver's side, which somehow augments and extends the received work, in other words creates an etymologically rigorous *author-ization* (*auctor* as the root of both *author* and *augmentation*). The cultural pirate only deserves redemption thanks to this creative augmentation.

From product to re-product

The most cited and renowned of Walter Benjamin's works[1] can still be read today, without much effort, as the first treatise on multimedia cultural piracy. Let us briefly recall the text. First, Benjamin reminded us that the reproduction of images dates back to the age-old tradition of minting coins and the serial manufacturing of bronze and terra-cotta pieces. This copying of images by the hundreds was perfected thanks to such technological developments as xylography, contemporary with printing, and much later, toward the end of the 18th century, lithography. However, none of these techniques were even remotely capable of reaching the quotas achieved by photography in the mid-19th century. In fact, throughout this journey, starting with photography and moving on through film, the very concept of 'original' itself obviously loses consistency: the original is already a copy, and the distance between future copies and the first is irrelevant. The work is no longer at its place of origin, nor does it show evidence or traces of such an origin (which is what is meant by 'original'), but instead, it exists precisely at the time and place of its distribution, where neither its accuracy (guaranteed by technology), nor its origin (converted into a fetishism which increases its exchange-value, but not the aesthetic pleasure which the copies can also provide) play any essential role.

Benjamin seems to laud, in any case in a prudent and subtle manner, artwork which is able to break away from its sacred origins, with its own specific time and place, and special and specialized officiants. In other words, he praises artwork which, while still being a work of art, does not claim to be an original, but is diffused around the world as reproduction, reaching the masses to whom art and culture had previously been inaccessible. Furthermore, Benjamin foresaw the concept of 'mass narcissism' as an effect of technical reproducibility. In cinema halls, the masses are not only witness to an imaginary and inaccessible world, but also to a world they themselves occupy, filling the streets on marches and demonstrations, on strike or in celebration; attending mass events, political rallies, sporting events; even fighting in wars. Obviously, the full magnitude of this is not something that the demonstrators themselves could appreciate, nor could they replay it at will. Neither could they form part of a causal history in which they were collectively included as protagonists – masses as actors in a narrative.

Faced with the anguish felt by his friend Adorno, Benjamin intuitively knew that a new dawn awaited the arts. In addition, by no means had arts such as painting, theater, or music suffered due to inventions like photography, film, and industrial phonography. It was possible for the painter, playwright, and composer to incorporate these new technologies into their work, and in so doing, to adapt their creations to the requirements imposed by reproducibility. All of these factors could serve not only as sources of motivation, but also for the projection of works unto previously unreachable audiences.

The aura of the original, 'the unique phenomenon of a distance, however close it may be', is lost in reproduction, according to Benjamin (1969: 221-230). As he states in *The Arcades Project*, reproduction sees the aura give way to the trace, which is a sign of intimate possession, and at the same time, of irretrievable loss (1999b: 447). The aura is the authentic and singular existence of a work of art; it is what gives an account of its material origin, as a thing in the world, and of a tradition from which said work is nourished and upon which said work has an effect, becoming a part of that tradition. Be it manual or technical, reproduction omits these qualities of the original work and the aura, in which they reside, disappears. The aura is what cannot be reproduced, what cannot be pirated: 'there can', as Benjamin puts it, 'be no replica of it'. So, what happens if the mere concept of 'original' loses meaning in a photochemical cultural production (as a static or moving image) which is essentially (not optionally) reproducible and therefore not anchored to a time and a place, to an epiphany, or to the uniqueness of its expression, but is, rather, a nomadic production? (1969: 224, 244).

Benjamin noted the turning point which photography and film brought to aesthetics, phenomenology, and even ethics of reproduction. Photography and film are technical reproductions which undermine the notion of 'original', and which switch the focus of interest from the work as a singularity that physically retains the creator's touch to a vision of the work as a multipliable and liberated piece which removes distinctions between original and copy, between early and late, between here and there and therefore, Benjamin suggests, removes distinctions between creator and audience. The nature of the new arts in technical reproducibility is, precisely, to remove itself from the ritual, the uniqueness and concentration, the time and place, the privileged audience, and instead, project itself to an undefined space and moment, and to a completely unknown audience – a mass audience 'whose sense of the universal equality of things has increased to such a degree that it extracts it even from a unique object by means of reproduction' (1969: 223).

When using such methods, the author is aware that he or she is working to promote traffic, public access, and convenient availability, as well as a process, a flow, and an audience of potential consumers of copies. Does the aura itself become reproducible, leaving the original, if there is one, without any claim to a stake? Does technical reproduction, the shredding of the aura, become its hiding place?

It is true that Benjamin's position with regard to the destruction of the aura is ambivalent. He tackles the subject in 'The Work of Art...' and on three other occasions,[2] to the point where it can be said without exaggeration that his reflections on the aura permeated the intellectual output of the last ten years of his life. Benjamin oscillated between a 'liquidationist' and an 'elegiac' attitude to the aura, just as he oscillates in his writings between a specific conception (the aura upon the arrival of photography and film) and another, more general (one could say 'experiential') conception, between an aesthetic and an ethical vision. In any case, and seeking to reconcile these perspectives, we could say that, for Benjamin, it is not so much that the aura can be derived from some objects (paintings and theatrical productions) and not from others (photographs and films), but rather, that there is a fundamental category of experience, memory, and perception which imbues people's ways of looking at the world, at others, and at works of art, and that said category is now disappearing under the weight of new technologies in technical reproducibility, which is both an opportunity and a danger. We could say that 1) an aura becomes less a property of the *object* and more a quality of the *subject* of the perception, a special sensitivity that allows this subject to perceive the world and works of art auratically, and 2) what is important, in this instance, is attitude, the *use* the subjects make of their ability to look and see in each case (Costello, 2005).

Let us consider for a moment a fully 'auratic' example: *The Scream* by Edward Munch. Curators of the Munch Museum in Oslo doubt that they will ever be able to repair the damage the painting suffered during its theft and subsequent recovery. The board was wet in some areas, and the painting had deteriorated so much that it seems it will be difficult to ever restore its original tonalities. This example, though unfortunate, gives pause for thought. On the one hand, Munch is considered a careless and almost even negligent painter in the completion of his works, often considering them finished, even when they showed signs of accidental marks or scratches. Who knows if the painting we were familiar with was not the result of luck and chance, even more than artwork usually is? The incidence of its theft was the most passionate adventure of its entire life as an artistic object, beyond the boring comfort of the Norwegian museum, where it was held under controlled temperature, humidity, and lighting conditions. No one dares to question whether the event of its theft and recovery has been lucrative for the museum and added to the painter's renown: this event is an added value to Munch's biography and the countless interpretations of his work. It is comparable in some ways to the lost head of the Winged Victory of Samothrace and the mutilated arms of the Venus de Milo.

The difference is that we have known Munch's painting in its (relative) completeness and integrity, while these statues have reached us and become part of the history of art with their beautiful defects. The painting, contrary to these statues, has been copied and photographed thousands of times, and had been reproduced a million times over on postcards, picture cards, posters, t-shirts, etc. prior to its deterioration. Thus, the curators must turn to these copies, born of technical reproducibility, in order to restore the initial appearance of the board as far as possible, in such a way that it will be the reproduction that will serve as proof of expertise in restoring the original, and not the original – now not so original and not so suggestive of its origin, but rather, corrupted by the circumstances of its theft. The reproduction is therefore the guarantee of accuracy. In a way, the copies are now more authentic than the original itself, more loyal to the author's will when he decided his work was completed. Munch created up to four different versions of the painting, two of which – not one – were stolen, in 1994 and 2004, and recovered soon afterwards. The differences between these versions are clearly distinguishable, though Munch did not identify any one as superior to the others. Was Munch himself trying out a type of 'serial' process in the creation of his own original work? Was he reproducing himself in a chirographic sense? Was Munch the first copier of *The Scream*? His own first pirate?

This anecdote, to which so many equivalents can be found in the history of painting, outlines the paradox which Benjamin had to confront, and which must still give us pause for thought today. The paradox of a photograph which can unquestionably crush the aura with the disquieting (but incomplete, frustrated) likeness it presents to us and with the (viscous, not friendly) closeness it imposes, but which is often that which is responsible for preserving that aura, that which testifies to something that the damaged original can no longer guarantee. And not only this, it is also responsible for *feeding* the aura, for exalting it: is it not true that the photograph of a work of art, which allows it to be reproduced in catalogs for museums and exhibitions, in encyclopedias, textbooks and history of art essays, and which has recently multiplied its dissemination and global circulation through the Internet, is far from an insignificant factor in the ever-renewed prestige, the topicality of said work? (Malraux, 1947/1978).

Let us consider for a moment the differences between, on the one hand, this act of actual theft and attempted piracy (as the thieves undoubtedly intended to trade in the stolen work) and, on the other, an act of online pillaging. Obviously, we must condemn the theft or destruction of an original, which is not only a criminal act, but also an irreparable loss for art as an institution and heritage. But what are we to say about the *multiplication* of an original? Does it call for the same judgment? Internet pillaging obviously involves digital copies, rather than a unique and irreplaceable original. And digital copies are, as we shall see, qualitatively different from chirographic copies: the practice of 'secondary' copying (copying in an attempt to supplant the original, to usurp its prestige) no longer exists. This secondarization of copying has no meaning in the digital world, as we are dealing with identical duplicates, rather than copies. Digital copying is a form of transportation which does not, however, move what has been copied from its original place, which does not seek to supplant but which in any case seeks a circulation that is difficult to restrict (Bunz, 2007). A circulation, yes, but also a rewrite, an alteration which, again, does not suppose the corruption of the original. Let us suppose that the thieves of the Munch paintings had been a mixture of admirers and frustrated painters. And they had wanted to add their own brush strokes to the original, to in a way renew Munch, update him. It seems absurd, yes, but this is what hundreds of Internet pirates are and what they do, as can be seen by anybody who types 'The Scream' into Google Images. From Macaulay Culkin to Homer Simpson, from Tarzan to Eric Northman (the latter being one of the stars of the series *True Blood*), from the mask used by the killer in the *Scream* saga (named, by no coincidence, after the Munch painting) to Senator Harry Reid – they have all been lifted by outside hands into the place of that anguished face, to varying degrees of success and creativity. New faces which perhaps (coincidences of this type have been seen before) occupy just the spot in which the corruption of the canvas due to its theft and handling could be most pronounced. And this is in a playful way, one that does no harm to the original held in Oslo, which will be restored (or not) thanks to photographs. Furthermore, it is in a way which poses no threat either to the history of the painting (nor, admittedly, does it substantially improve it), or to the copyright held by Munch's heirs, should there be such a thing.[3]

Reproducible arts and the reproducibility of the arts

With great insight, Benjamin defined a point of inflection not so much between the chirographical and technographical arts (painting and photography, respectively), but rather between arts for the purpose of producing an original and arts in which the notion of original loses value in favor of a multitude of 'copies' available to the public. The issue is not, strictly speaking, a matter of technology: our notion of 'technological' is history-based, but, upon further reflection, chirography also requires technology, whether paintbrush, stage, pen, chisel, flute, or violin. An artistic genius has never been hindered by these more or less refined technical instruments, which have allowed his or her self-expression through the modeling of a material, but rather, the test of his or her art has been precisely his or her ability to dominate the techniques required to bring imagination to life in the form of artwork.

The crux of the matter lies in the development and perfection of technology and the skills for reproduction – all reprographic techniques, in the broadest sense, from the press to the laser printer, photographic, sound/music, cinematographic, and also broadcasting-related technologies (radio, television, video, Internet) which appear to offer a point of convergence or overlap with production-related technologies and skills.

We refer to the critical moment in which, for example, a camera points its lens at paintings exhibited in museums, at sculptures, at monuments and buildings, and thereby allows their reproduction through illustrated cards (Malraux, 1978), or the moment in which a musician's live performance is reproduced at a distance or recorded (Szendy, 2008).

But then, what Benjamin documents and theorizes about is precisely that period in the history of technology at the service of creation during which the line between production and reproduction blurs. Paradoxically, this occurs to the point where reproduction both 'precedes' production and becomes its ultimate purpose: something is produced bearing in mind how it will look or sound once it is reproduced and the devices, supports, and reproductive formats with which it will be reproduced. The creator is perfectly aware that of the whole he or she produces, the only part that counts is the part that goes on to be reproduced – let's call it the 'reproduct': the negatives from which positive images will be created, enlarged, and eventually exhibited or published; the takes that will become the final shots in the film; the recorded chords and vocalizations which will compose the corresponding soundtrack. Meanwhile, these same reproduction techniques do not simply involve a carefully thought-out selection or reduction of the whole that was recorded before the camera or microphone, but they also provide a mine of expressive resources which alter (by stylizing, hyper-realizing, dramatizing, ridiculing, cleaning, equalizing, synthesizing, and sampling) what has been saved on photographic film, motion picture reels, sound recordings, or digital archives.

The record industry provides a clear example. Doesn't a pop or rock artist compose a song or collection of songs to be recorded on an album in a studio where technical manipulations and virtuosities are carried out that are impossible during a live performance? Also, don't we often yearn to adapt a live concert performance, the 'copy', to the recording we have listened to previously, our original? Even when we seek a different experience at the live concert, a more direct musicality, isn't this live concert itself often recorded for marketing purposes, whether as an audio (a music CD of the *live* concert) or audiovisual product (a reproducible DVD for viewing on the TV or computer screen)? The performance's dynamics concerning time and space are subjected to the needs of the sound or video recordings. Just to make things even more complicated, isn't this video recording projected live on giant screens for the public *in situ*? A crowd so large that, for the majority, the only option is to watch the live broadcast of the performance, in this case not on television, but on *proxivision*, in a rigorously etymological sense. Isn't it true that the *live* retransmission, in using multiple cameras and audio takes, offers a different experience, but one which is probably richer in sound and visually than that enjoyed by the front-row spectator at the foot of the stage? The other spectator (the ambivalent one) is able to experience the real presence of the artist and his or her work (the aura?), as well as the contagious mood of a multitudinous congregation, all while receiving the detail and quality provided by audiovisual reproduction technologies.

Nevertheless, this paradoxical precedence and preference of the recording or retransmission of the performance does not only occur in pop music. A classical music composer or performer may prefer a recording, i.e., performing for a recording device under favorable conditions, over a live public performance. Let's take Stravinski and Glenn Gould as two opposing paradigmatic cases. In the early 20th century, due to his concerns about the distortions that his written, perhaps interpreted albeit unrecorded, work could suffer at the hands of Hollywood (e.g., the arrangements of *The Rite of Spring* for *Fantasia*), Stravinski struggled between preventing such manipulation and his general disapproval of mechanical recordings and personally controlling said recordings, or in other words, of establishing an approved version of his work which would prevent or discredit as mere rearrangements all of those which, whether he liked it or not, would eventually be produced by the music or film industry. Conversely, Glenn Gould detested exhibiting his performance-based virtuosities and preferred to lock himself away in a recording studio and transform the production of records into his 'art'. In other words, Gould decided to take advantage of the fact that technical reproducibility could finally separate the musical performance from the listening experience, after centuries of necessarily coinciding, and thus edit the recording that mediated between the two to create a montage of different performances, perhaps even recorded at different times.[4] The same is true for music lovers: for them, it can no longer be a live performance by the conductors Menuhin, Bernstein, or Von Karajan that they adore, but rather, the recordings of these performances which, without a doubt, create a musical experience that is different from attending a live performance and, in their judgment, unquestionably superior to any later performance, whether recorded or live. Most likely this is due to cultural fetishism, fanaticism, and perhaps an excessive admiration, that represent, even amongst *connoisseurs*, a guarantee for technical reproduction: the recorded performance, experienced and enjoyed strictly as such, becomes the standard for excellence of any other performance, whether recorded or live.

Benjamin was precociously aware of this major aspect of 20th-century culture, society, and technology, which opens up a joyful, or at least hopeful, perspective, precisely in the mid-1930s, a time when culture, society, and technology offered little in the way of hope. Furthermore, Benjamin also seems to propose, often between the lines, that technical reproducibility, which in a certain sense corrupts originality and the aura, is capable of relocating and reconstructing this elsewhere, perhaps at the receptor's end – but let us not get ahead of ourselves. The main point is that Benjamin advocates the intimacy and mutual support that exists between productive and reproductive technologies, as well as the initial impact this undoubtedly has on the diffusion, circulation, and (surely) ownership of the work of art.

From re-product to post-product

Let us take a step forward: what happens in the case of digital works of art? As noted by Michael Betancourt:

> Every digital reproduction is identical to every other; digital objects are stored as a form of information, rather than limited as physical objects inherently are; thus the digital state can be understood as a form of instrumental language – instructions for executing the 'retrieval' that is a specific digital (art) work. (2006: para. 9)

Digital objects are radically different from physical objects. Betancourt distinguishes between a 'digital object' materially present to our senses and a 'digital work,' i.e., 'a series of binary signals recorded by a machine and requiring a machine to render this unseen "code" readable to humans'. This separation between the digital file in binary code form, which is limitlessly copyable, and its effective retrieval using a device which displays it in the form of a still or moving image, or as text, music, or whatever, is a way of resurrecting the aura – the 'aura of the information', in this case. While the material aspects of the digital work appear to be characterized as ephemeral, lasting no longer than the phenomenological encounter with its presentation, the aura of information suggests that the digital itself transcends physical form: the digital work as immortal. An immortality that is no longer associated with the uniqueness of an original which acts as a warranty for all its copies, but with precisely the proliferation of identical instances. A digital master which lives on in the successive textual bodies in which it materializes, across different spaces (surfaces of expression) and times (the evolution of digital technologies in both hardware and software).

It is a paradoxical aura, which resides in a reproducible binary code that is limitlessly copyable (although illegible to humans) and that, depending upon the device in which it is embodied, makes its effective presentation contingent, ephemeral. Moreover, it is, as Betancourt notes, an aura that separates physical materiality from the context of the tradition in which it was produced and, instead, highlights both the contexts of its effective reception and, further still, those of its use, as envisaged by Benjamin. It is an aura which makes sacred the digital but not the digitalized, as this use often anticipates – and even encourages – the transformation of what is received: manipulation of the basic binary code. This creates an obvious problem with accumulation and intellectual property: access must be regulated, more so than ownership. And once access has been regulated, the conditions of the derived work must be established. Now, we are not only dealing with the confusion between production and reproduction, but also between *reception* and *postproduction*. Let us look at some examples:

1) Music fans not only play the tracks of an acquired product as often as they like, they can also select their favorite songs, rename and recompile them at will, producing a new, if unedited, set of tracks, or even edit or sample them, post-producing the product to create personalized listening on a CD or an MP3 player's playlist. This practice, which became known in the industry as 'sampling' in the 1950s (with sampler albums being compilations of various artists from the same label), is now a prerogative of the listener. But the concept went from being an anthology of

tracks to being the creation of a new tune through mixing existing tracks, something which is also within reach of the user. Two or three tunes would be mixed to produce a musical mashup, a hitherto-unheard mix of previously released and recognizable tunes.[5] Video clips are another format much favored by the fans of singers and groups, as well as (on the crossover) by lovers of audiovisual creation. There are, of course, 'official' clips, but there are also anime music videos (AMV), an entire category of alternative clips, and amateur clips, as well as a universe of home-produced clips which employ images from highly diverse sources set to music, ranging from tributes to the most outrageous parodies. There are also lip-dubs (or mass motion sequence shots with playbacks of hit songs) in which members of a collective generally choreograph a routine around a song.[6] And new categories of music videos are being created all the time, driven by emulation and even competition. Listeners are transformed into arrangers, their instruments come between the instruments (the 'musical' instruments) used for production, the competent performers thereof, and their own listening. Is this, then, an interposition or a continuity of said instruments?

2) Painting enthusiasts can download an image from the Internet or scan a printed copy, modify, rename or label it at will, thereby appropriating it (without necessarily avoiding any reference to the 'original'). The aforementioned painting by Munch is available on the Internet in hundreds of different ways, as we have pointed above, with hundreds of variations on the subject, whether they be for the better or for the worse. Photo enthusiasts act similarly, using photographs taken by others or from an image bank and applying computer graphics to these materials. The humoristic dimension of these collage techniques is self-conscious, as if the creators want to insure that the process of 'cut and paste' underlying the joke remains evident. Interactive humor, funny photos, maniphotos, phanimation, celebrity soundboards, and PowerPoint humor are recently coined words describing these techniques (Shifman, 2007).

3) Movie-buffs and home moviemakers not only play movies and make home videos or DVDs, they also edit, add sound, dub, insert subtitles

or signs, visual or sound effects, and design their own trailers. It is also popular to compile anthologies of favorite scenes, organized by director, actor, genre, or subject.[7] A host of *ad hoc* terms is already in circulation to describe all this audiovisual productivity on the part of the user: synchros, i.e., split screens with windows showing simultaneous actions viewed at different points in time;[8] recaps, i.e., summaries of a TV season, for example, using a selection of dramatic highlights, often with a voiceover or explanatory subtitles to link the scenes together;[9] unofficial trailers; alternative endings; interstitial stories which 'fill in' the gaps of another product (what did so-and-so from such-and-such series do during the missing two years?); spoilers, or unauthorized previews of an essential element of the plot or its denouement, some rather tongue-in-cheek;[10] false trailers for non-existent films, or trailers in which the sound, logos, or montage paradoxically change the genre of a well-known film; and homemade clips at the boundary between the music and the video industry, made by amateurs.

4) Readers of e-books, or of digitalized literary texts in general, show a tendency toward underlining, annotating, and criticizing these texts. This is obviously nothing new: we readers have been doing so since the dawn of writing. What characterizes the current time is the obsession with sharing these selected quotes, impressions, comments, and comparisons with other earlier or later texts by adding to the original, thus extending and diffusing them. The task of Google Books to digitalize all the books in the world is complemented by the joint, collective, but no less titanic task of giving these books their commentary, their replica, their gloss. In the most elaborate cases, even with parodies, sequels, and prequels, this can mean picking up threads which are intimated but not developed, or following up with secondary characters who are relegated but show promise.

5) First, bloggers (more selective) and then social networkers (more frequent and usual), the apex of this electronic Babel, combine the aforementioned multimedia skills and multiply circulation. We are dealing with telematic activity and interactions between individuals and groups that do not simply feed off a product, but moreover, off a *productivity* that is in

a process of continuous construction and acquires a precarious stability at the moment in which it is accessed, only to be modified the next time, by our hand or by that of another. Furthermore, the increasingly advanced skills involved in browsing, production, postproduction, and circulating all these different kinds of files give rise to a tidal wave of user-generated content which encroaches upon all the aforementioned media (music, illustration, photography, animation, audiovisual productions, written texts, etc.) and sets them working synergistically through transmedia fictional universes which are as complex as they are, quite consistently, joint and collaborative.[11]

All of this does not strictly enter the dominion of the habitual Internet user; it also falls within the still institutionalized artistic practices themselves – in other words, the fields of literary, plastic, cinematographic, or musical arts – which have replicated this vast (post)productivity of the 'sampler' (Bourriaud, 2005) or 'remixer' (Manovich, 2005) in their works.

Thus: *product, re-product* and, finally, *co-product? post-product? trans-product? e-product?* A product which is not only in transit, but is being remade while it transits and because it transits. Said digital transit, then, represents the happy encounter of the aura of an origin with the imprint of the reproduction, as discerned by Benjamin. All this is accompanied by the successive imprints of multiple reproductions which will keep on coming, one after the other. Of course, some will only be reproduced as streamings, downloads, or copy-and-pastes of an identical digital master, but others will be veritable edits, as authentic author-izations: the *auctor*, in the etymological sense, was the person who augmented (*augmentation* and *author* come from *augere*, to increase, also giving rise, in a way, to author-ize).[12]

Strictly speaking, more than being confusing, what production/reproduction and reception/postproduction do is share, to a great extent, the same instruments and same actions. Acclaimed musicians, moviemakers, videographers, press editors, publicists, and plastic artists increasingly and decisively practice the technique of presenting the Internet-based public, sometimes organized into very active communities, their partial or completed works for the purpose of receiving feedback, reactions, proposals, collaboration – all user-generated content (Jenkins, 2006b). Lev Manovich questions whether, in this digital era, culture will not end up being divided into discrete units designed to be copied and integrated within larger modules, like LEGO bricks. Blocks which contain all of the information required in order to be easily attached to others, to be adapted to facilitate this attachment, and also to record, at any given moment, the historical sequence of loans which, as a whole, result in the product as it stands. Bricks which, moreover, are displayed in a quasi-unlimited showcase in such a way that users can endorse them and express their support for the changing contents. In other words, he foretells a 'cultural modularity' in which, paradoxically a priori, there is no minimum delimited vocabulary (given that the modular seems to require a finite series of minimal units, the combination of which results in an exponential variety). This modularity does not reduce the total number of units to be combined, but rather, it allows the modification of each unit during each use, thereby guaranteeing an innovative final result (Manovich, 2005).

From the DJs of the 1980s to the current *geeks* who remix and fine-tune cultural products that are in circulation, such as photographs, songs, films, television series, videogames, and their corresponding promotional subproducts (trailers, clips, promos, etc.) and return them to the Internet, edited but remixable (*lip-dubs, mashups, public movies*), all the fan culture in general assumes a modular logic (Jenkins, 2006a, 2006b). These interventions are, to a great extent, ironic and parodic (Shifman, 2007). On the one hand, they recognize (and do not try to hide) this assembly of preformed parts, citations, allusions, and intertextual gestures, and on the other, they give value to a democratized creativity of diffuse and jointly-owned authorship.[13]

From experience to experiment

Recently, cultural objects in their most noble form seem to aim to be 'appropriated' by the reader, listener, or spectator, not only as the object of their contemplation, but also as an operation; not only as an experience, but also as an experiment. They are definitely more open to being manipulated and handled; they offer a moment of reading, listening, or contemplating, surely, while at the same time, there is an invitation to write, compose, and design, to implicate oneself through participation and co-production. In addition, we could say that modern technologies which act as the means of support for cultural goods – literature, painting, film, music – have substantially modified our way of understanding how to deal with them.

Cultural experience was, before, a *circumscribed* activity, exclusively applied to an object, and therefore *intense* and almost always *intimate*. Meanwhile, today, a valued cultural experience is one that does not seem to fix its attention on one particular point, unraveling it in detail, but rather, it follows a trajectory which jumps from one point to another, stopping at any specific point only long enough to gather momentum to move on to the next interconnected point. It's not a matter of diving down into the depths to recover a hidden, though identified, treasure, but rather, it is one of quickly surfing along the surface's intermittently emergent crests, which may crash over us and swallow us up if we stop too long.[14]

If we look closely, this is precisely how Internet works, with a hypertextuality that *mines* (or *contaminates* or *sows*) each text with links that lead to all kinds of other texts, inviting us to jump from one to another without having even, perhaps, finished reading the text displayed before us, and which is already disappearing from view (although always recoverable) in our search for another which grabs our attention, and so on. This same experience of connection is what hierarchizes Google searches: the list of results is not ordered so much according to how many times the word we are searching for appears in the text, but rather, according to how many documents are linked to the text we are presumably searching for, and which will therefore prove to be the most useful to us, precisely because these are the most connected documents on the Internet. Therefore, these documents have the most interconnections between pieces of knowledge that form a series which is practically infinite, but which is especially *broad* and *attractive* at certain points (Battelle, 2006).

In today's panorama, a heterogeneous public is presented with an elaborated, but as yet unfinished and open-ended, product, presented both as a 'figure', and as the possibility for 'configuration'; as finished pieces, and as an instruction manual for building something previously unknown, foreseen but not present. Enjoyment of the product is achieved not so much through mere contemplation, but rather, by creating a finished product, albeit it a provisional one, as there always exists the possibility of recovering the original condition and opting for a different reconstruction – a finished product. The placement of an 'order', to the contrary of what occurred during times of patronage, does not happen at the beginning of the work, but upon its completion; it is not an order from a client to a cultural producer, but rather, from the cultural producer to the client, who appropriates the work not merely by purchasing it as part of a lot identical to one acquired by many other buyers, but by finishing it through an appropriation which is not strictly commercial in nature and which presupposes (and this is the essence of the business) the client's access to similar instruments used in its production by the issuing entity. This is the case with many current artistic approaches which take the idea of 'open work' to its ultimate consequences, not only as regards interpretative closure (mental), but also regarding physical participation and intervention (interactive installations, video art), and involving entertainment-related technologies (karaoke, videogames, virtual reality, video game consoles) and, in general, cultural experiences in which digitization, interactive computerization, and advanced interfaces intervene. If we include connection to the Internet, this opening-up of the process is multiplied exponentially, and it is even more evident that 1) reception and consumption are potentially creative (and digital platforms actively promote this creative participation), 2) this user-generated content circulates freely, open to new creative reappropriations, and 3) the increase in culture owned by others neither undermines nor threatens our own, but rather reinforces it through cooperative exchanges (*Creative Commons* and *copyleft* licenses, P2P protocols for file sharing, circulation of free software, etc.).

If, as Morin yearned for in the 1960s, the cultural industry were to consist of a collection of mechanisms and operations through which cultural *creation* was transformed into *production*, then the new paradigm of production, which transfers completion and even endorsement of the productive process to the reception of the product itself by a multitude of possible destinations (perhaps partially predetermined, but with a great degree of uncertainty nevertheless), should be christened with a name that accounts for this mutation (Rodríguez-Ferrándiz, 2011). Terms such as *postproduction* (Bourriaud, 2005), *remixability* or *software culture* (Manovich, 2005), *mass self-communication* (Castells, 2009), amongst others, have been proposed and already circulate. The old pairs of creation/enjoyment or production/consumption are insufficient and fail to consider the complexity of the situation.

Conclusions

Since Benjamin, we have become used to speaking of an author's work as a *production*, and of the cultural industry as offering *reproductions* which lack the aura of an original that was directly manipulated by its author. This was a prerogative of cultural production over other types of industrial manufacturing: no one would even think of considering a soft drink can or an automobile off a Ford-type assembly line as either a *reproduction* or a *copy*, but rather as a product (Lash & Urry, 1994). However, we do so with books, records, DVDs, or the publishing of pictorial works. We have already observed that Benjamin was precisely aware of how photographic or cinematographic copies jeopardized the notion of original. And we have observed how digital reproducibility extends and radicalizes this tendency by definitively shattering the hierarchy of original then copy, by consecrating digital files as auratic treasures which are no less valuable for having been reproduced and copied, and which are, at the same time, open to recreative manipulation, open to use (and abuse).

In brief, what we have explored here is the extension of the phenomena: not only do production and reproduction converge, but they both also converge with reception and postproduction. Not only is production carried out bearing in mind reproduction, but it also depends on reception and postproduction. Nevertheless, it is not merely a matter of the *lector in fabula* or the *spectator in spectaculo*, in other words, prefiguring the model receptor in the text. The intended receptor is not only contemplative, but also participative: he or she must be capable of intervening in, manipulating, and (provisionally) finishing the product. Therefore, it is not a matter of merely acquiring the product (a possessive piracy, as in the accumulative logic of libraries, record or video collections, which are often inactive and inert – ROM, HD, or downloading logic, by the person accumulating the material just in case there's time later to watch, read, or listen to it, who foresees enjoyment but might not be able to fulfill this desire). Rather, it is a matter of doing something with it, a piracy which does not just involve collecting treasures, but reminting the coins, adding the pirate's own stamp, and making them available to others by recirculating them, for free, a type of piracy which conciliates appropriation and conviviality – RAM, access and streaming logic by someone who does actually watch, listen, or read what he or she acquires, and does not merely accumulate for accumulation's sake, but enjoys the material. It is this enjoyment that produces a comment, a recommendation, a critique or an intervention – the (authorized) consumer as postproducer, to paraphrase, once again, Walter Benjamin.

Original source and licence

International Journal of Communication 6 (2012), 396–412 1932-8036/20120396. Copyright © 2012 (Raúl Rodríguez-Ferrándiz). Licence: CC-BY-NC-ND. Available at http://ijoc.org.

References

Adorno, T. W. (1991) *The Culture Industry. Selected Essays on Mass Culture* J. Bernstein (ed.), London: Routledge.

Battelle, J. (2005) *The Search: How Google and Its Rivals Rewrote the Rules of Business and Transformed Our Culture.* New York: Portfolio.

Benjamin, W. (1969) 'The Work of Art in an Age of Mechanical Reproduction', in H. Arendt (ed.), *Illuminations.* New York: Schocken Books, 217-251.

Benjamin, W. (1999a) 'Little History of Photography', in M. W. Jennings, H. Eiland, & G. Smith (eds), *Walter Benjamin: Selected Writings,* Vol. 2. Cambridge, MA: Belknap Press, 1927-1934.

Benjamin, W. (1999b) *The Arcades Project.* Cambridge, MA: Harvard University Press.

Betancourt, M. (2006) 'The Aura of the Digital' *CTheory,* td041. Retrieved from http://www.ctheory.net/articles.aspx?id=519.

Bourriaud, N. (2005) *Postproduction: Culture As Screenplay: How Art Reprograms the World.* New York: Lukas & Sternberg. Retrieved from http://www9.georgetown.edu/faculty/irvinem/theory/Bourriaud-Postproduction2.pdf.

Buck-Morss, S. (1989) *The Dialectics of Seeing: Walter Benjamin and the Arcades Project.* Cambridge, MA: MIT Press.

Bunz, M. (2007) 'The Digital Copy'. Retrieved from http://www.mercedes-bunz.de/english/the-digital-copy — no longer available.

Carroll, N. (1998) *A Philosophy of Mass Art*. Oxford: Clarendon Press.

Castells, M. (2009) *Communication Power*. Oxford: Oxford University Press.

Costello, D. (2005) 'Aura, Face, Photography: Re-reading Benjamin Today', in A. Benjamin (ed.), *Walter Benjamin and Art*. London: Continuum, 164-184.

Eco, U. (1994) *The Limits of Interpretation*. Bloomington, IN: Indiana University Press.

Eiland, H. (2003) 'Reception in Distraction', *boundary 2*, Spring 2003, 30 (1): 51–66. doi:10.1215/01903659-30-1-51.

Gould, G. (1990) *The Glenn Gould Reader*, Tim Page (ed.) New York: Vintage Books.

Gumbrecht, H. U. & Marrinan, M. (eds.) (2003) *Mapping Benjamin: The Work of Art In the Digital Age*. Stanford, CA: Stanford University Press.

Isenberg, N. (2001) 'The Work of Walter Benjamin in the Age of Information'. *New German Critique*, 83, 119-150.

Jenkins, H. (1992) *Textual Poachers: Television, Fans and Participatory Culture*. London: Routledge.

Jenkins, H. (2006a) *Convergence Culture: Where New and Old Media Collide*. New York: New York University Press.

Jenkins, H. (2006b) *Fans, Bloggers and Gamers: Exploring Participatory Culture*. New York: New York University Press.

Kaufman, R. (2002) 'Aura, Still'. *October*, 99, 45-80.

Koepnick, L. (2002) 'Aura Reconsidered: Benjamin and Contemporary Visual Culture', in G. Richter (ed.), *Benjamin's Ghosts: Interventions in Contemporary Literary and Cultural Theory*. Stanford, CA: Stanford University Press, 95-117.

Lash, S. & Urry, J. (1994) *Economies of Sign and Space*. London: SAGE Publications.

Malraux, A. (1951/1978) *The Voices of Silence*. Princeton, NJ: Princeton University Press.

Manovich, L. (2005) 'Remixability and Modularity'. Retrieved from http://manovich.net/index.php/projects/remixability-and-modularity.

Manovich, L. (2008) 'The Practice of Everyday (Media) Life'. Retrieved from http://manovich.net/index.php/projects/the-practice-of-everyday-media-life.

Patt, L. (ed.) (2001) *Benjamin's Blind Spot: Walter Benjamin and the Premature Death of Aura*. Topanga, CA: Institute of Cultural Inquiry.

Rodríguez-Ferrándiz, R. (2011) 'From Cultural Industries to Leisure and Creative Industries: The Boundaries of the Cultural Field'. *Comunicar* 36, 149-156. Retrieved form http://www.revistacomunicar.com/index.php?contenido=detalles&numero=36&articulo=36-2011-18.

Scolari, C. A. (2009) 'Transmedia Storytelling: Implicit Consumers, Narrative Worlds, and Branding in Contemporary Media Production'. *International Journal of Communication*, 3: 586-606.

Shifman, L. (2007) 'Humor in the Age of Digital Reproduction: Continuity and Change in Internet-based Comic Texts'. *International Journal of Communication*, 1: 187-209.

Szendy, P. (2008) *Listen: A History of Our Ears*. New York: Fordham University Press.

Notes

1   'The Work of Art in the Age of Mechanical Reproduction' was written in 1936, but not translated into English until 1969, in a book edited by Hannah Arendt, *Illuminations* (Benjamin, 1969: 217–251). That was the year of the Berlin Olympics, Picasso's 'Guernica', Riefenstahl's 'Triumph of the Will' and Chaplin's 'Modern Times' – in other words, when old technologies were new. Benjamin's work has yielded a vast bibliography over the past 20 years, particularly after the publication of *The Arcades Project* (Benjamin, 1999b). Many relevant works can be found in the article by Isenberg (2001), while *New German Critique* magazine has devoted several issues to the author: 17 (1979), 39 (1986), and 83 (2001). With regard to technical reproducibility in Benjamin, see Buck-Morss (1989), Carroll (1998), Kaufman (2002), Koepnick (2002) and several essays in Gumbrecht and Marrinan (2003) and Patt (2001).

2   One such occasion, which predates that quoted, is his 'Little History of Photography' (1931/1999: 507–530), with the other two – subsequent – occasions being 'On some motifs in Baudelaire' (1939/1968: 155-200), particularly Epigraph XI, and some of the texts by the convulte J (Baudelaire) of *The Arcades Project* (1999b: 228-386), which date from a similar period to the aforementioned text (between 1937 and 1940).

3   Umberto Eco devotes several chapters of *The Limits of Interpretation* to both serials of a work (#5 'Interpreting Serials') and forgeries (#12 'Fakes and Forgeries'; Eco, 1994). While Munch's serials are similar to what Eco describes in the case of De Chirico (non-identical copies by the author which are but slight variations on the same theme), the 'textual poachers' we are dealing with, whether analog (Jenkins, 1992) or digital (Jenkins, 2006b), practice an intertextuality which does not seek to plagiarize, falsify, or supplant, but rather, to play.

4   Gould argued that one should be free to 'edit' a sonata by Beethoven or a fugue by Bach, cut into it unrestrictedly and apply post-production techniques: '[I]n this way the composer, the *performer and, particularly, the listener, would be better served*' (Gould, 1990: 359). In fact, as Gould himself would admit, the *Fugue in A minor* from volume I of *The Well-Tempered Clavier* included in the record edited by CBS does not correspond to a unique recording of his, but is a rearrangement of two different recordings.

5   *Riders on the Storm* by The Doors and *Billy Jean* by Michael Jackson are mashed up here, in *Billy Jean on the Storm*: http://www.youtube.com/watch?v=BMLFrwK7EYA.

6   One such example is the University of Quebec, with *I Gotta Feeling* by the Black Eyed Peas: http://www.youtube.com/watch?v=-zcOFN_VBVo.

7   Selected fragments of the entire film catalog of Quentin Tarantino: http://www.youtube.com/watch?v=6bdovgjn7BY&feature=related. See also The murder scenes, one after the other, in The Sopranos: http://www.youtube.com/watch?v=JhFeZZflUj4.

8   Using the film *Elephant* by Gus Van Sant, for example, http://www.youtube.com/watch?v=HZ7aAuGukps.

9   Such as the 6th season of *Lost*: http://www.youtube.com/watch?v=AOHVuJC101Y. See also this recap of *The Sopranos*: http://www.youtube.com/watch?v=AsgRwxx7au0.

10 Like this from the Fine Brothers: '100 Movie Spoilers in 5 Minutes'. Pared-down economic resources employed with a fine irony: http://www.youtube.com/watch?v=hN5avIvyIDw.

11 In other words, so-called *transmedia storytelling*, which is described as the professional *strategy* for producing (and promoting) industrial culture (Jenkins, 2006a; Scolari, 2009) consisting of expanding a fictional universe through different media (film, TV, comics, books) and platforms (blogs, forums, wikis, social networks), has its replica in the *tactics* of users, who create an entire parallel and complementary narrative, colonizing the unoccupied narrative spaces, the virgin lands of this universe. Television

series such as *Lost* (ABC, 2001-2006) and *True Blood* (HBO, 2008-), among many others, and also franchises of publishing or movie origin (*Harry Potter, Lord of the Rings, Pirates of the Caribbean*) have not only been expanded through different media and platforms, but have also stimulated creativity in the form of user-generated content. Production teams have often reused, in terms of narrative, what was originally amateur content submitted free of charge online. Three consequences can be highlighted of this strategy-tactics mix in transmedia storytelling: 1) the potential for enjoyment which can be generated by this way of audiences viewing, understanding, and participating; 2) audiences' increased skills and abilities for transmedia surfing; and 3) the adoption and adaptation of the logic of games into mass-media fiction, so that fictions are a place not only of contemplative and essentially passive enjoyment, but also of active enjoyment which demands working with the products, circulating them, enriching them, connecting them with other fictional universes – a tendency toward resolving them like a game.

12   Let us note that almost all of the definitions of digital piracy in circulation (OED, Webster's, Wikipedia) stress that it is the *unauthorized* reproduction or use of something, such as a book, recording, computer program, film, etc. It is paradoxical that condemnation of *unauthorized* copies now has little to do with the actual author who is being copied and more to do with the entity that holds the rights (the publishing house, record label, film distributor). And, by contrast, that the person who challenges this authority often becomes the author (let's say *aug-men-tor*) of the author, in that etymological sense of augmenting or extending an existing work without thereby corrupting it or seeking to arrogate ownership or rights. The condemnation of digital piracy indiscriminately lumps together the action of pirates who trade commercially with works subject to copyright and the action of users who appropriate the work to recreate it, augment it, give it new meaning and a new direction, and then share their product. To identify such piracy, which is often non-venal transit and recreation, with theft – as is done in an unskippable anti-piracy film included in some movie DVDs – is unfair.

13   An urgent question must be raised at this point. It would be naive to ignore the fact that the percentage of users who effectively participate creatively in this postproductivity is, while growing, relatively small. Manovich provides a pertinent figure: in 2007, only between 0.5 and 1.5% of users of the most popular sites classified as social media (Flickr, YouTube, Wikipedia) contributed with their own content. But for the same year, research conducted by Michael Wesch shows that commercially produced videos comprised only 14% of YouTube content, with the remaining 86% made up of user-generated content. Small but highly active communities drive much of this. An added complication, noted by Manovich (2008): how to

draw the dividing line between professional and amateur products? Is it that professionals cannot imitate the 'carelessness', the homemade touch of regular users? Is it that industry professionals (software or hardware manufacturers, Internet or mobile phone service providers, the companies behind the social media) cannot hide what they are, but use contributions to promote profitable traffic to these pages?

14 By the mid-1930s, Benjamin was already speaking of that disconcerting mix between the voracity of cultural and aesthetic stimuli from the public, and (at the same time) the inconstancy, impatience, and dispersed average attention span: 'The film makes the cult value recede in to the background not only by putting the public in the position of the critic, but also by the fact that at the movies this position requires no attention. The public is an examiner, but an absent-minded one' (1969: 240-241). Not only do we find the urgency of pronouncing an opinion here (a non-expert but nevertheless firm opinion), but also the will to participate, for now, in the print culture:

> For centuries a small number of writers were confronted by many thousands of readers. This changed toward the end of the last century. With the increasing extension of the press, which kept placing new political, religious, scientific, professional, and local organs before the readers, an increasing number of readers became writers – at first, occasional ones. It began with the daily press opening to its readers space for 'letters to the editor'. And today there is hardly a gainfully employed European who could not, in principle, find an opportunity to publish somewhere or other comments on his work, grievances, documentary reports, or that sort of thing. Thus, the distinction between author and public is about to lose its basic character. The difference becomes merely functional; it may vary from case to case. At any moment the reader is ready to turn into a writer. (Benjamin: 1969: 231-232)

See Eiland (2003) on these aspects of Benjamin's work.

CHAPTER 17

The Gestural Image: The Selfie, Photography Theory and Kinaesthetic Sociability

PAUL FROSH

A selfie, whatever else it might be, is usually a photograph: a pictorial image produced by a camera.[1] This banal observation informs widespread understandings of the selfie as a cultural category: 'A photograph that one has taken of oneself' (Oxford Dictionaries Word of the Year, 2013: 1). Yet despite the selfie's obvious photographic provenance, little scholarly research has drawn systematically on the intellectual resource most closely associated with the aesthetics of its host medium: photography theory.

In a way this is unsurprising. The selfie is the progeny of digital networks. Its distinctiveness from older forms of self-depiction seems to derive from *non-representational* changes: innovations in distribution, storage and metadata that are not directly concerned with the production or aesthetic design of images. As the 2013 Oxford Dictionaries definition continues, the selfie is typically 'taken with a smartphone or webcam and uploaded to a social media website'. It is these innovations that are thought to distinguish the selfie: 'Instantaneous distribution of an image via Instagram and similar social networks is what makes the phenomenon of the selfie significantly different from its earlier photographic precursors' (Tifentale, 2014: 11).

Recent research on transformations in personal photography *in general* has been largely provoked by these non-representational developments (Lasén and Gómez Cruz, 2009; Lister, 2013; Nightingale, 2007). Their influence has even prompted Gómez Cruz and Meyer (2012) to proclaim the arrival of a new, 'fifth moment' in photography history. And where aesthetic developments are foregrounded, they too appear to be driven by device functions not principally concerned with image production or design. Hence the immediacy, ephemerality and incessant performativity of contemporary everyday photographs are primarily explained with reference to the combined ubiquity, mobility and connectivity of smartphone devices (Murray, 2008; Van Dijck, 2008; Van House, 2011).

Once non-representational technological changes are made analytically pre-eminent, what role remains for an aesthetically-oriented and medium-specific intellectual tradition like photography theory? In fact, the recent prominence of non-representational practices echoes a recurrent tension in photography theory that has long divided scholars: between an 'ontological' commitment to the (largely semiotic) 'essence' of the medium, which tends to privilege the discrete photographic image as an object of aesthetic analysis, and historical conceptualizations of photography as a fluctuating constellation of different devices, material cultural practices, and representational forms (Batchen, 1997). This tension between aesthetic object and socio-technical practice is even evident in two of the adjective-noun compounds recently coined in contemporary photography theory itself: the networked image (Rubinstein and Sluis, 2008) and algorithmic photography (Uricchio, 2011).

The selfie affords a productive vantage point on this tension. On the one hand it appears to constitute an aesthetic and representational innovation in everyday photography, potentially offering a degree of resistance to non-representational emphases (similar claims could be made for popular applications like Instagram and Hipstamatic). Moreover, as a photographic genre, it invites attention to the pictorial conventions underpinning generic identity: after all, one cannot recognize an image *as* a selfie without looking at what it represents.[2] Yet as with genre more broadly, representational criteria alone are insufficient (Mittell, 2001). Understanding that a particular image is a selfie (rather than just a photograph of, say, a face) requires viewers to make inferences about the non-depictive technocultural conditions in which the image was made (Frosh, 2001). It requires, among other things, that these viewers have been adequately socialized through having seen, taken or heard tell of selfies.

The selfie thus foregrounds representational change while putting the very term 'representation' in quotation marks as a contingent variable. This makes it a timely 'theoretical object' (Verhoeff, 2009), a concrete phenomenon that is good to think with about contemporary photography and representation in general. The selfie prompts us to ask how it can be explained using concepts fashioned to illuminate the traditional aesthetics of photography, and how it might reconfigure those concepts to forge new directions for theorizing both photography and digital culture.

In what follows, then, I propose to animate the conceptual fecundity of the selfie by engineering some brief encounters with a number of terms in photography theory: *indexicality*, *composition* and *reflection*. Together these encounters will weave an argument – perhaps surprising, given its emergence from a visually-oriented body of thought – that the selfie is a 'gestural image', and that we should not understand its aesthetics purely in visual terms. Rather, selfies conspicuously integrate still images into a techno-cultural circuit of corporeal social energy, which I will call 'kinaesthetic sociability'. This circuit connects the bodies of individuals, their mobility through physical and informational spaces, and the micro-bodily hand and eye movements they use to operate digital interfaces.

Indexicality

Indexicality is the conceptual bedrock of traditional photography theory. Based on Peirce's notion of the index as a sign that stands for its object through physical or causal connection, it designates the sense that photography is distinctive because what it depicts had, necessarily, to be located in front of the camera at the moment the photograph was taken. The photograph is described as an 'emanation' (Barthes, 2000) of the referent, or a 'quotation' (Sontag, 1977) from reality, since it is produced by light-sensitive material reacting to the light reflected from the spatio-temporal field exposed before the lens.

The supposed loss of photographic indexicality in a putative 'post-photographic' era of digital image simulation was loudly debated in the 1990s (Mitchell, 1992; Robins, 1996). Recent revisions question the simple analogue-digital binary, with claims that the substitution of photo-electronic and computational processes for photochemical and darkroom ones need not have eroded – though it may subtly have altered – photography's indexical quality (Soderman, 2007).

Given this intellectual commotion, what can we learn from the selfie about photographic indexicality that has not already been said? Two things: first, that the selfie as an index is less the trace of a reality imprinted on the photograph than of an action enacted by a photographer; second, that the selfie exploits indexicality in favour of connective performance rather than semantic reference. These two things are intertwined, and they reconfigure photography in relation to distinct dimensions of indexicality that are often fused, which Doane (2007) calls 'index as trace' and 'index as deixis' (see also Niessen, 2011). The former dominates traditional photography theory, casting the photograph as equivalent to a footprint in the sand: a material trace or imprint created by 'contact' with its object, the photograph foregrounds the temporal relation of pastness with its original event. Yet Doane claims that 'index as deixis' is equally important. Deixis is the pointing finger, directing attention onto a present object: as Barthes says, 'the Photograph is never anything but an antiphon of "Look", "See", "Here it is"'. (Barthes, 2000: 5). The connection to deictic language – 'this', 'that', 'here', 'now', and personal pronouns 'I', 'you' etc. – is especially revealing. These terms acquire sense in reference to a present context of discourse which constantly changes: where 'here' is altered from one execution to another. The index as deixis operates in the temporality of the mutable present, rather than of the salvaged past.

Like much everyday digital photography the selfie tips the balance between these forms of indexicality. The advent of photography as a 'live' medium, utilizing digital networks to connect interlocutors in space rather than in time, brings it closer to a conversational practice that draws images and their referents into the immediate moment of discursive interaction (which applications like WhatsApp and especially Snapchat both promote and exploit). It also turns the temporal oscillation of the photograph as trace (Durand, 1993) – between the 'now' of viewing and the 'then' of the depicted scene – into a spatial oscillation between a proximal 'here' and a distal 'there'. The selfie is a form of relational positioning between the bodies of viewed and viewers in a culture of individualized mobility, where one's 'here' and another's 'there' are mutually connected but perpetually shifting (Garcia-Montes et al., 2006). It continually remolds an elastic, mediated spatial envelope for corporeal sociability.

But the selfie does more than this: it deploys both the index as trace and as deixis to foreground the relationship between the image and its producer, since its producer and referent are identical. It says not only 'see this, here, now', but 'see me showing you me'. It points to the performance of a communicative action rather than to an object, and is a trace of that performance. This performance is embodied. As Jerry Saltz observes: '...selfies are nearly always taken from within an arm's length of the subject. For this reason the cropping and composition of selfies are very different from those of all preceding self-portraiture. There is the near-constant visual presence of one of the photographer's arms, typically the one holding the camera' (Saltz, 2014: 4).

The selfie, then, is the culmination and also the incarnation of a *gesture* of mediation. It is an observable 'sensory-inscription' (Farman, 2012) of the body in and through technological means. The body is inscribed in part into an already existing order of interpersonal signification – gestures have meanings in face-to-face interactions – but it is also inscribed as a figure for mediation itself: it is simultaneously *mediating* (the outstretched arm executes the taking of the selfie) and *mediated* (the outstretched arm becomes a legible and iterable sign within selfies – of, among other things, the 'selfieness' of the image). In order to understand more about how the selfie communicates this sensory inscription, another term needs to be brought into play.

Composition

Visual composition usually refers to the arrangement of elements within the space of a picture and their orientation to the position of the viewer (Kress and van Leeuwen, 2004: 181). One key feature of conventional photographic composition that remained relatively unchanged across the analog-digital divide is the spatial separation between photographed objects and the photographer's body. The depicted scene is produced from a position *behind* the camera, a position almost always occupied by the photographer and subsequently adopted by the viewer. Although there is a venerable history of photographic self-portraiture (Lingwood, 1986), literally 'putting oneself in the picture' (Spence, 1986) relies on technological 'work-arounds' like timers or remote control devices, the use of reflective surfaces, or a human proxy. Taking a conventional photograph means, as a rule, not being in it.

This 'backstage' of image-production generates a linear gaze through the apparatus of the camera towards those being photographed. It also encourages a directorial performance of spatial evacuation: photographers shooing unwanted objects off-frame as potential interferences.

Traditional camera design and use – of both analogue and digital devices – means that the camera is not just a machine for making pictures: it is a barrier between visible photographed spaces and undepicted locations of photographing and viewing. Composition, the integration of elements together 'into a meaningful whole' (Kress and van Leeuwen, 2004: 181), is thus based on a foundational *cleavage* between seeing and being seen, directing others and being (com)posed. Such compositional separation tends to underpin asymmetrical power-relations between viewer and viewed (Beloff, 1983; Frosh, 2001; but see Rose, 2010 on the complexity of these relations), drawing its scripts from broader disciplinary 'scopic' regimes shaping social relations (Jay, 1988; Sekula, 1989; Tagg, 1988).[3]

Three features of smartphone design enable the selfie to challenge this spatio-representational segregation: they can be held and operated relatively easily by one hand, they display an image of the pre-photographic scene large enough to be viewed at arm's length, and the inclusion of front- and back-facing cameras. The first consequence of this challenge is that the photographing self is easily integrated into the depiction. The space of photographic production/enunciation is effortlessly unified with the space of the picture itself, and *not* photographing oneself as part of an event or scene becomes an aesthetic, social, political and moral choice (Andén-Papadopoulos, 2014; Becker, 2013) rather than a sine qua non of the photographic act. Group-selfies are particularly striking examples of this transformation, where the photographer is usually at the forefront of a mass of faces and bodies, visibly participating in the process of composing the image as it is taken.[4]

Additionally, the unified space of production and depiction becomes a field of embodied inhabitation. The camera becomes quite literally *incorporated*, part of a hand-camera assemblage, whose possibilities and limitations are mutually determined by technical photographic parameters (available light, field of view, angle, etc.) and the physical potential and constraints of the human body. The most important embodied constellation consists of 1) moving one's outstretched arm holding the smartphone or tablet at a calculated angle before the face or body, 2) the sensorimotor co-adjustment of those body parts which are to be photographed (frequently the face and neck, and 3) the visual and spatial coordination of these two in composing the image to be taken via the device's screen. The very term 'composition' is reconfigured through this constellation. To 'com-pose' acquires a hyphen: no longer does it refer to the arrangement of elements in a representation whose origin it hides, but to the act of *posing together*, mutually emplacing the photographing body and the depicted figure (the famous Oscars Ellen DeGeneres shot). The dominant figuration of the body shifts from the still, invisibly-directed pose of others in traditional everyday photography, to the dynamic, visible, self-animated gestural action of limbs and faces in selfies. That the body is both the platform and the limitation of this new kind of self-depiction is evident from the deliberately extreme examples of photographic pyrotechnics assembled by projects like the 'Selfie Olympics', as well as in reflexive images of oneself taking a selfie.[5]

These 'athletic' examples remind us that taking selfies is not natural to the body: it is an acquired skill and requires practice, the attainment of limbic and manual dexterity (activating the right button/icon to take the picture while often holding the device at extreme angles to maximize headspace), and the calibration of the body to technical affordances and desirable representational outcomes. The selfie is both expressive and disciplinary: this is the duality of most kinds of sensory inscription. Just as the moving body is the platform for the smartphone, so the device is the picturing agency that motivates, justifies and disciplines the body's performance. These two faces of embodied technicity are inherent, and frequently explicit, in ordinary (i.e., non-athletic) selfies, combined – as I have mentioned – in the visible arm gesture or in its implied presence.

Yet that gesture not only 'composes' technicity and embodiment in the moment of image-production: it also constitutes a deictic movement of the body that draws attention to the immediate context of image-viewing, and to the activity of a *viewer*. The suggestive power and versatility of this deictic movement of the photographing gesture towards the viewer is vividly demonstrated in 'Around the World in 360 degrees: 3 Year Epic Selfie' by Alex Chacon, a three-minute video stitching together the photographer's video selfies taken as he traversed '36 countries in 600 days using 5 motorcycles'. A key feature of the film is the use of the outstretched arm, and especially the prosthetic limb of a stick camera-mount, to create a visual-corporeal lexicon of direct kinetic relations between Alex's body and the viewer: walking alongside, hand-on-shoulder, moving counter-balance, circular dance, to name only a few.[6] These (and other) gestures invite the viewer to infer and adopt a physical position in relation to the photographer. Manifested in the suggestion of bodily contact, they propose a particular kind of sociable interaction: the act of accompanying, and the subject-position of companionship.

Murad Osmann's Instagram series 'Follow Me' provides a converse yet parallel example of how a deictic gesture can generate kinetic relations between viewer and viewed.[7] In this project each image is based on an identical formal template, the intrusion of the photographer's arm as he (and by implication, the viewer) is led by the hand by a young woman, always seen from the back in a different location. Unlike the broad lexicon of deictic and kinetic visual figures in Chacon's film, Osmann's series demonstrates the power of a single gesture of implied physical movement and sociable companionship sustained across multiple iterations. As with Chacon's project, however, the outstretched arm (or prosthetic stick mount) doesn't just show the photographer depicting himself. It also draws the viewer in as a gesture of inclusion, inviting you to look, be-with, and act.[8]

Reflection

Oliver Wendell Holmes famously observed that photography is a 'mirror with a memory' (Holmes, 1859/1980: 74). This may have been metaphorically apposite to photography in general, but as we have seen it was not literally applicable to most cameras. The popular iconography of the selfie literalizes Holmes' trope: rather than forming a barrier between photographer and viewed, the smartphone camera produces a reflective image for beholding oneself, apparently resembling nothing so much as a pocket makeup mirror.

It is all too easy, then, to conceptualize the selfie's gestural invitation to look through a voyeurism-narcissism model of mediated performance (Abercrombie and Longhurst, 1998): as others have noted, the accusation of narcissism is one of the most common themes in public discourse about selfies.[9] While there is an enticing self-evidence to the accusation, it is often unnecessarily reductive: with important exceptions like Mendelson and Papacharissi's (2010) analysis of Facebook 'self-portraits', it tends to block further thought – regarding both selfies and narcissism – and frequently ignores its own gendered assumptions linking young women with fickle self-obsession.

Other interpretative extensions of the visual trope 'reflection' provide food for thought. The first, and most obvious, is that the selfie is a reflexive image. Reflexive texts are usually understood to direct attention to the conditions and context of their own presence, activity, or efficacy: they are expressly self-referential (Stam, 1992). With regard to the selfie, this observation itself has two applications. One is that the selfie is self-referential *as an image*. It makes visible its own construction as an act and a product of mediation. Losh (2014) calls this 'transparent mediation': parallel terms would include 'hypermediacy' (Bolter and Grusin, 1999). Not every selfie is reflexive in this sense, though the popular subgenre employing mirrors and screens suggests the achievement of playful, generic self-consciousness.

More prosaically, and perhaps more significantly, selfies are a genre of *personal* reflexivity. This is true of all selfies by definition: they show a self, enacting itself. Selfies extend the photographic grammar of everyday communication: they are an instantly recognizable visual correlate to the linguistic self-enactment routinely performed by reflexive verbs. Indeed, their ability to combine transparent mediation and personal reflexivity reveals the very instability of the term 'self' as a deictic shifter, fluctuating between the self as an image and as a body, as a constructed effect of representation and as an object and agent of representation.

Tied to techno-cultural conditions of synchronous connectivity with others, the self-enactment elicited and shown by selfies is simultaneously mediated, gestural and sociable. These three features combine in the invitation to the viewer implicitly made by the outstretched arm. They also converge through a further twist in the trope of 'reflection': the centrality of imitation and mirroring to human cognition, emotion and communication. Psychological work on imaginative projection and mental simulation (Currie and Ravenscroft, 2002), neurological research on mirror neurons (Gallese, 2005), and aesthetic scholarship on make-believe as the basis for mimesis (Walton, 1990), despite important differences between them, connect human responses to representations with sensory and mental processes that imitate depicted states – especially, though not exclusively, the motor activity of the body. Put very crudely, responses to representations are built upon embodied simulation of what is shown: neurological and/or unconscious mental processes that perform bodily and sensory imitations 'offline'.

These ideas, though contested within their various fields, are extremely fertile for thinking about the selfie as a gestural invitation to distant others. They enable us to conceptualize the selfie as a *sensorimotor* (rather than merely sensory) inscription of a bodily gesture into a still image that summons us to do more than look. The selfie invites viewers, in turn, to make conspicuously communicative, gestural responses. Sometimes, viewers respond to selfies in kind, taking reactive selfies that themselves summon further response: here sensorimotor mirroring is almost literally achieved. In most cases, however, the action is displaced into other physical movements that execute operations via the social media platforms on which the selfies are seen: 'like', 'retweet', 'comment'. Like the selfie, such operations are also performed through sensorimotor actions – actions that are semi-conscious yet habitual to the degree that we might even call them 'reflex': fingers swiping and tapping apps on touchscreens, or scrolling, moving and clicking a mouse attached to a desktop computer. In Osmann's 'Follow Me' series, for example, viewers cannot literally follow the woman's outstretched arm into the image, but the kinetic power of the gesture redirects this sensorimotor potential to a different operation of the hand, and a substitute performance of following: clicking on the 'Follow' icon next to the photograph in the Instagram interface. As a gestural image, then, the selfie inscribes one's own body into new forms of mediated, expressive sociability with distant others: these are incarnated in a *gestural economy of affection* as the 'reflex' bodily responses by which we interact with our devices and their interfaces, through the routinely dexterous movements of our hands and eyes.

Conclusion: the selfie, the phatic body and kinaesthetic sociability

We have moved far from the primarily visual terms of traditional photography theory and the conventional uses of indexicality, composition and reflection. These terms have been steered towards recent conceptualizations of photography as an embodied performance and a material practice (Edwards, 2012; Larsen, 2005), intersecting with accounts of the corporeality of digital culture and its organization of affection (Hansen, 2004). The motivation behind this rethinking of core terms is not mere theoretical whimsy. Rubbing these concepts against the grain of the selfie reveals their enduring productiveness for thinking about photography. It also reanimates photography theory as a truly aesthetic project, in that it is concerned not just with visual semiotic modes, but with broader somatic and sensory dimensions of cultural experience and practice.

That practice is sociable. 'The impulse to sociability distils, as it were, out of the realities of social life the pure essence of association, of the associative process as a value and a satisfaction' (Simmel, 1910/1997: 125). The selfie – deictically indexical, inclusively com-posed, reflexive and reflex – alters and deepens the relationship between photographic mediation and the impulse to sociability.

Two final observations will clarify this claim. The first is that the selfie is linked to phatic communion, 'a type of speech in which ties of union are created by a mere exchange of words' (Malinowski, 1923: 315), whose primary purpose is the production, expression and maintenance of sociability. Miller (2008) argues that contemporary networked culture accentuates a phatic culture of non-substantive communication mediated across distances: his examples are primarily drawn from the banal verbal messages on Twitter and other social network services. The selfie represents a parallel process to this mainly verbal phenomenon: the production of the *mediated phatic body* as a visible vehicle for sociable communication with distant others, who are expected to respond.

Response is crucial: phatic exchanges stage sociability as a binding affective energy transferred between individuals in interpersonal settings, and response is an embodied social reflex – it is hard not to perform it. Highly ritualized and yet profoundly routinized, phatic utterances demand to be requited (Coupland, Coupland and Robinson, 1992). Failure to acknowledge the nod of a passing acquaintance or her casual 'how are you?' is easily perceived as an expression of non-recognition and social exclusion. Yet how are mediated exchanges of responsive phatic energy made possible through the representational form of a still photograph?

This is where the second observation becomes important. The selfie is a pre-eminent conductor of embodied social energy because it is a *kinaesthetic* image: 1) it is a product of kinetic bodily movement; 2) it gives aesthetic, visible form to that movement in images; 3) it is inscribed in the circulation of kinetic and responsive social energy among users of movement-based digital technologies. As a kinaesthetic image, then, the selfie makes visible a broader kinaesthetic domain of digital culture that is relatively overlooked as an object of analysis. This is the limbic, gestural register, overtly apparent in games systems like Wii and Kinnect, that creates a circuit for mediating social and corporeal affective energy by intersecting with two other registers of embodied technicity: 'the mobile' – the mediated mobility of whole bodies in physical and augmented space provided by locative technologies (the body as a single moving data point), and 'the operative' – the habitually nimble coordination of hands and eyes used for navigating the virtual space of interfaces (body parts as media operators). The selfie is thus a new phatic agent in the energy flow between bodily movements, sociable interactions and media technologies that have become fundamental to our everyday, routine experience of digital activities: part of what Hjorth and Pink (2014), following Ingold's work, call digital 'wayfaring'. It is a sign not only of digital photography's agency as a form of popular depiction, but of the further transformations of everyday figural representation as an instrument of mediated, embodied sociability.

Original source and licence

An earlier version of this piece was published in *International Journal of Communication*, vol. 9 (2015). http://www.ijoc.org. Licence: CC BY-NC-ND.

References

Abercrombie, N. & Longhurst, B. (1998) *Audiences: A Sociological Theory of Performance and Imagination*. London: SAGE Publications.

Andén-Papadopoulos, K. (2014) 'Citizen Camera-Witnessing: Embodied Political Dissent in the Age of 'Mediated Mass Self-communication', *New Media and Society*, 16 (5).

Barthes, R. (2000) *Camera Lucida: Reflections on Photography*. London: Fontana.

Batchen, G. (1997) *Burning with Desire: The Conception of Photography*. Cambridge: MIT Press.

Becker, K. (2013) 'Gestures of Seeing: Amateur Photographers in the News', *Journalism* (December 12) online.

Beloff, H. (1983) 'Social Interaction in Photographing', *Leonardo*, 16 (3).

Bolter, J. D. & Grusin, R. (1999) *Remediation: Understanding New Media*. Cambridge: MIT Press.

Crary, J. (1992) *Techniques of the Observer: On Vision and Modernity in the Nineteenth Century*. Cambridge: MIT Press.

Coupland, J., Coupland, N. & Robinson, J. (1992) '"How Are You?" Negotiating Phatic Communion', *Language in Society*, 21.

Currie, G. & Ravenscroft, L. (2002) *Recreative Minds: Imagination in Philosophy and Psychology*. Oxford: Oxford University Press.

Doane, M. A. (2007) 'The Indexical and the Concept of Medium Specificity', *Differences*, 18 (1).

Durand, R. (1993) 'Event, Trace, Intensity' in *Discourse*, 16 (2).

Edwards, E. (2012) 'Objects of Affect: Photography Beyond the Image', *Annual Review of Anthropology*, 41.

Farman, J. (2012) *Mobile Interface Theory: Embodied Space and Locative Media*. New York: Routledge.

Frosh, P. (2001) 'The Public Eye and the Citizen Voyeur: Photography as a Performance of Power, *Social Semiotics*, 11 (1).

Gallese, V. (2005) 'Embodied Simulation: From Neurons to Phenomenal Experience', *Phenomenology and the Cognitive Sciences*, 4.

Garcia-Montes, J. M., Caballero-Munoz, D. & Perez-Alvarez, M. (2006) 'Changes in the Self Resulting from the Use of Mobile Phones, *Media, Culture and Society*, 28 (1).

Gómez Cruz, E. & Meyer, E. T. (2012) 'Creation and Control in the Photographic Process: iPhones and the Emerging Fifth Moment of Photography', *Photographies*, 5 (2).

Hansen, M. (2004) *New Philosophy for New Media*. Cambridge: MIT Press.

Hjorth, L. & Pink, S. (2014) 'New Visualities and the Digital Wayfarer: Reconceptualizing Camera Phone Photography and Locative Media', *Mobile Media and Communication*, 2 (1).

Holmes, O. W. (1859/1980) 'The Stereoscope and the Stereograph', in A. Trachtenberg (ed.) *Classic Essays on Photography*. New Haven: Leete's Island Books.

Jay, M. (1988) 'Scopic Regimes of Modernity', in H. Foster (ed.), *Vision and Visuality*. Seattle: Bay Press.

Jay, M. (1995) 'Photo-Unrealism: The Contribution of the Camera to the Crisis of Ocularcentrism', in S. Melville and B. Readings (eds.), *Vision and Textuality*. London, UK: Macmillan.

Kress, G. & van Leeuwen, T. (2004) *Reading Images: The Grammar of Visual Design*. London: Routledge.

Larsen, J. (2005) 'Families Seen Sightseeing: Performativity of Tourist Photography', *Space and Culture*, 8 (4).

Lasén, A. & Gómez Cruz, E. (2009) 'Digital Photography and Picture Sharing: Redefining the Public/Private Divide', *Knowledge, Technology and Policy*, 22 (3).

Lingwood, J. (ed.) *Staging the Self: Self-portrait Photography 1840s-1980s*. London: National Portrait Gallery.

Lister, M. (2013) *The Photographic Image in Digital Culture*. Abingdon: Routledge.

Losh, E. (2014) 'Beyond Biometrics: Feminist Media Theory Looks at Selfiecity', *Selfiecity* at http://selfiecity.net/#theory.

Malinowski, B. (1923) 'The Problem of Meaning in Primitive Languages', in C. K. Ogden and I. A. Richards (eds.), *The Meaning of Meaning*. London: Routledge and Kegan Paul.

Mendelson, A. & Papacharissi, Z. (2010) 'Look at Us: Collective Narcissism in College Student Facebook Photo Galleries', in Z. Papacharissi (ed.), *A Networked Self: Identity, Community and Culture on Social Network Sites*. New York: Routledge.

Miller, V. (2008) 'New Media, Networking and Phatic Culture', *Convergence*, 14 (4).

Mitchell, W. (1992) *The Reconfigured Eye: Visual Truth in the Post-photographic Era*. Cambridge: MIT Press.

Mittell, J. (2001) 'A Cultural Approach to Television Genre Theory', *Cinema Journal*, 40 (3).

Murray, S. (2008) 'Digital Images, Photo-Sharing, and Our Shifting Notions of Everyday Aesthetics', *Journal of Visual Culture*, 7 (2).

Niessen, N. (2011) 'Lives of Cinema: Against Its 'Death'', *Screen*, 52 (3).

Nightingale, V. (2007) 'The Cameraphone and Online Image Sharing', *Continuum: Journal of Media and Cultural Studies*, 21 (2).

Oxford Dictionaries Word of the Year 2013. Retrieved from http://blog.oxforddictionaries.com/press-releases/oxford-dictionaries-word-of-the-year-2013.

Robins, K. (1996) *Into the Image: Culture and Politics in the Field of Vision*. London: Routledge.

Rose, G. (2010) *Doing Family Photography: The Domestic, the Public and the Politics of Sentiment*. Farnham: Ashgate.

Rubinstein, D. & Sluis, K. (2008) 'A Life More Photographic: Mapping the Networked Image', *Photographies*, 1 (1).

Saltz, J. (2014) 'Art at Arm's Length: A History of the Selfie', (January 27) *Vulture.com* at http://www.vulture.com/2014/01/history-of-the-selfie.html.

Sekula, A. (1989) 'The Body and the Archive', in R. Bolton (ed.), *The Contest of Meaning: Critical Histories of Photography*. Cambridge: MIT Press.

Simmel, G. (1910/1997) 'The Sociology of Sociability', in D. Frisby & M. Featherstone (eds.), *Simmel on Culture: Selected Writings*. London: SAGE Publications.

Soderman, B. (2007) 'The Index and the Algorithm', *Differences* 18 (1).

Sontag, S. (1977) *On Photography*. New York: Doubleday.

Spence, J. (1986) *Putting Myself in the Picture*. London: Camden Press.

Stam, R. (1992) *Reflexivity in Film and Literature: From Don Quixote to Jean-Luc Godard*. New York: Columbia University Press.

Tagg, J. (1988) *The Burden of Representation: Essays on Photographies and Histories*. London: Macmillan.

Tifentale, A. (2014, February 14) 'The Selfie: Making Sense of the "Masturbation of self-image" and the "Virtual mini-me"', *Selfiecity* at http://selfiecity.net/#theory.

Uricchio, W. (2011) 'The Algorithmic Turn: Photosynth, Augmented Reality and the Changing Implications of the Image', *Visual Studies*, 26 (1).

Van Dijck, J. (2008) 'Digital Photography: Communication, Identity, Memory', *Visual Communication*, 7 (1).

Van House, N. A. (2011) 'Personal Photography, Digital Technologies and the Uses of the Visual', *Visual Studies*, 26 (2). doi:10.1080/1472586X.2011.571888

Verhoeff, N. (2009) 'Theoretical Consoles: Concepts for Gadget Analysis', *Journal of Visual Culture*, 8 (3).

Walton, K. (1990) *Mimesis as Make-believe: On the Foundations of the Representational Arts*. Cambridge: Harvard University Press.

Notes

1   The author would like to thank Zohar Kampf, Ifat Maoz, Amit Pinchevski, Limor Shifman and Julia Sonnevend for their readings of an earlier version of this article.

2   The need for at least basic representational criteria is evident from the sampling design of projects like *Selfiecity* (http://selfiecity.net/#dataset): 'To locate selfies photos, we randomly selected 120,000 photos (20,000-30,000 photos per city) from a total of 656,000 images we collected on Instagram. 2-4 Amazon's Mechanical Turk workers tagged each photo. For these, we asked Mechanical Turk workers the simple question "Does this photo show a single selfie?"'.

3   Significant controversies about the historical stability of visual modes in modernity are elided here for lack of space. Crary (1992) is well known for disputing any simple claim of continuity between the photographic camera, 19th and 20th century visual regimes, and the 'camera obscura' model of vision that preceded them. Jay (1988) associates photography with two different 'scopic regimes' connected with painting, and also argues that photography simultaneously strengthens and undermines modern 'ocularcentrism' (Jay, 1995).

4   Ellen DeGeneres' group Oscar selfie from 2014 is a perfect illustration of this point: http://www.smosh.com/smosh-pit/photos/30-hilarious-pics-selfie-olympics.

5   See 'The 31 Best Selfies From The First Annual Selfie Olympics' on Distractify, http://old.distractify.com/news/the-best-selfies-from-the-first-annual-selfie-olympics-i-cannot-believe-how-far-people-took-it.

6   Alex Chacon 'Around the world in 360° - 3 year epic selfie': https://www.youtube.com/user/chaiku232.

7   Murad Osmann #followmeto Times Square, http://instagram.com/muradosmann.

8   Purists may question whether Osmann's images are really selfies. The photographer's arm is a perpetual visual synecdoche for his presence in his own images: hence if they are not 'true' selfies they are sufficiently close to be of relevance. Thanks to Gefen Frosh for help on this point.

9   For a critique of the popular (and scholarly) charge that the selfie is narcissistic, see *The Carceral Net*: http://thecarceralnet.wordpress.com.

CHAPTER 18

The New Technological Environment of Photography and Shifting Conditions of Embodiment

Mika Elo

In 1889 George Eastman, the founder of Eastman Kodak Company, introduced the No. 1 Kodak camera with the catchy slogan 'you press the button, we do the rest'. While photography still involves pressing the button the 'we' and the 'rest' have transformed significantly during the last few decades. In the age of information, 'photography has come to exist within a new technological environment', as Martin Lister aptly puts it (2007: 251). This shift has wide-reaching cultural consequences that also involve our bodily existence, even if no significant changes can easily be recognized at the level of the trigger finger.

It is a widely recognized fact that images are involved in thinking processes. Their status, however, has been heavily disputed. The figurative elements of thinking have been seen now as a sign of weakness of thinking, now as its innermost strength. Logical empiricism and early romanticism could be used to mark the two extremes in this regard.

Thinking, however, does not only rely on imaginative elements that refer to our bodily experience; it also takes place in the body. Body is the place where the intellect and the senses come together and constitute meaningful thinking. Referring to Immanuel Kant's 'transcendental aesthetics' we could say that the body schematizes. It makes an 'image' of reality, and, at the same time, takes part of it as an image-like unit. Further, the question as to whether and how thinking finds its place in images is a theme taken up by several philosophers and media theorists. It is all but self-evident how to demarcate the place of thinking with regard to living and non-living bodies and the images they, in one way or another, embody.¹

In the discussions concerning the relations between image, body and thinking, interestingly enough, attention has often been turned to photography. In Jacques Rancière's discussion of the pensiveness of images, photography constitutes a paradigmatic example (2009). In *How Images Think* Ron Burnett takes up photography as a good example of intelligence programmed into images (2004). Jean-Luc Nancy, in turn, has paid attention to an analogy between the Cartesian *cogito* and photography (2005). He writes: 'Every photograph is an irrefutable and luminous *I am* ... Like the other *ego sum*, this one is made explicit as an *ego cogito*. Photography thinks ...' (Nancy, 2005: 105, emphasis in the original). Nancy also insists on the inseparability of body and thinking in Descartes: 'for Descartes, the *res cogitans* is a body' (Descartes, 2008: 131).

Against this background it seems that image, body and thinking relate to each other in a circular way: both body and thinking make use of images, both images and bodies think, and both thinking and images involve a body. Should one break this circle or should one dive into it? I choose the latter: I dive in, since I think that this seemingly vicious circle can be turned into a productive one, even if it soon becomes obvious that one touches here upon the limits of conceptualization.

I want to ask how photography contributes to this frame of 'bodily schematism'. I will focus on the question of haptic realism and the way it builds on the interplay of three aspects of embodiment that I would like to call (1) physical body, (2) phenomenological body and (3) libidinal body. The notion of 'haptic realism' refers here to the peculiar role that touching (both in tactile and in affective terms) plays in representations that are considered realistic. Using these terms, I will develop a hypothesis that aims at indicating how a certain shift in the cultural status of touching might contribute to reshaping the 'photographic' conditions of embodiment in the age of information.

Photographic distance and proximity

It has become one of the commonplaces of recent media theoretical debates to state that digital media transform the frame of human experience. It is not difficult to find a consensus on this general level of the diagnosis of a shift. It is easy, for example, to agree on the fact that digital media are changing our sense of time and space – the conditions of our bodily existence – in many ways. Distance and proximity, both in physical and mental sense, take new forms. The task of theoretically articulating the details and the transformation mechanisms of experience that is at stake here is, however, a much more complicated matter and leads to numerous questions and debates.

In these debates photography is often claimed to be an outmoded medium as we live in digital or even post-digital culture. Photography is, however, booming like never before, both in terms of quantity of images produced and multiplicity of new photographic technologies and practices. In its current state of rapid transformation and diversification photography shows rich cultural potential, a situation comparable to the first decades after the invention of photography in 1839. As a consequence, photography research is facing new challenges and gaining new importance.

Today, photographic technologies are linked to new production and publishing structures that alter the ways photographs circulate. This has multifaceted social, economical, political and theoretical consequences that are difficult to decipher. What to think, for example, of the fact that with the help of metadata that accompanies the digital image, moments of capturing, processing, presentation and distribution can be automatically interlinked in ways that go beyond visual mastery of spatiotemporal relations? To use Lev Manovich's terms, it would seem that digitally mediated photographs are part of another kind of 'cultural interface' or 'cultural software' than film-based photography (2001). The cultural status of photographic images is undergoing a transformation. My question will be: how to articulate this in terms of 'bodily schematism?' How are the intimate connections between body, thinking and photography currently changing?

The sense of touch offers a productive starting point for an enquiry into these questions. The highly ambivalent role that touching has in western thinking is symptomatic of the tensional relation between physiological, mental and technical aspects of sentience. Touch twines together physical and psychical movements and intensifies them in pleasure and pain. To touch is always, in one way or another, to touch a limit, to push it and to test it, and, in the same instance, to attest to it. Touch is sentience at the limits, and thus an exemplary figure of reconfiguration.

In contrast to other senses, at least seemingly, the sense of touch makes the sensing and the sensed coincide. When I see a stone, it is 'out there' and does not see me, but when I touch that stone, it is 'right here' and touches me. This sense of concreteness and immediacy lends the sense of touch a certain credibility. A seen stone can be made of plastic even if it looks just like a stone, but when I touch it I can feel the material. It is due to this fullness of touching that the tactile metaphor of 'grasping' can stand for 'fully understanding something'. From this point of view the sense of touch appears as uncomplicated and immediate. On closer inspection, however, its status as a sense is rather difficult to grasp. In fact, it is more appropriate to speak of *senses* of touch, since touching exceeds the tactile world and encompasses also immaterial aspects of experience. Due to its multifaceted characteristics touch also challenges representational thinking in many ways (Elo, 2012).

Photographs make this evident in a poignant way when they touch us at the same time as they withdraw themselves from the realm of tangibility and meanings. As Margaret Olin points out, there is a tension between the ways in which photographs involve looking and touching: 'the two activities seem to alternate like a blinking eye, as though we cannot do both at the same time' (Olin, 2012: 2). This implies that our grasp of photographs does not take place in the light of knowledge only. One might recall here also the thought-provoking claim that Roland Barthes makes in *Camera Lucida*, according to which 'a photograph is always invisible' (Barthes, 1981: 6). Visibility falls short of explaining the ways in which we relate ourselves to photographic images. A photograph is touching when it provokes speech by being mute, and when it opens up a space for thinking by a gesture of closing itself off, by being individually separate and distinct. In other words, photograph's entry to the realm of representations is mediated besides vision also by a distant touch – not unlike an eye contact that seizes the gaze only as absent (Olin, 2012: 3).

Touching is a moot point in western conceptions of embodied experience due to its peculiar role as a mediator between the material and immaterial aspects of reality. Different conceptual articulations and arguments, however, almost invariably share the 'haptocentric' idea that touching is a way of locating and guaranteeing the contact between different elements of experience (Derrida, 2005). On this basis, reality is understood as being-in-touch-with-something-real. The matter is further complicated by the fact that the different parties to this contact have many names in our tradition: soul, mind, psyche, reason versus body, flesh, sensuality, etc. Correspondingly, the contact itself has been studied from the point of view of religion, intuition, reflection and synapses.

Touch, as a mediator between processes of signification, affectivity and materiality, figures prominently also in discourses on photography. Various forms of contact play an important role, especially whenever photography is inscribed into the tradition of 'true images' (*vera icon*) or 'self-generated images' (*acheiropoietoi*). Variations of this scheme can be found in Henry Fox Talbot's ideas of 'natural magic', C. S. Peirce's 'indexical' sign function, André Bazin's 'objectivity', and Roland Barthes's discourse on 'punctum' (Geimer, 2011: 28-30). With regard to the digitalization of photography the role of touching in its relation to seeing is, however, highly ambivalent. This is not quite unexpected, since, in the experiential horizon of digital technology, the status of touch as a guarantor of tangible reality would appear unstable, as a great deal of what we consider real is anything but tangible – even when we find it touching. At the same time, touch as tactility plays an important role in various forms of interface design. There the implicit aim is to functionalize touch and to integrate it into a system of digital mediations in order to increase the sense of instantaneity and realism. In these settings, touch tends to become represented as a sense that works in synchrony with vision offering a support for optical intuitionism. The question arises of how to relate tangibility to the conceptual, affective and mental dimensions of touch or feel.

In the 1990s much of the discussion concerning the digitalization of photography focused on questions of difference between the digital and the analogue. Digitalization was often seen as a fundamental shift comparable to the invention of phonetic writing (Stiegler, 2002) or that of central perspective (Mitchell, 1992). These debates led to various reconsiderations of the peculiar convergence between notions of photographic realism and discourses of indexicality (Frohne, 2002; Green and Lowry, 2003; Wortmann, 2003). Today, as photography has come to exist within a new technological environment, questions of connectivity, mobility and metadata are also starting to play an important part in considerations of the photographic 'reality effect'. In Frieder Nake's terms, we could say that at the same time as there are ever more invisible indices on the 'subface' that are made operative in the construction of photographic 'reality effects', the digital 'surface' is modelled on photographic looks familiar from film-based photography (Nake, 2008). Photoshop filters such as 'film grain' and 'lens flare' are in this respect telling examples.

What strikes me in these debates is the way in which most conceptions of photographic evidence tend to rely on ideas of continuity and causality. Photographic 'reality effect' – regardless of whether it is held to be a result of context-related signification or material mediation – seems to be modelled on the 'haptocentric' idea according to which the 'real' is something we can grasp mentally or touch physically, and, ideally, both in a synchronous way. In short, the rhetoric of photographic realism builds, in one way or another, on the continuity of chains of reference.

At first glance there would seem to be a clear contrast between mental continuity and sensuous contiguity, between the sign and the trace. On closer inspection, however, we can discern that the trace-like character of the photographic image relies, in the last instance, on some kind of authorization, an 'authorizing legend' that establishes the continuity of chains of reference (Wortmann, 2003). It is telling that even if photographs (and the various layers of metadata attached to them) can be used as pieces of evidence in court, they cannot replace a testimony. The photographic trace needs to be authorized, i.e. 'culturally generated' (Wortmann, 2003: 222). The other side of the coin is that signification processes need to be embodied, i.e. bundled and incorporated, in order to be effective.

Haptic realism

I would go as far as to claim – this is my hypothesis – that the very notion of photographic realism is 'haptocentric' in the sense that it tends to function as a vehicle for reproducing the idea of touch as an objective sense, i.e. as haptic sense operating in the realm of physical bodies. In short, visual capture combined with perceptual and cognitive recognition tends to objectify bodies.

This operation tends to conceal something that we, following Bernhard Waldenfels, could call the 'pathic moment' of touching (Waldenfels, 2002: 14-16). The term 'pathic', derived from the Greek word *pathos*, refers to sensibility, affectedness and suffering. Inherent to the term, although normally ignored, is the concrete sense of being exposed to something excessive and unexpected that can even leave painful marks, such as wounds. In a word, 'pathic moment' refers to exposedeness that is implicated in all forms of touching.

Following Waldenfels it can be argued that as regards the phenomenological body, touching constitutes a prototype of 'pathic experience' (Waldenfels, 2002: 71). It is the felt sense of being in the world, of being exposed: to touch is always also to be touched. Although touching is contact with the touched, there remains something inaccessible and withdrawing, something even untouchable inherent to the touched. This withdrawal lends to the contact an affective tension: the touched becomes touching. In other words, touching is over-determined by otherness as strangeness, and it turns out to manifest traits of a 'foreign-sense', with respective ethical significance (Waldenfels, 2002: 64). This elemental asymmetry tends to be ruled out when touching is studied in terms of immediacy and symmetry of a contact.

As a prototype of 'pathic experience' touch turns out to be a complex field of sensing and feeling. In short, it is the making sense of various encounterings. This elementary function implies that when we consider the sensory distance, we cannot take the separateness of sensor and sensed as our point of departure, because to be exact, they are only articulated as such in touching. Furthermore, the question what should be invested in the positions of sensor and sensed is historical. To be able to study the suspension of sensory distance we must take into account 'phenomenotechnics', i.e. the technical and technological conditions of each particular time, since the experiences of distance and proximity are also always articulated in relation to them (Waldenfels, 2002: 361-2). This shows how the pathic structure of touch brings out the elemental role of technics in the constitution of experience.

My hypothesis is that in the 'haptic realism' the photographic contact is conceived of in terms of immediacy and continuity, despite its obvious asymmetry. This takes place predominantly in the name of visibility. This implies that, as 'hapto-visual' appropriation, photography tends to reduce different dimensions of touch to tactility, that is, to an order where all distinctions are made between the same and the other and where there is the structural possibility for a third party to assess these distinctions. In contrast to this realm of objective contact between visible surfaces of physical bodies, touch as exposedness has to do with existential integrity, a depth, from which any objectifying third party is excluded. This pathic moment of touching is about separation between own and alien, between self and stranger, and remains a matter of singular experience. Touch as a pathic sense is a sense of exclusion of a third party.

'Haptic realism' would thus be about conflating or confusing these two orders. It would be about equalizing the ways in which distinctions between the same and the other can be made and the ways in which a self separates itself from a stranger. In other words, in haptic realism phenomenological bodies would, tendentiously, be modelled on physical bodies. Here photography builds on a long tradition, since this kind of haptocentric conception of the sense of touch has been operative in western thinking from Plato to Husserlian phenomenology as, for example, Jacques Derrida has painstakingly shown (2005).

The tendency to confuse these registers derives form the visual accuracy of photography as light-writing. This has consequences as regards both material mediation and signification processes. With regard to material mediation, the optical laws of light-writing suggest a natural link between the iconic and the indexical aspects of the depiction. As regards signification processes, in turn, the visual accuracy of the photographic image makes it more tempting to look through the image and see it as a visual representation of an absent thing than to see the image as a strange presentation that brings forth something which finds its origin in the image itself. In both cases there is a tendency to conflate iconicity and indexicality, and to measure photographic evidence in terms of visual likeness.

Formatting embodied experience

Digital forms of photography both reaffirm and destabilize this link between iconicity and indexicality. On the one hand, the relation between the 'subface' and the 'surface' tends to be conceived of (and programmed) in terms of hapto-visual appropriation. On the other, the affective tension potentially involved here turns out to be non-programmable. I try to explicate this ambivalence with regard to the third aspect of embodied experience that I introduced at the outset: the libidinal body.

Here I would like to take up the interesting argument made by Cathryn Vasseleu that digital technologies contribute to the 'formalization of touch' by instituting touch as an objective sense – with the objective of making contact and staying in touch (Vasseleu, 1999: 159).² According to her, digital technologies tend to prioritize haptic appropriation and grasping by detaching the objective side of touching from its affective qualities. The result is an enhanced polarity between two interacting modes of touching: hypersensitive 'ticklishness' that is detached from all functional object relations and 'haptic touch' exemplified by the omnipotence of the finger as regards the horizon of real-time telecommunication. This has implications for the libidinal body. This is also the decisive point where I see that digitality changes something in the intricate interplay between image, body and thinking that I call 'bodily schematism'.

In so far as 'ticklishness' is a domain of tactile experience that is out of self-coordinatable control, it cannot have any pre-programmed function in digital telecommunication networks, since these are built on the idea that being in contact equals perception that one is in touch with someone or something. It nevertheless plays an important role in digital tactility.

The enhanced polarity between the two modes of touching that Vasseleu discerns can be seen as a symptom of a transformation of tactile experience that finds its articulation also in the new technological environment of photography. This enhanced polarity becomes tangible in situations where the feedback structure of an interface is engaging at the same time as it lets the lability of the mediated contact come to the fore. Various forms of visual live streaming and instant photo sharing could be used as examples of this.

The psychodynamics of these operations can be studied in terms of Freudian vocabulary. In his article on denial, Sigmund Freud foregrounds parallels between thinking and perceiving by suggesting that they are both based on a 'palpating impetus' (*tastender Vorstoß*), that is, a feeling and testing of the limits between inside and outside. This tactile process of demarcation offers a basis for psychic structures and various defence mechanisms, such as denial. Freud states that repressed representations can enter into the consciousness under the precondition that they are denied. Denial is a process of rationalization that disconnects affectivity from representation. The integration of repressed representations into consciousness takes place only on an intellectual level, and the affective implications of the repressed are cut off (Freud, 1999: 12–15).

Denial depends on an intellectual judging function (*intellektuelle Urteilsfunktion*), which concerns questions of inclusion and exclusion (13). The ego decides if something is to be taken in or excluded. The reverse side of this intellectual decision is something Freud calls 'reality testing' (*Realitätsprüfung*) (14). The ego tests if an intellectually accepted and thus internalized representation also reappears in perceived reality. What is at stake in both functions is a decision between the inside and outside. The subjective exists only inside, whereas everything that counts as objective must exist outside as well. This double operation of internalization and reality testing makes sure that the relation between the inner representations and their counterparts in outer reality can be mastered.

Against this background, 'haptic realism' in digitally mediated photography can be understood as denial of the ambivalence of touch. It is an operation that secures the division between the inside and the outside by representing the affective and physical aspects of contact as relatively autonomous dimensions. Hereby, tactility is prioritized and made into the paradigm of touching. Further, as a media technological form of denial 'formalization of touch' appears as a 'reality test' that contributes to consolidating those patterns of communication and affective behaviour that fit to its formats.

Following Bernard Stiegler one could also take up Freud's nephew Edward Bernays' theory of industrial manipulation of libido, according to which 'the fight against economic crises required harnessing consumers' desire to lead them to consume things they did not need' (Stiegler, 2011: 224). As the facilitation of the passage from need to desire this 'harnessing' allowed for the manipulation of the desire itself, because the passage is constituted by phantasm, i.e. the realm of objects that has reality only in the framework of desire. In other words, the harnessing of consumers' desire is like set design as regards the staging of the desire in a phantasm. For Stiegler, the central question is, who is in control of this set design? In his analysis, the globalized culture industry has led to intensified exploitation of libidinal energy that accelerates the decomposition of desire into drives. In his scenario, finance capitalism itself, epitomized by the short-term investments of the stock market, becomes drive based. '[T]he rule of the short term is the rule of the drive. The drive wants everything right away: it wants immediate satisfaction' (Stiegler, 2011: 226).

With regard to the new technological environment of photography, the phantasmatic structure of the libidinal economy becomes tangible, if we think of the ways in which various forms of interactivity that involve photographic images endow the user with a sense of power at the same time as the status of the objects gained access to remain suspended. Typically, the developers of multimodal interfaces set as their goal not only the richness and realism of sense feedback but also the pleasure that the user can experience. The idea is to have everything related to the system smoothly to hand. When this happens, the pathic moment of touch and the ethical dimensions of feedback remain in a dead angle. The focus is on feedback that affirms recognition and forms in its functionality a circle that feeds the sense of selfpower.

Conclusion

The difference between 'haptic realism' in film-based and in digitally mediated photography, according to the initial analysis presented here, would thus lie in their different ways of enhancing hapto-visual appropriation. Whereas the haptic realism of film-based photography tends to reduce touch to tactility by modelling phenomenological body on physical body, digital environments add to this an affective shortcut by customizing information with regard to the physical body (and its metonymic figure, the omnipotent finger). In their new technological environment photographs engage the viewers, or perhaps more precisely *the users*, more and more often by being hotspots. With regard to the tensional relation between vision and touch this implies that it is the affective link between the user's body and digital information that tends to motivate the visual appearance of media contents in digital culture, whereas in pre-digital visual culture the most powerful substrate of affectivity was made up by visual appearances. In both cases the pathic moment of touching tends to be concealed. In Stiegler's vocabulary, this kind of tendency is regressive: it marks the destruction of desire and the passage to the level of unbounded drives. This process takes the form of a 'disordering of the aesthetic' that, despite of its regressive tendency, opens up also the possibility for a 're-constitution of a new libidinal economy' (2011: 227-35).

The rather schematic and hypothetical argument I have presented here has the implication that when analysing photographic truth claims and reality effects we should take into account not only technological formats but also conceptual, affective and sensuous processes of formatting. As I have indicated, a careful consideration of the multiple senses of touch operative in haptic realism offers a productive starting point for this. Against this background, the new technological environment of photography appears as a site where the ambivalent tendencies of touch are negotiated. Photographic interfaces, i.e. the ways in which photography faces the body, provide something like an 'aesthetic horizon' for the experience in the age of information by engaging the contradictions of our time at the level of the senses.[3] The way in which these processes are intertwined in and through photographic images makes up the highly ambivalent and historically variable setting of photographic conditions of embodied experience.

Original source and licence

M. Elo (2013) 'The New Technological Environment of Photography and Shifting Conditions of Embodiment', in A. Fisher, J. Golding & D. Rubinstein (eds), *On the Verge of Photography: Imaging Beyond Representation*. Birmingham: ARTicle Press, 87-102. Permission to republish granted.

References

Anzieu, D. (1989) *Le Moi-peau, Paris: Bordas. The Skin Ego*. New Haven: Yale University Press. Trans. Chris Turner.

Barthes, R. (1981) *Camera Lucida. Reflections on Photography*. New York: Hill and Wang.

Belting, H. (2011) *An Anthropology of Images: Picture, Medium, Body*. New Jersey: Princeton University Press.

Boehm, G. (2007) *Wie Bilder Sinn erzeugen. Die Macht des Zeigens*. Berlin: Berlin University Press.

Bredenkamp, H. (2010) *Theorie des Bild-Akts*. Frankfurt am Main: Suhrkamp.

Burnett, R. (2004) *How Images Think*. Cambridge: MIT Press.

Derrida, J. (2005) *On Touching – Jean-Luc Nancy*. California: Stanford University Press.

Elo, M. (2012) 'Digital Finger: Beyond Phenomenological Figures of Touch', *Journal of Aesthetics and Culture*, vol. 4, doi: 10.3402/jac.v4i0.14982.

Freud, S. (1999) 'Verneinung' in *Gesammelte Werke*, vol. XIV (eds), A. Freud et al. Frankfurt am Main: Fischer Verlag.

Frohne, U. (2002) 'Berührung mit der Wirklichkeit. Körper und Kontingenz als Signaturen des Realen in der Gegenwartkunst' in H. Belting et al. (eds), *Quel Corps?* Munich: Wilhelm Fink Verlag.

Geimer, P. (2011) 'Self-Generated Images', in J. Khalip & R. Mitchell (eds), *Releasing the Image: From Literature to New Media* (California: Stanford University Press.

Green, D. & Lowry, J. (2003) 'From the Presence to the Per-formative: Rethinking Photographic Indexicality', in D. Green (ed.) *Where is the Photograph?* Kent and Brighton: Photoworks/Photoforum.

Hansen, M. B. (1999) 'The Mass Production of Senses: Classical Cinema As Vernacular Modernism', *Modernism/Modernity* 6 (2).

Head, H. & Holmes, G. M. (1911) 'Sensory Disturbances from Cerebral Lesions', *Brain*, 34 (2-3).

Kant, I. (2007) *Critique of Pure Reason*. London & New York: Penguin.

Krois, J. M. (2011) *Bildkörper und Körperschema*. Berlin: Akademie Verlag.

Lister, M. (2007) 'A Sack in the Sand. Photography in the Age of Information', *Convergence: The International Journal of Research into New Media Technologies* 13 (3).

Manovich, L. (2001) *The Language of New Media*. Cambridge: MIT Press.

Merleau-Ponty, M. (1945/1962) *Phenomenology of Perception*. London and New York: Routledge.

Mitchell, W. J. (1992) *The Reconfigured Eye: Visual Truth in the Post-Photographic Era*. Cambridge: MIT Press.

Nake, F. (2008) 'Surface, Interface, Subface: Three Cases of Interaction and One Concept', in U. Seifert, J. Hyun K. & A. Moore (eds), *Paradoxes of Interactivity. Perspectives for Media Theory, Human-Computer Interaction, and Artistic Investigations*. Berlin: Transcript.

Nancy, J. L. (2005) *The Ground of the Image*. California: Stanford University Press.

Nancy, J. L. (2008) *Corpus*. New York: Fordham University Press.

Olin, M. (2012) *Touching Photographs*. Chicago and London: University of Chicago Press.

Rancière, J. (2009) *The Emancipated Spectator*. London and New York: Verso.

Stiegler, B. (2002) 'The Discrete Image', in *Echographies of Television*, J. Derrida & B. Stiegler. Cambridge: Polity.

Stiegler, B. (2011) 'The Tongue of the Eye: What "Art History" Means', in J. Khalip & R. Mitchell (eds), *Releasing the Image: From Literature to New Media*. California: Stanford University Press.

Vasseleu, C. (1999) 'Touch, Digital Communication and the Ticklish', *Angelaki* 4 (2).

Waldenfels, B. (2002) *Bruchlinien der Erfahrung. Phänomenologie Psychoanalyse Phänomenotechnik*. Frankfurt am Main: Suhrkamp.

Wortmann, V. (2003) *Authentisches Bild und authentisierende Form*. Cologne: Von Halem Verlag.

Notes

1   'Bodily schematism' and 'embodiment' have been conceived from numerous points of view. On the one hand, thinking has been seen as an embodied phenomenon, and on the other, a certain 'schematicism' has been linked to body. About 100 years ago, Henry Head and Gordon Morgan Holmes introduced the notion of body scheme in neurology (1911), and this notion has figured in many ways in the biological sciences ever since (Callagher, 2005). On the side of the humanities Jacques Lacan's theory of the 'mirror stage', Didier Anzieu's (1989) theory of 'skin-ego' and Maurice Merleau-Ponty's (1962) phenomenology of perception have been widely influential in studies of different aspects of embodied experience. Interesting attempts to articulate the dynamic exchange between bodies, images and thinking can be found also in contemporary 'image science', or, *Bildwissenschaft* (Belting, 2011; Boehm, 2007; Bredenkamp, 2010; Krois, 2011).

2   Vasseleu refers to Immanuel Kant's *Anthropology* and the ambivalent position *Berührung* (referring both to tactility and affectivity) takes there

with regard to the distinction between objective and subjective senses (Vasseleu, 1999: 155).

3   I borrow the very useful term of 'aesthetic horizon' from Miriam Bratu Hansen. According to her analysis of early twentieth century mainstream film culture, so-called 'classic cinema', 'not only traded in the mass production of the senses but also provided an aesthetic horizon for the experience of industrial mass society' (Hansen, 1999: 70). It 'engaged the contradictions of modernity at the level of the senses' and contributed to the 'mainstreaming' of the emergence of mass culture (70).

CHAPTER 19

Authorship, Collaboration, Computation? Into the Realm of Similar Images

Katrina Sluis

Photographers may think they are bringing their own aesthetic, epistemological or political criteria to bear. They may set out to take artistic, scientific or political images for which the camera is only a means to an end. But what appear to be their criteria for going beyond the camera nevertheless remain subordinate to the camera's program.

(*Vilém Flusser, Towards a Philosophy of Photography*).

I feel like everyone sort of has the same photos.

(*Hannah, respondent in a 2008 Facebook study*).

In 2011, Google added a 'search by image' feature to its suite of search products. Capitalising on advances in computer recognition, the tool enabled users to find images with similar 'visual fingerprints' spread across the web. On Google's search blog, Johanna Wright, Director of Search Product Management, described its value as follows: 'You might have an old vacation photo, but forgot the name of that beautiful beach. Typing [guy on a rocky path on a cliff with an island behind him] isn't exactly specific enough to help find your answer. So when words aren't as descriptive as the image, you can now search using the image itself' (Google: Inside Search). Being able to search 'visually' was the latest method through which one might overcome the fallibility of human memory in an age of accelerating data. Its launch presented Google as an indispensable aide, collaborator and confidante for your digital lifestyle. Or, as Google VP Marisa Meyer phrased it: 'Your best friend with instant access to all the world's facts and a photographic memory of everything you've seen and know' (Google: Official Blog).

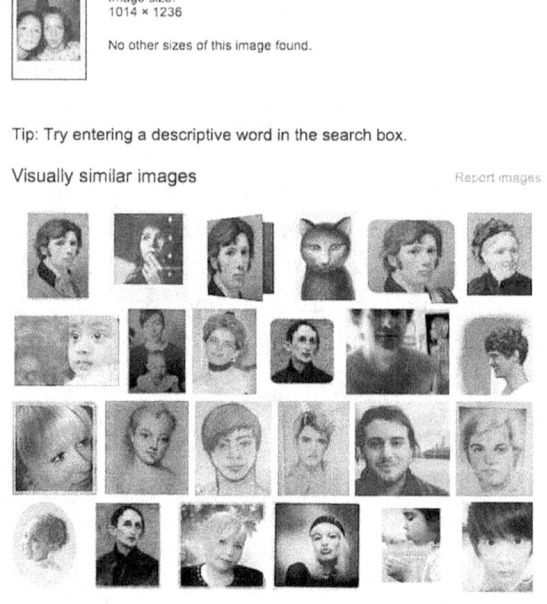

Figure 19.1 Erica Scourti, 'search by image' from *So Like You*, 2014

Through the magic of pattern-recognition algorithms, Google would be there to help you recall names and locations, and create novel vectors between your snapshots and billions of others in only milliseconds. By temporarily unifying groups of dispersed images hosted on remote web servers, the tool offered itself up as a kind of networked, protological vision machine. Just as image tagging had transformed Web 2.0 platforms, here was a technology that offered a new navigational paradigm for the image 'cloud'. But, whereas tagging was an important part of the social life of platforms such as Flickr, with 'reverse image search' it became possible to plot a course through a web of images using the ordering logic of the machine's gaze. Think your #srsly #cute #scottishfold #cat is unique? Think your enhanced high-dynamic-range photo of the Franz Josef glacier viewed from the altar window of Waiho church in the South Island of New Zealand is unique? Think again. The grouping, aggregating and tracking online of images 'visually' made it possible to discover images that were *just like yours*, and escape the image-language problem of previous archival taxonomies.

Authorship and collective labour in an image cloud

Perhaps unsurprisingly, it was not in the potential imag(in)ing of collective memory but in the arena of rights management that Google's reverse image search was quickly co-opted by photographers. Professionals and amateurs alike praised the tool for its ability to track an image's reuse online in order to 'catch copyright crooks' and 'recover what is rightfully yours'. Rather than sending photographers into a spiral of angst around the cultural politics of reproduction, 'search by image' became the Holy Grail for a community intent on defending its authentic creativity against an information economy that valorises the real-time exchange of multiple, simultaneous, orphaned images.

But the question of how to be acknowledged as an author – with all the economic and social capital that entails – is not just limited to professional photographers in network culture. The pursuit of self-realisation through creative digital labour has been a defining feature of social media in an era characterised by hyper-individualism (observe the rise of the 'selfie') and hyper-consumption (observe the rise of the 'selfie, holding my new boutique pet'). Within neoliberal culture we are all invited to endlessly re-invent ourselves, turn our life into a work of art and, in the process, make ourselves transparent to software and to each other. How, then, might it be possible to be recognised as a unique individual with a creative voice when Instagram has made everyone's photos look the same?

In considering this paradox, it is worth returning to a question that has haunted photography since its inception: is photography a technology of reproduction or a tool for artistic expression? The problem with the latter, as critics point out, is that the collective labour that makes photographic reproduction possible (from design and marketing to manufacturing and display) is rendered invisible when the photograph is limited to a creative act originating in the mind of an individual photographer. And despite the increasing automation of photography, this model of modernist authorship persists in the rhetoric of consumer electronics manufacturers, museums, and university photography courses alike. But when the act of viewing, searching or tagging an image online potentially changes its visibility, velocity and legibility, the separation of author from audience, individual from crowd becomes extraneous. Not least because today's web architectures have become 'social machines' in which the boundaries between computations performed by machine logic and those that result from human sentiment are increasingly interwoven.

Collaborating with machines

It is precisely this meshwork of humans and non-humans, images and code that the artist Erica Scourti attends to in her practice. Setting out to test the limits of self-expression in a fully mediated culture, her work explores the tension between the desire to be (or believe oneself to be) authentic and singular within it. Subjecting her life to the gaze of the machine (and keenly aware of the implicit narcissism), Scourti has collaborated with security experts, software platforms, Googlebots and other network users in her search for self-knowledge. Informing her approach is an understanding that sharing the digital detritus of our lives may connect us to a host of interested and interesting unknown people, in ways that ultimately require us to be readable to others (and their non-human agents) too.

In *Life in AdWords* (2012–13), Scourti wrote and emailed her diary to her Gmail account over a year, collecting the keywords that Google had scanned and harvested for targeted advertisements. She read the results to her webcam wherever she happened to be that day, creating video portraits of her life as mined and understood by Google's algorithms. Rather than a document of authentic or quotidian experience, Scourti explains that her diary became a compilation of 'clusters of relevant ads, making visible the way we and our personal information are the product in the "free" Internet economy'. Hijacking and making visible the commercial exploitation of personal data, the project uses the intimate mode of the

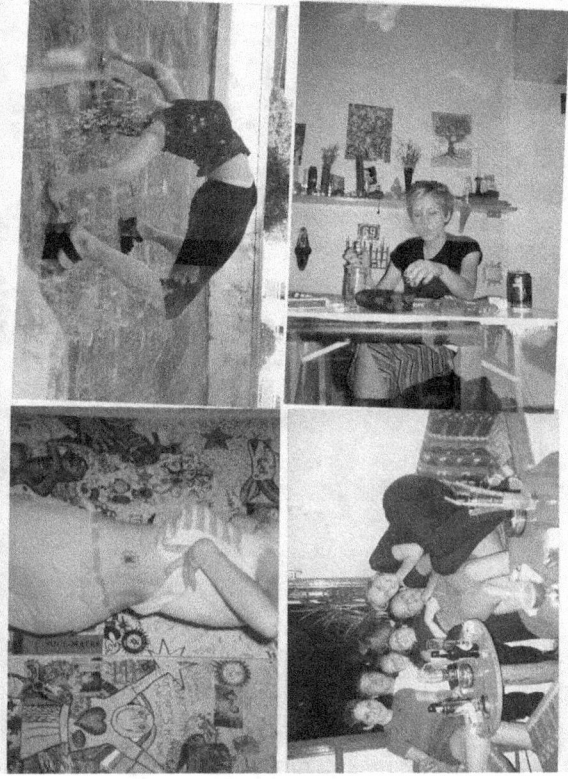

Figure 19.2 Erica Scourti, from *So Like You*, 2014

webcam confession in order to raise the question of whether there is any area of life that can't be assimilated and commodified through the power of computer analytics.

In approaching her commission for Brighton Photo Biennial 2014, Scourti set out to discover what happens when statistical correlations are used to delineate existing links between things and direct relationships between people. Beginning with the specificity of her own personal memory – in the form of documents, love letters, snapshots and other ephemera – she used Google's 'search by image' function to create a version of her own life through the discovery of thousands of other images that visually resemble it. Brought into this process was an array of network users who gained a temporary closeness with Erica not through shared interests but through the statistical similarities determined by Google's

288 Katrina Sluis

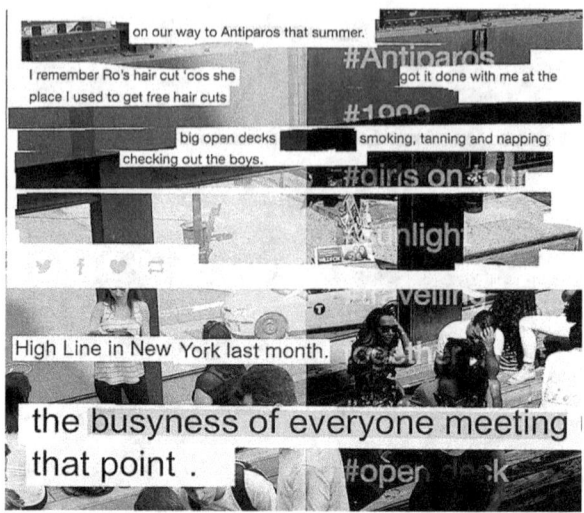

Figure 19.3 Erica Scourti, from *So Like You* Tumblr, 2014

VisualRank algorithm. Her investigation into the mediation of the self through software also has links to the increasingly popular paradigm of the statistically derived or quantified self – in which one's own identity makes sense as part of a wider demographic. With this in mind, Scourti asks us to consider how this tension between the individual and the collective be staged in relation to the images we capture and continuously share? What does it mean to open oneself up to metadata? What possibilities become available when you acknowledge software as a collaborator in the reflexive project of the self?

Scourti's work helps to highlight the way that a photograph's value might not lie in the specificity of its content but in its legibility to machines and the data generated around it. Whilst photographers continue to demand control of their intellectual 'property', ownership and monetisation of the data that accumulates as a by-product of our collective creativity remain less contested. This is, of course, what Getty understood when it decided to give away its image assets for 'free' – with the condition that we permit it to harvest information about the photograph's use. This reflects a paradigm shift in which there is less value to be extracted from individual images than from the relations between them. These relations tell us much about audience sentiment, patterns of consumption and potential future demand for images. The situation has wider implications for culture, as data-driven decision-making becomes the latest business meme to cross over into UK arts policy. One wonders if, in the future, it will be Getty and not the gallery that will serve as an example of what an audience-responsive, market-driven, image-serving organisation might look like in tune with the public's cultural desires.

Original source and licence

An earlier version of this text was published as (2014) 'Authorship, Collaboration, Computation? Into the Realm of Similar Images', with Erica Scourti, *Photoworks, Brighton Photo Biennial*: 150-159. © Katrina Sluis. Permission to republish granted.

References

Flusser, V. (2000) *Towards a Philosophy of Photography*. London: Reaktion Books.

Google: Inside Search, 'Search by text, voice, or image', http://insidesearch.blogspot.co.uk/2011/06/search-by-text-voice-orimage.html. Accessed on 18 June 2014.

Google: Official Blog, 'The future of search', http://googleblog.blogspot.co.uk/2008/09/future-of-search.html. Accessed on 18 June 2014.

CHAPTER 20

The Horrors of Visuality

Rob Coley

PART I

[T]he supernatural has returned – not in the guise of answered prayers or divinely sanctioned holy wars, but via the panoply of media objects that satellite us and that are embedded into the very material fabric of our bodies, cities, and lives. (Thacker, 2014: 95).

Monstrous Media

In his terrifying essay-cum-horror-story on the then nascent logic of 'control', Gilles Deleuze warned of a power that writhes and flexes like the 'coils of a serpent' (Deleuze, 1992: 7). Speculating on the transformative implications of the digital, he told of an ontological power, an adaptable power performed in complex systems of mediated communication, a power no longer restricted by the space-time of modern institutions. In this story, a monstrous control operates in the form of computational stimuli, functioning socially and biologically, infiltrating bodily relations so as to cultivate an addiction to its influence. The aim of such a power is not to fix or restrict radical energies but to manage or generate such processes by massaging relational potential, by mediating the becoming of the world.

Here, in three short essays, I briefly consider how the 21st century actuality of such a monster might demand an adjustment in the study of visuality. To begin, it is important to stress that this does not mean supplementing 'visual culture' with 'new media'. Indeed, the apparent newness of new media, so highly venerated by the culture industries, is a problematic designation, to say the least. There is often nothing particularly *new* about new media – media continually rework their older forms, continually revisit and transmute their own past. Instead of asserting claims to newness, the role of the digital should rather be seen as lying in its tendency to refocus attention on what media *do*, on the transformative powers of media, on the ability of media to invisibly affect the overall 'conditions of possibility' (Galloway et al., 2014: 1). In a society of control, any study of visuality must therefore also be a study of media, and this means taking on 'media and mediation as conceptual objects in their own right' (Galloway et al., 2014: 2).

In doing this, the canonical issues and concerns of photography studies, and visual culture studies more generally, do not suddenly become irrelevant, but the way in which these issues are approached must change. This is precisely because the fundamental paradoxes of mediation make the task of theorizing visuality today so challenging, to say nothing of the disappearing possibilities for 'countervisuality'. Specifically, though visuality is understood here, with Nicholas Mirzoeff (2011), as a matrix of power that is undoubtedly visual in its expressions and symptoms, it is also now clear that the activities of visuality are enacted prior to, or beyond, representation. Moreover, in the 21st century, contact with, and experience of, visuality can be increasingly understood to function on the basis of what, in Deleuzian terms, we might call a 'disjunctive synthesis' of the pure immediacy and total opacity of mediation. In cultivating this relation between materiality and abstraction, it is a power that domesticates and exploits paradox.

In this context, mediation is something that cannot be examined discretely, in the way that media objects tend to be studied. This is to insist on a departure from studies of media long preoccupied with an opposition between technological determinism and social constructivism. In this opposition, agency is understood to lie either with technical machines which causally determine the future form and function of society, or with the humans who produce and use technologies to wield such power through various representations. It is on the basis of such disciplinary investments that, even in recent attempts to radically reassess the concept of visuality, media is still understood as a series of technical objects that maintain and uphold dominant ideologies. However, with the increasingly seamless integration of such objects into the social habits of everyday activity, it seems that any act of *counter*visuality must begin by addressing 'modes of mediation *that refuse bi-directionality, that obviate determinacy, and that dissolve devices entirely*' (Galloway et al., 2014: 10). Beyond representation, this is a question of belief – belief in what psychical researcher William James called 'the reality of the unseen', belief in the communication of something incommunicable, in a truth which exceeds the conventions of rationalism. The digital prompts us to reconsider our belief in a realm we had long since given up on. And so, to confront the monster, countervisuality must tactically aspire to make flesh creep (James, 1982: 63).

From beyond

McKenzie Wark (2012: 68) gives shape to such a tactic by calling for the identification of weird moments, anomalous irruptive events, when the paradoxes of control reveal an 'after image', a peripheral glimpse of the monster. One suitably weird moment occurred in December 2013, when a now infamous image was made public via the official Twitter account of the Office of the Director of National Intelligence (ODNI), an agency headed up by retired lieutenant general James Clapper, principal advisor to Barack Obama on issues of national security. Set against an emblematic starfield, the illustration depicts a giant cephalopod seizing hold of the planet Earth (figure 20.1). One of its arms, or tentacles, grips hold of the planet, while others stretch and unfurl. The creature glowers, which is to say, in anthropomorphic terms, that it wears an evil expression. Emblazoned below it is the motto, 'Nothing is beyond our reach'. As revealed by follow-up photographs tweeted from the ODNI account, this menacing creature is the official insignia of the latest in a series of spy satellites launched under the auspices of the National Reconnaissance Office, the US government agency responsible for satellite intelligence (figure 20.2). Further tweets gave updates on the favorability of rocket launch from Vandenberg Air Force Base, along with a link to a gallery of images produced by the organization which provides space launch services for the US government. A video of the launch itself was later posted on the Facebook page of the 30th Space Wing. 'Anyone stay up late to watch?' asked the ODNI in a tweet.

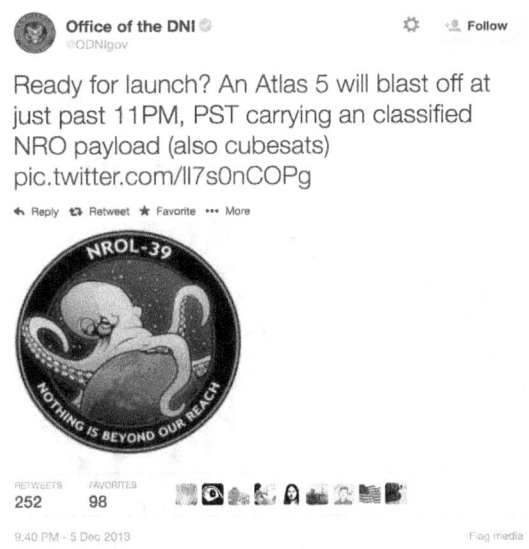

Figure 20.1. The ODNI unveil the NROL-39 logo. Image from ODNI Twitter account, original available at: https://twitter.com/ODNIgov/status/408712553179533312, accessed February 4, 2014.

The oblique announcement is at once transparent and opaque, open and secret. In this odd exercise in public relations, in which something that remains invisible is branded, the announcement publicizes and draws attention to an event – a blast off – while revealing only that the event is classified. The same paradox is central to artist Trevor Paglen's *Symbology* series. Traversing restricted landscapes and tracking classified objects, Paglen's work attempts to map what his sources and informants call the 'black world'. *Symbology* is an ongoing project to collect the heraldic patches and insignias designed for secret military units. Among these cryptic logos (or 'gang colors', as one of Paglen's sources puts it), there are tongue-in-cheek references to popular conspiracies concerning Area 51 (as seen in the bug-eyed faces of alien 'grays'), together with examples of frat boy humor (as seen in the recurring presence of a character from MAD magazine). But there is also a dominance of occultural iconography – the wizard, the serpent, and the all-seeing eye familiar to mystical practice. Moreover, the evil world-dominating cephalopod also appears in Paglen's series of patches (figure 20.3).

294 Rob Coley

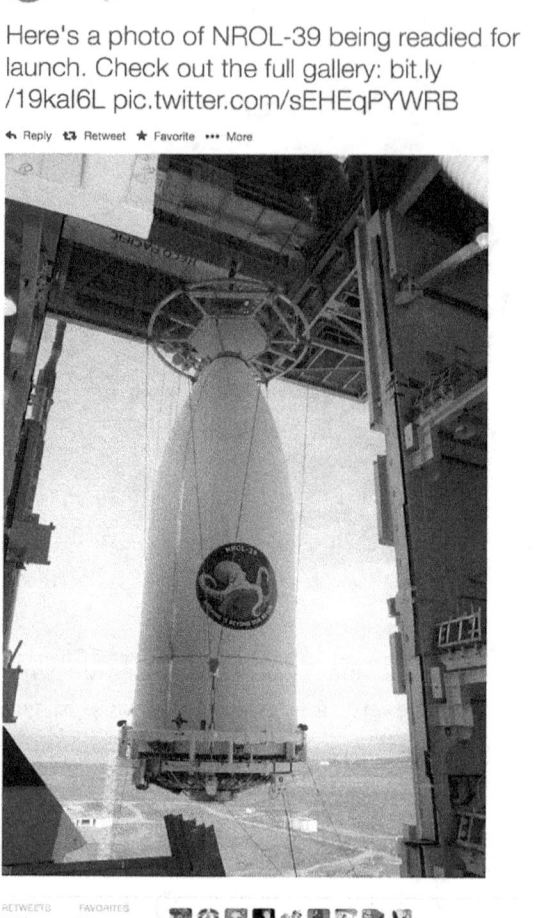

Figure 20.2. The NROL-39 payload, ready for mating with an Atlas V booster rocket. Image from ODNI Twitter account, original available at: https://twitter.com/ODNIgov/status/408715995008598016, accessed February 4, 2014.

The real paradox of this image lies not only in its communication of something that must not be communicated, but also in its communication of something that cannot be communicated. It is weird because

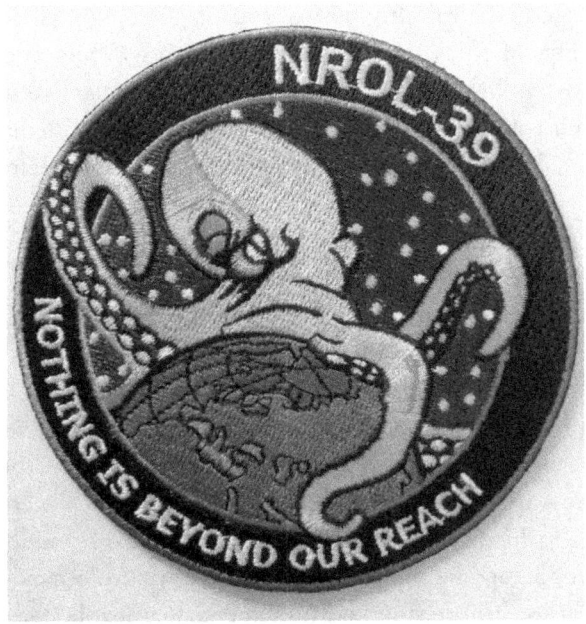

Figure 20.3. Image by Trevor Paglen. Original available at: https://twitter.com/trevorpaglen/status/390580113840283648/photo/1, accessed February 4, 2014.

it provides a creeping glimpse of a power 'from beyond'; as an image, it 'works too well', it communicates 'more than we bargained for' (Thacker, 2014: 102). This is, however, the paradox that conditions all mediation, and to consider it more closely we must grasp the monster's tentacle.

Problematized ontology

For novelist China Miéville, the tentacle is 'the default monstrous appendage of today', and it 'signals the epochal shift to a Weird culture' (2008: 105). Today, weird fiction, once relegated to the status of supernatural pulp horror, is accorded classic status and revered by a new generation of writers, fiction and non-fiction alike. Indeed, in contemporary cultural theory, references to the work of H. P. Lovecraft – the key proponent of what Miéville calls haute-weird – are so widespread as to practically constitute a field in itself. The genre's earlier form came in something of a radical break from the conventions of Gothic storytelling, with monstrous cephalopods, and their multiplicity of suckers, first taking hold of the pre-Weird writings of Jules Verne and Victor Hugo. While myths and legends of monsters have always been a part of the collective imaginary of the sea, in the 19th century major technological developments altered the way in which the sea was represented, and in which it reflected new anxieties about a changing world (Grant, 2013: 24-30). It was, though, only in the 20th century, with Lovecraft's Kraken-inspired Cthulhoid creatures, that an emergent media culture began to be conceived as a Weird culture, a culture in which the human's centrality and dominance over the nonhuman was increasingly thrust into a state of crisis.

Of course, the Lovecraftian Weird is itself paradoxical. On one hand, the writer's unsettling narratives express an explicit desire to escape the mechanistic prison house of human space-time, while, on the other, this desire remains inseparable from 'a loathing of the alien materialisms he conjures up in his fiction' (Lockwood, 2012: 75). The sudden encounter with a cephalopodic monster offers an escape from meaning; it is, in Miéville's terms, 'unprecedented, unexpected, unexplained, unexplainable – it simply is'. Yet at the same time, this encounter threatens and overwhelms the stable aesthetic of the human. Such is the power of the humble octopus. Once identified by the pattern recognition procedures of human perception (having previously employed camouflage and mimicry to remain hidden in plain sight), the creature is recognized as a possible form. And yet this form is horrifying precisely because it transgresses the solidity and specificity we normally associate with being: 'The octopus is problematized ontology' (Miéville, 2008: 109). It expresses the potentiality of a weird world, a 'cosmic outsideness', as Lovecraft put it, in which the outside is immanent to – within and beyond – the human (Lovecraft, 1933).

In the 20th century, problematized ontology is central to the early development of a weird culture. As Dean Lockwood suggests, it is marked by the departure of the octopus from the sea and its institution within the network. In his account, the evolution of a 'networked, tentacular' horror is inseparable from the evolution of media. Specifically, 'the affective core' of Lovecraft's writing took shape in the immediate context of 'the new wireless traffic in media messages', namely early commercial broadcasting (Lockwood, 2012: 80). The radio set, ensconced in the living room, is 'invasive, tentacular and alien', a whisper in the darkness (Lockwood,

2012: 81). The development of broadcast radio marks a shift from an oceanic model of media, one in which early wireless communication is conceived as a vast sea of noise, a roiling flux in which it is possible to become lost, to a network model of media in which radio captures and controls a mass audience. Yet, in harnessing the transformative 'waves of forces' that create and destroy, in subjecting the forces of a Dionysian world, Nietzsche's 'monster of energy', to control, there is something about our contemporary network culture that retains the vastness of the ocean. Today, our relations with media can unmoor old dualistic certainties and produce an encounter with the systems of feedback embedded within everyday life. In such encounters, human life – previously understood as a separate determining force – is revealed as part of an assemblage of forces, a supernatural composition of processes both human and nonhuman. It is this 'weird media', as Thacker (2014: 133) puts it, that 'indicates a gulf or abyss between two ontological orders', between the natural and the supernatural.

In part 2, I will begin to outline how a horrifying encounter with such an abyss might be formulated in the critical practice of countervisuality.

PART II

> Once again, the secret world won... And once again, the border between the black and the white dissolved. Everything became gray. It was hard to tell where one world ended and the other began. (Paglen, 2010: 273)

Weird media

Trevor Paglen describes his practice of countervisuality in terms of adjusting attentional habits and perceptual tendencies. To identify weird glitches in the system of control, he emphasizes the need to remain attuned to its occlusions. 'It's difficult to figure out what goes on behind the restricted airspaces, the closed doors, the cover stories, and the official denials of the Pentagon's black world' (Paglen, 2008: 4). This black world is one of closely guarded secrets, a covert world that, for the most part, remains entirely hidden. From time to time, though, Paglen suggests, 'the black world peeks out into the "white" world, and those paying attention can get a fleeting glimpse' (11). This is not, however, a process of enlightenment, or simply a consequence of having seized the right to look. Indeed, Paglen's black and white worlds seem all too dualistic for the soupy miasma of mediation and its weird paradoxes.

Let us instead imagine a countervisuality more directly inspired by supernatural horror. For Thacker, horror is the mode of thought most suited to an increasingly unthinkable world. It seizes upon the paradoxical moments 'in which thinking enigmatically confronts the horizon of its own possibility' (Thacker, 2011: i). As he describes it, dominant modes of thought and perception presume the world to be a human world: for us, governed by us. Alongside this subjective, human-centric world, we also acknowledge an objective nonhuman world-in-itself that exists in an 'already-given state', that is, until the very moment that we perceive it and transform it into a world for us (Thacker, 2011: ii-iii). Arguably, these are the dominant terms by which visuality has been conceived up to now, that is, by focusing on the formation of a world picture, on a comprehensive representational object. For Thacker, though, horror confronts a third category beyond the subjective and objective world – a world without the human (Thacker, 2014: 113). This is a hidden, occulted world that cannot co-exist with the human-centered world, a world that can only become perceptible 'after' the human. The horror in question, then, is one of *negation* – it does not express the emotional fear of a human in a human-centered world, but a horror produced in the confrontation of the very limits of the human. It is a communication with or mediation of something from beyond that, simultaneously, remains a communication breakdown, a failure to mediate anything more than a void. Its irruptive power is generated by the mediation of lacunae, blind spots. Its weirdness is an event, a perceptual encounter with something for which our habitual patterns of recognition cannot prepare us.

In Thacker's terms, this weird space-time is a 'magic site', a place in which 'the hiddenness of the world presents itself in its paradoxical way' (Thacker, 2011: 82), which is to say that what is revealed is the site's own hiddenness. In horror fiction the magic site is, on occasion, specifically constructed by humans as a device through which an occulted world might be accessed. It is, though, usually produced spontaneously or accidently, without design. Moreover, it is not 'black'. Rather, as Thacker describes, such sites manifest the occulted world as mists, fogs and slime. Magic sites are marked by their betweenness: by formless clouds both material and immaterial, by oozing states that inhabit both liquid and solid form, by grayness. If black and white worlds are separate worlds set in opposition, a gray world is one in which such categories are in open communication with one another. And yet, this does not mean that grayness is simply a ratio of black and white. On the contrary, it is produced by the careful composition of a multiplicity of colors, a spectral *prism*, it is the color of the whole.

Ancient revelations

We now know about PRISM. We know about the collection of data from the servers of Microsoft, Yahoo, Google, Facebook and Apple. We know about Boundless Informant, the NSA's tool for metadata analysis, for the real-time examination of data flows. In the UK, we also know about the government's Tempora project, we know about 'Mastering the Internet' and 'Global Telecoms Exploitation', the project's component parts. For Geert Lovink, such enlightenment is a rude awakening – the Snowden revelations bring to an end three decades of naïve media rhetoric and celebration. The revolutionary dreams of cyberculture, in which 'media' becomes synonymous with 'future', are exposed as a waking nightmare: 'The values of the internet generation have been dashed to pieces: decentralization, peer-to-peer, rhizomes, networks. Everything you have ever clicked on can and will be used against you' (Lovink, 2014). Affirmative Deleuzian-inspired discourses of acceleration – collective flights toward future trajectories – are exposed as the very energies, which feed the monster of control. Futures have been foreclosed.

By contrast, for Wark, although the Snowden documents illustrate a current form and strategy of power, there is nothing radically new about these revelations. The dialectic of escape and capture has been integral to every era of communication – surveillance has always been part of telephonic networks, just as it was part of the networks of express mail that preceded them (Wark, 2014). Indeed, this would all seem to confirm current theories of visuality. Take, for example, the science-fictional images of the NSA's Information Dominance Center (figure 20.4). Last

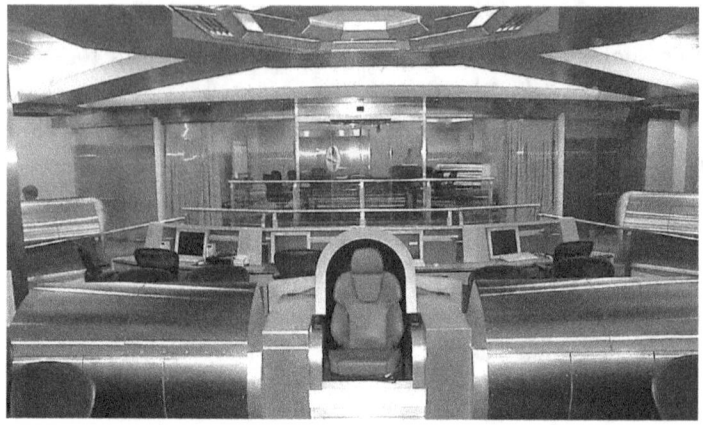

Figure 20.4. The NSA's Information Dominance Center. Image by DBI Architects, original linked at: http://www.theguardian.com/commentisfree/2013/sep/15/nsa-mind-keith-alexander-star-trek [no longer accessible].

year, the journalist Glenn Greenwald published excerpts from the architect's brochure of the Center based at Fort Belvoir in Virginia. The document notes that designers were asked to model the space on the command bridge from Star Trek's Enterprise. The space was fitted out with 'chrome panels, computer stations, a huge TV monitor on the forward wall, and doors that made a "whoosh" sound when they slid open and closed. Lawmakers and other important officials took turns sitting in a leather "captain's chair" in the center of the room and watched as [NSA chief General Keith] Alexander, a lover of science-fiction movies, showed off his data tools on the big screen' (Greenwald, 2013). The architect's brochure goes on to state that 'the prominently positioned chair provides the commanding officer an uninterrupted field of vision to a 22'-0" wide projection screen,' while the primary function of the center 'is to enable 24-hour worldwide visualization, planning, and execution of coordinated information operations'.

Such power would seem directly aligned to the historical legacy of visuality, a term Mirzoeff (2011) traces to 19th century historian Thomas Carlyle. For Carlyle, visuality is an authoritarian perceptual activity, one that endows the heroic commander with a power both techno-scientific and mystical.[1] In this account, visuality's truth-giving authority worked precisely against the kind of grayness produced by excitable states of social flux and disequilibrium. Visuality was a force that shone 'like a polestar through smoke-clouds, dust-clouds, and all manner of down-rushing and conflagration' (Carlyle, 1841). It would, then, be easy to take images of the NSA's Information Dominance Center as confirmation of the continuing operation of a visuality that functions to maintain transcendent order, that ensures future order remains bound to a certain truth and realism, while the irrationalities of other, virtual potentials remain closed off. And yet, the danger of reducing all of visuality's current manifestations to mere iterations of its historical form – wielded by a commander – is that it remains all-too-human in its conception.

Indeed, following the Snowden leaks, we now also know that the vast majority of data intercepted from fiber-optic cables is unexamined by humans.[2] It is software that sieves metadata, that conducts complex pattern analysis, that searches for 'triggers' (MacAskill et al., 2014). Here, as Deleuze warned us (Deleuze, 1992: 5), the individual becomes the 'dividual', the network subject, depersonalized as packets of potential. Moreover, the gray infrastructure of distributed computing through which such power is exercised – wi-fi networks, apps, system protocols, passwords, verification procedures, traffic routers and switches, firewalls – is an assemblage of biological and technological actors, 'a restless expanse of multihued contaminations, impurities, hybridity, monstrosity, contagion, interruption, hesitation, enmeshment, refraction, unexpected relations, and wonder' (Cohen, 2013a: xxiv). There is, though, something neutral, something bland about this technological unconscious: this 'gray media'. Its unspectacular operation, its 'dull opacity of devices and techniques', mostly eludes our attention (Fuller and Goffey, 2012: 1). And yet, grayness is not flat or uniform – it is dynamic, it remains in continuous transition. These states of disequilibrium are, as Mirzoeff insists, the strategic environment for visuality's new cultural counterinsurgency, but the newness of this mode of power is not what concerns us here.

What makes revelations about PRISM so terrifying is, instead, the disclosure of something older, something more ancient. PRISM is an attempt to command and coordinate prismatic multiplicity, this spectrum of possible relations and agencies, human and nonhuman. It aims to manage escape and capture systematically, which is to say non-dialectically, extracting and generating difference from a single set of relations – relations from which no godlike perspective is possible. It therefore reveals to us what we were already. It reveals the alien immanent to the human. It reveals our instability, our in-betweenness. It reveals that 'we are media' (Kember and Zylinska, 2012: 13).

In the third and final part of this essay series, I will reflect further on the vitality of this gray middleness and propose that practices of counter-visuality must remain immanent to its weird processes.

PART III

> *Conflict with time* seems to me the most potent and fruitful theme in all human expression. (H. P. Lovecraft: 1933)

Shades of gray

In the Deleuzian horror story, control operates on the basis of modulation. It is a power both supple and subtle, adjusting from one moment to the next. Media theorists Matthew Fuller and Andrew Goffey take the idea of modulation seriously. For them, processes of mediation create 'a troubling opacity and thickness in the relations of which they are a part'. These are processes 'with an active capacity of their own to shape or manipulate the things or people with which they come into contact' (Fuller and Goffey, 2012: 5). The consequence is that mediation generates 'opaque zones', the compositional form of which Fuller and Goffey describe in terms of grayness.

Typically, grayness is conceived in anthropocentric terms, that is, as a depletion of life, as a running down of energy and vibrancy, as an absence of human vitality. A gray world is a post-disaster world, a world in which the human is all but snuffed out (Cohen, 2013b: 270). In the collective imaginary of the 21st century, gray is the color endured by surviving humans scratching out an existence in the aftermath of a secular apocalypse. What remains missing from such imagery, though, is a certain gray vitalism. As Jeffrey Jerome Cohen argues, gray is a process rather than a color, and in this sense the liminality of the gray should not center on the human: 'The gloaming is a place of life, but not necessarily of those sublime forms we expect life to assume' (Cohen, 2013b: 271-2).

The grayness of mediation is vital; it is comprised of generative forces, of world-making processes, but human life is just one amongst many of these interrelated energies. A certain grayness characterizes the human's ontological entanglement with its technical environment, whereby the apparently natural division between human and machine is dissolved. In the gray, technology can neither be defined as a tool for our use nor as something that uses us. More importantly, for the human, the world has always been gray – grayness has always been 'an intrinsic condition of being-in, and becoming-with, the technological world' (Kember and Zylinska, 2012: 1). The human has never been an autonomous agent, there is what Bernard Stiegler has called an 'originary technicity' to the human, always outside and beyond itself, open to the nonhuman.

The materiality of grayness, of gray relations, is continually variable, continually shifting: grayness thins and congeals, darkens and lifts. It is a rushing, an undulation, a noise. Noise is something that is impossible to get a distance on, something that infects you, that you cannot be rid of. Noise is that which cannot or will not be confined to the usual hermeneutic categories. So it is that noise is 'indelibly associated with horror' (Hainge, 2013: 85). In the standard cybernetic model of mediation, noise is the unwanted corruption of a transparent connection between sender and receiver. In such a model, mediation is understood in terms of a device connecting two self-contained and previously separate points. It is only by occluding noise that 'meaning' can occur. But in the ancient fug of gray, noise is always present – it cannot be distinguished or separated out from 'information'. Noise is medial, it expresses the relation between actual and virtual; noise is 'the trace of the virtual out of which all expressive forms come to be, the mark of an ontology which is necessarily relational' (Hainge, 2013: 13-14). It is, then, the breakdown in conventional models that gives rise to the horror. With no clear senders or receivers, our existence in the world appears less hospitable, less validated by meaning. We are left with nothing but an oceanic middle, a cosmic middle in which we suddenly find ourselves (Thacker, 2014: 87-90). For Lockwood (2012: 80), this constitutes a 'media sublime' – not as rapturous transcendent sublime, but an immanent-transcendence, a sublime as the infective propagation of alien affect into the everyday.

In a society of control, the media sublime again serves to describe weird encounters, those fleeting moments when it is briefly possible to perceive the powers of modulation in effect. As an 'affective and perceptual condition', as a low level buzz, an atmosphere, grayness constitutes 'a changeable but often unnoticed background – unnoticed until an environmental shift occurs' (Fuller and Goffey, 2012: 12). Usually, gray media have little aesthetic charge, they calibrate human activity on a pre-individual level, on a low boil, a simmer of not entirely burnt out producers and not entirely addicted users. Their unconscious background of routines and algorithms assuage perceptual and affective intensity just as they preserve a consistent liveliness (Fuller and Goffey, 2012: 14). But there are necessarily glitches in the continuity of this system – more forceful movements of power into the ontogenetic processes of life itself, movements that leave vague impressions on conscious perception. More importantly, it is possible to instigate such horror in ways that glitch conventional belief in the world and confront the sensation that 'the scratching from "outside" is already inside, infecting, running rampant, warping and deforming human life' (Lockwood, 2012: 76).

Cosmic countervisuality

In his own response to the opaque powers of control, Deleuze famously called for 'circuit-breakers', for 'vacuoles of noncommunication' (Deleuze, 1995: 133). Today, in the midst of an increasingly loquacious and performative century, how are we to understand such a tactic? Are we to fall silent? On the contrary – as Wark (2014) cautions, 'secret' communication only serves to attract greater attention. Vigilant, surreptitious, or false behaviours, which impair algorithmic control, might allow some room to manoeuvre, but an escape to transcendent privacy remains a bourgeois fantasy. Silence is too moral, too human. Any countervisuality must be immanent to the weird and noisy middle of mediation.[3] This is to believe in our existence within what Deleuze (Deleuze, 1995: 133) called a 'cramped space', a bottleneck, though cramped need not indicate something small – we might imagine the horror of being cosmically cramped. Indeed, this is, at least in part, the approach Trevor Paglen takes in another recent project.

In November 2012, the communications satellite EchoStar XVI launched from a base in Kazakhstan and joined the hundreds of other spacecraft now in geosynchronous orbit around the earth. In this narrowly defined region of space, in which there is no atmospheric drag, the craft will continue to circle the earth for millions, even billions of years. It will remain stable, never falling back to earth. It is now part of 'humankind's longest-lasting material legacy', ensuring that, long after all human life on the planet has winked out, it 'will remain encircled by a thin ring of long-dead-spacecraft' (Paglen, 2012: 6). In the years leading up to its launch, Paglen conceived the idea of attaching to the satellite an archival disc micro-etched with one hundred photographs. The work, titled The Last Pictures, is a collection of images that will outlast the species that produced them.

On one level, the work is a product of the Anthropocene, namely the present era in which human activity is understood to affect all life on the planet. This is made clear in the selection of images which, although occasionally weird (figures 20.5 and 20.6), generally attest to a political and environmental crisis. The first photograph shows the back of Paul Klee's *Angelus Novus*, an image famously described by Walter Benjamin (1968: 257-58) as depicting the angel of history, who looks at the mounting wreckage of the past as he is blown backwards into the future by the storm of progress. Paglen's set of images compels us to adopt the angel's view of recent history, comprised as it is by pictures of the Occupy movement, a nuclear explosion, battery farming, a disappearing glacier, cloned livestock, drone warfare, and high frequency trading. But for Paglen, who is conscious of the project's conceptual affinity with *haute*-Weird, the work is also 'a future alien artifact', made for a future in which humans are the 'ancient aliens' (Paglen, 2012: 7). Accordingly, the artifact confronts that which Lovecraft (1933) described as 'the most profoundly dramatic and grimly terrible thing in the universe', namely, time. It destabilizes anthropocentric time in favor of an 'utterly foreign' and 'deeply unearthly' time (Paglen, 2012: 6, 3).

It was, after all, only in the 20th century that human knowledge grasped with any certainty the 'deep time' of the Earth, encountering a new concept of planetary history that spans billions of years. The sheer scale of this temporality entirely shatters humanist narratives of progress, narratives in which man continuously develops and commands ever more sophisticated machines. Deep time is entirely alien to us, it exceeds our powers of imagination. It is in this sense that *The Last Pictures* invokes a cosmic perception, a terrifying view of the world after the human.

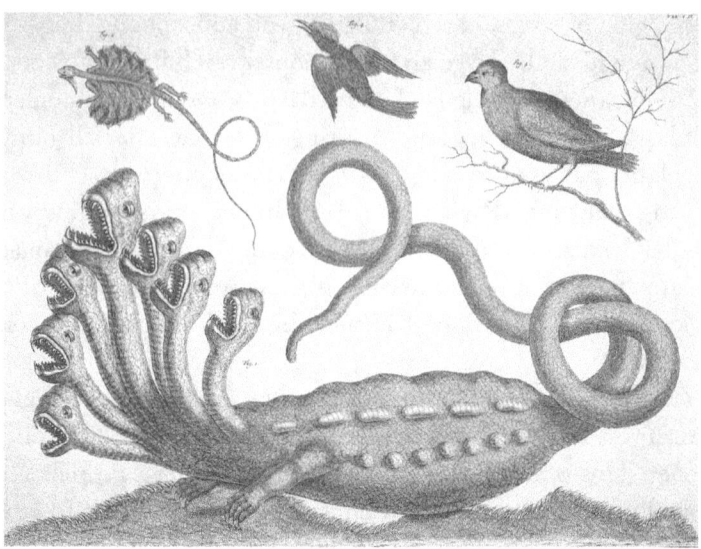

Figure 20.5. 'Lernaean Hydra, Albertus Seba's Thesaurus' (as featured in Trevor Paglen's The Last Pictures). Image from Wikipedia Commons: http://commons.wikimedia.org/wiki/File:Albertus_Seba_-_Hydra.jpg [accessed April 15, 2014].

Paglen's work is not about control society but it does force us to think reflexively about our relations with nonhuman agents. Importantly though, the images – apparently selected to represent the challenges, complexities and crises of human existence on and with the planet – play a different role in this process. In spite of the lengthy deliberations, interviews, research and debate, which led to their inclusion, the individual images actually function most effectively as a series of negations, as failures. In other words, where the work necessarily fails in its curatorial attempt to 'render the inaccessible accessible', to capture an artifactual portrait of human life, it does reveal something else; in its cosmic sensibility it does begin to 'make accessible the inaccessible – in its inaccessibility' (Thacker, 2014: 96). The work not only evokes the limits of representation but the limits of perceptual experience, the limits of expression. The work is a *scream*.

For Deleuze, the scream is a disharmony of the senses through which perception can be transformed (Deleuze, 2014: 15). It is a 'spasm', the body's attempt to escape itself, to break from the frameworks of recognition that inhibit other perceptions, other visualities. The scream resolves

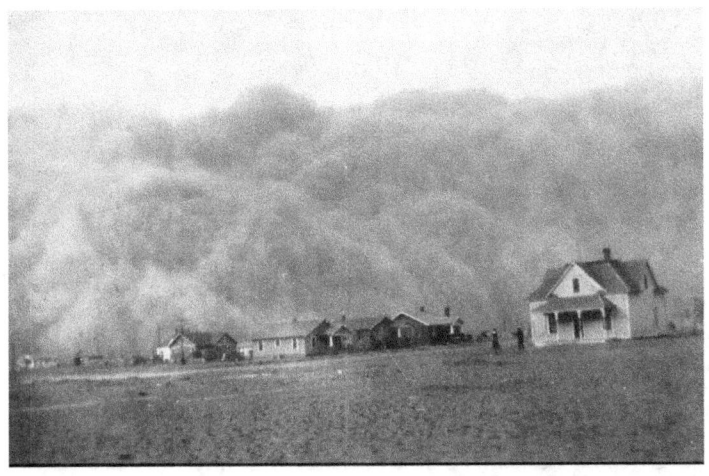

Figure 20.6. 'Dust Storm, Stratford, Texas' (as featured in Trevor Paglen's *The Last Pictures*). Image from US Department of Commerce, National Oceanic and Atmospheric Administration: http://www.photolib.noaa.gov/bigs/theb1365.jpg [accessed April 15, 2014].

nothing, creates nothing, but it does express a perception of opacity in and of itself. In this we can begin to imagine how seizing upon the right to scream might produce an ethico-aesthetic sensibility to that which is beyond the human. We can begin to formulate new tactical possibilities for confronting a visuality that is not simply visual. For in the end, while the sublimity of the scream is born of fear over the demolition of the unified human subject, of a perception of connectedness as terrifying overconnectedness, it also testifies to an excitable awe at radical relationality, to a sudden wonder at perceiving a multiple and collective subject. It welcomes, as much as it fears, becoming monstrous.

Original source and licence

Photomediations Machine, 30.06.2014, http://photomediationsmachine.net/. © Rob Coley. Permission to republish granted.

References

Benjamin, W. (1968) 'Theses on the Philosophy of History', in *Illuminations* (ed.), H. Arendt. New York: Schocken Books.

Carlyle, T. (1841) *On Heroes, Hero-Worship, and the Heroic in History*. Available at: http://www.gutenberg.org/files/1091/1091-h/1091-h.htm.

Cohen, J. J. (2013a) 'Ecology's Rainbow' in J. J. Cohen (ed.), *Prismatic Ecology: Ecotheory Beyond Green*. Minneapolis and London: University of Minnesota Press.

Cohen, J. J. (2013b) 'Grey', in J. J. Cohen (ed.), *Prismatic Ecology: Ecotheory Beyond Green*. Minneapolis and London: University of Minnesota Press.

Deleuze, G. (1992) 'Postscript on the Societies of Control', *October* 59: 7.

Deleuze, G. (1995) *Negotiations*. New York: Columbia University Press.

Deleuze, G. (2004) *Francis Bacon: The Logic of Sensation*. London and New York: Continuum.

Fuller, M. & Goffey, A. (2012) *Evil Media*. Cambridge, MA: MIT Press.

Galloway, A., Thacker, E. & Wark, M. (2014) *Excommunication: Three Inquiries in Media and Mediation*. Chicago: University of Chicago Press.

Grant, S. (2013) 'Monsters and Myths: The Manifestation of Man's Deepest Fears', in A. Farquharson & M. Clark (eds), *Aquatopia: The Imaginary of the Ocean Deep* London: Nottingham Contemporary/Tate.

Greenwald, G. (2013) 'Inside the Mind of NSA Chief Gen Keith Alexander', *The Guardian* 15 September. Available at: http://www.theguardian.com/commentisfree/2013/sep/15/nsa-mind-keith-alexander-star-trek. Accessed on 19 November, 2013.

Hainge, G. (2013) *Noise Matters: Towards an Ontology of Noise*. London: Bloomsbury.

James, W. (1982 [1902]) *The Varieties of Religious Experience: A Study in Human Nature*. London: Penguin.

Kember, S. & Zylinska, J. (2012) *Life After New Media: Mediation as a Vital Process*. Cambridge, MA: MIT Press.

Lockwood, D. (2012) 'Mongrel Vibrations: H.P. Lovecraft's Weird Ecology of Noise', in M. Goddard *et al.* (eds), *Reverberations: The Philosophy, Aesthetics and Politics of Noise* London: Continuum.

Lovecraft, H. P. (1933) 'Notes on Writing Weird Fiction' [online] available at: http://www.hplovecraft.com/writings/texts/essays/nwwf.aspx. Accessed on 7 April 2014.

Lovink, G. (2014) 'Hermes on the Hudson: Notes on Media Theory after Snowden' *e-flux* 54. Available at: http://www.e-flux.com/journal/hermes-on-the-hudson-notes-on-media-theory-after-snowden/.

MacAskill, E. et al. (2014) 'GCHQ Taps Fibre-optic Cables for Secret Access to World's Communications', *The Guardian* 21 June. Available at: http://www.theguardian.com/uk/2013/jun/21/gchq-cables-secret-world-communications-nsa.

Miéville, C. (2008) 'M.R. James and the Quantum Vampire', *Collapse* IV: 105.

Mirzoeff, N. (2011) *The Right to Look: A Counterhistory of Visuality*. Durham: Duke University Press.

Nietzsche, F. (1968) *The Will to Power*. New York: Vintage.

Paglen, T. (2008) *I Could Tell You But Then You Would Have to Be Destroyed by Me: Emblems from the Pentagon's Black World*. Brooklyn: Melville House Publishing.

Paglen, T. (2010) *Blank Spots on the Map: The Dark Geography of the Pentagon's Secret World*. New York: New American Library.

Paglen, T. (2012) *The Last Pictures*. Berkeley and Los Angeles: California University Press.

Thacker, E. (2011) *In the Dust of This Planet: Horror of Philosophy*, vol.1. Winchester and Washington: Zero.

Thacker, E. (2014) 'Dark Media', in *Excommunication: Three Inquiries in Media and Mediation*, A. Galloway, E. Thacker & M. Wark. Chicago: University of Chicago Press.

Wark, M. (2012) *Telesthesia: Communication, Culture & Class*. Cambridge: Polity.

Wark, M. (2014) 'Where Next for Media Theory?' Public Seminar 9 April. Available at: http://www.publicseminar.org/2014/04/where-next-for-media-theory/#.Uokyqce9MXw.

Notes

1 Similar assertions could be made of DARPA's much discussed Total Information Awareness project, which came with its own Illuminati-inspired mystical insignia.

2 The story's source states that, 'The vast majority of data is discarded without being looked at... we simply don't have the resources'.

3 It is in similar terms that Fuller and Goffey commend 'gray immanence for gray media' (2012: 13).

Notes on Contributors

Kimberly K. Arcand is a scientist and co-author (with Megan Watzke) of *Your Ticket to the Universe: A Guide to Exploring the Cosmos* (Smithsonian Books, 2013).

David Bate is a practising photo-artist. He is Professor of Photography at the University of Westminster and director of its Photography Research Group. He was co-founder of Accident and Five Years Gallery in London, and is co-editor and co-founder of the academic journal *photographies*. His recent publications include the photobook *Zone* (Artwords, 2012) and the widely used book *Photography: Key Concepts* (Berg, 2009).

Rob Coley is a Lecturer in the School of Media at the University of Lincoln. His PhD thesis (awarded in 2013) explored an immanent, ontological mode of visuality. He is the author, with Dean Lockwood and Adam O'Meara, of *Photography in the Middle: Dispatches on Media Aesthetics and Ecologies* (forthcoming with Punctum Books) and, with Dean Lockwood, of *Cloud Time* (Zero Books, 2012).

Charlotte Cotton is a curator and writer. She is the author of *The Photograph as Contemporary Art* (2004) and founder of *Words Without Pictures* and *Eitherand.org*. She has held various curatorial positions, including curator of photographs at the Victoria and Albert Museum, London, and head of the Wallis Annenberg Department of Photography at the Los Angeles County Museum of Art. She has been a visiting scholar at Parsons, The New School for Design, New York and CCA, San Francisco.

Joseph DePasquale is an astronomer working for the operations team for NASA's Chandra X-ray Observatory at the Harvard-Smithsonian Center for Astrophysics.

Alexander García Düttmann is Professor at Berlin University of the Arts. He is a philosopher with an interest in aesthetics and art, but also in moral and political philosophy. He frequently collaborates with artists: in 2004 the chamber opera *Liebeslied/My Suicides*, for which he wrote the libretto, and which featured music by Paul Clark and photographs by Rut Blees Luxemburg, opened at the Institute of Contemporary Arts, London. His most recent book publications include *Naive Art: An Essay on Happiness* (2012) and *What Does Art Know?* (2015) (both in German).

MIKA ELO is Professor of Artistic Research and the Head of the Doctoral Programme of the Academy of Fine Arts, University of the Arts Helsinki. His research interests include theory of photographic media, philosophical media theory and epistemology of artistic research. He is the author of *Valokuvan medium/The Medium of Photography* and one of the main organizers of the Helsinki Photomedia conference series.

PAUL FROSH teaches in the Department of Communication and Journalism at the Hebrew University of Jerusalem. His publications include *The Image Factory: Consumer Culture, Photography and the Visual Content Industry* and *Media Witnessing: Testimony in the Age of Mass Communication* (with Amit Pincheski).

YA'ARA GIL-GLAZER is Head of the Department of Education and Visual Research at the Shpilman Photography Institute. Her research areas include modern and contemporary art and visual culture and its educational integration into social contexts; photography books and documentaries; the relationships between image and text; and historiography and the theory of photography. She is the author of *The Documentary Photobook: Social-Cultural Criticism in the U.S. during the Great Depression and the New Deal* (Resling, 2013)

LEE GRIEVESON is Reader in Film Studies at University College London. He is the author of *Policing Cinema: Movies and Censorship in Early Twentieth Century America* (University of California Press, 2004) and co-editor of several volumes, including *Inventing Film Studies*, *Empire and Film* (with Haidee Wasson, Duke University Press, 2008) and *Film and the End of Empire* (Palgrave Macmillan, 2011), both with Colin MacCabe.

AUD SISSEL HOEL is Associate Professor of Visual Communication in the Department of Art and Media Studies at the Norwegian University of Science and Technology. Her research explores the interfaces of art, science, and culture, focusing on topics such as face images, technologies of thinking, scientific vision, medical imaging, and visualization. Currently she is heading an interdisciplinary research project on neuroimaging.

KAMILA KUC is Postdoctoral Research Assistant in the Department of Media and Communications at Goldsmiths, University of London. She is also a curator and an experimental filmmaker. Co-editor (with Michael O'Pray) of *The Struggle for Form: Perspectives on Polish Avant-Garde Film 1916-1989* (Columbia University Press, 2014), she has curated programmes of experimental film for international film festivals and venues (New Horizons Film Festival, Poland; Experiments in Cinema, US). Her short films have been screened widely.

ZOLTAN G. LEVAY is a US-based scientist who was awarded a Space Telescope Science Institute Individual Achievement Award in November 1997 and the Association of Universities for Research in Astronomy (AURA) 1997 Service Award. He is a member of the American Astronomical Society (AAS) and the National Association of Photoshop Professionals (NAPP).

FRANK LINDSETH is Adjunct Associate Professor in the Department of Computer and Information Science at the Norwegian University of Science and Technology. He works on medical image computing and visualisation.

DEBBIE LISLE is Reader in International Relations at Queen's University Belfast. Her research engages with a number of contemporary debates in International Relations and beyond, most notably around issues of difference, mobility, security, travel, visuality, governmentality, biopolitics, materiality, technology, practice and power. She is the author of *Dangerous Routes: Entanglements of War and Tourism* (University of Minnesota Press, forthcoming).

RAFE MCGREGOR teaches at the Centre for Lifelong Learning at the University of York. He is the author of numerous publications about film.

ROSA MENKMAN is a Dutch art theorist, curator and visual artist specialising in glitch art and resolution theory.

MELISSA MILES is Associate Professor and Australian Research Council Future Fellow in the Faculty of Art, Design and Architecture at Monash University. Her most recent publication is *The Culture of Photography in Public Space* (co-edited with Anne Marsh and Daniel Palmer, Intellect and University of Chicago Press, 2015). Her research centres largely on the history and theory of photography. Along with photography, her research interests include feminist art practice, intercultural relations, and studies of witness and testimony in contemporary culture.

TRAVIS RECTOR is Professor of Physics and Astronomy at the University of Alaska, Anchorage. He is also an astrophotographer.

RAÚL RODRÍGUEZ-FERRÁNDIZ works at the University of Alicante. He is the author of numerous books on visual culture, including *Apocalypse Show - Intelectuales, Television y Fin de Milenio* (Biblioteca Nueva, 2001).

METTE SANDBYE is Head of Department and Associate Professor in the Department of Arts and Cultural Studies at the University of Copenhagen. She was the editor of the first Danish edition of history of photography (*Dansk Fotografihistorie*, 2004) and has published numerous books and articles on contemporary art photography and photography as part of the visual culture.

JONATHAN SHAW is the co-director of the Disruptive Media Learning Lab at Coventry University; visiting fellow at the Centre for Excellence in Media Practice at Bournemouth University; and Chair of the Association for Photography in Higher Education in the UK. His work blurs the boundaries between the still and moving image. He is the author of *NewFotoScapes*, an online multi-platform book.

AJAY SINHA is Professor of Art History at Mt. Holyoke College. He is the author of *Imagining Architects: Creativity in the Religious Monuments of India* (University of Delaware Press, 2000), and editor, with Raminder Kaur, of *Bollyworld: Popular Indian Cinema through a Transnational Lens* (Sage, 2005).

KATRINA SLUIS is a New Zealand-born artist, writer, curator and educator. She balances her present post as Curator (Digital Programme) at The Photographers' Gallery in London with her role as Senior Lecturer at London South Bank University. Prior to this, she lectured in digital photography at the University of New South Wales and the Sydney Gallery School.

OLIVIA SMARR, Stanford University, is a scientist who has worked NASA Goddard Space Flight Center.

ROSS VARNEY is Assistant Lecturer in Media at Coventry University. His research interests encompass the moving image, screen-based media, fan cultures, digital curation and open publishing. He has published co-authored papers for *The International Journal of Performing Arts and Digital Media* and the *Body, Space and Technology Journal*.

MICHAEL WAMPOSZYC is a designer, researcher and educator, currently working as Lecturer in Information Design and Graphic Design at the University of Portsmouth. He is the author of several theoretical and experimental publications on visual communication, typography and systems of notational iconicity. His work focuses on design research methodology and diagrammatics.

MEGAN WATZKE is an astronomer and co-author (with Kimberly K. Arcand) of *Your Ticket to the Universe: A Guide to Exploring the Cosmos* (Smithsonian Books, 2013).

JOANNA ZYLINSKA is Professor of New Media and Communications at Goldsmiths, University of London. The author of five books – most recently, *Minimal Ethics for the Anthropocene* (Open Humanities Press, 2014) and *Life after New Media: Mediation as a Vital Process* (with

Sarah Kember; MIT Press, 2012) – she is also a translator of Stanislaw Lem's major philosophical treatise, *Summa Technologiae* (University of Minnesota Press, 2013). She is one of the Editors of *Culture Machine*, an international open-access journal of culture and theory, and a curator of its sister project, *Photomediations Machine*. She combines her philosophical writings and curatorial work with photographic art practice.

www.ingramcontent.com/pod-product-compliance
Lightning Source LLC
Chambersburg PA
CBHW071018240526
45469CB00006BD/1963